SAM SHULSKY
ON INVESTING

New York Institute of Finance ● New York, New York 10005

Library of Congress Cataloging in Publication Data

Shulsky, Sam, 1907–
    Sam Shulsky on investing

    Includes index.
    1. Investments.   I. Title.   II. Title: On
investing.
HG4521.S548   332.6'78   80–17037
ISBN 0–13–790907–1

© 1980 by New York Institute of Finance
            70 Pine Street
        New York, New York 10005

Printed in the United States of America
10 9 8 7 6 5 4 3 2

This publication is designed to provide accurate and authoritative information in regard to the subject matter covered. It is sold with the understanding that the publisher is not engaged in rendering legal, accounting, or other professional service. If legal advice or other expert assistance is required, the services of a competent professional person should be sought.

—*From a Declaration of Principles jointly adopted by a Committee of the American Bar Association and a Committee of Publishers and Associations.*

PREFACE

Why One More Book?

In 1865, the very year the wartime president was assass-
inated, a nineteenth-century historian, L. P. Brockett, M.D.,
wrote and had published a volume titled simply *Life and
Times of Abraham Lincoln.* In the preface he asked, somewhat rhetorically to be sure, "Why, pray, add another to the
many memoirs of him already published?" And he then
provided his own answer: "Because, dear reader, there was
need of just *one* more."

Having been so close to the tragedy, perhaps Doctor
Brockett can be excused for underestimating Lincoln's impact on generations to come—in fact, on all history.

But today's readers who ask, "Why yet another book on
securities, on Wall Street, on the stock market, on investing,
on speculation?" are on far more solid ground. After all, they
have been relentlessly preached to on the stock market.
They have been overwhelmed with false promises of what
the market can do for them. They have been lectured for
years that "anyone can make a million dollars in stocks" and,
more often than not, they have consistently lost money
chasing that will o' the wisp. Honest brokers will tell you that
if as many as 1% of "average" stock market dabblers ever

took "real money" home they (the brokers) would be much surprised. Millions of copies of thousands of books, which over the years have promised that just any reader could make a million dollars by "trading convertible preferreds" or by "buying insurance stocks low and selling them high" have, of course, made money—for their authors.

I, too, hope to make money on this book. And possibly may if I can persuade enough investors and would-be investors that they might profit by buying and reading a book which *does not* promise everyone, or even *anyone* a stock market killing or a secret formula for achieving it. The ancient scientists and philosophers spent lifetimes seeking the "philosopher's stone"—a formula for changing low-grade metals into gold. They never found it . . . and no one has since. Neither has anyone discovered a royal road to stock market riches. Because there is none. There can be none. The purpose of this volume—and the justification for the question, "Why, pray, another stock market book?"—is to explain why there is no such formula, and yet to urge qualified investors to consider securities as a sensible method of putting one's money to work.

Such a "common sense" approach to investing might well be equated to the oft-given "common sense" medical advice to get enough sleep and eat a balanced diet—in a word, "dullsville." There is no evidence that over the years it has turned out beauty queens or six-figure contract football stars, even though it has worked well for millions of common sense citizens.

Similarly, a "common sense" approach to the stock market will not double your money in two weeks, will not transplant you from a modest home in the suburbs to a villa on the Riviera. But such an approach could help put your investable funds to work in a "common sense" manner in exactly the same sense that a man who works at a construction job wears a hard hat. There is no glamour involved. It is

not an exciting program but, rather, one which I've formula-
ted over more than 50 years of studying, reporting, and
investing money in securities.

More than 50 years ago—as a youngster who, in fact,
legally should not have traded stock—I bought my first
stock, 100 shares of a copper-mining stock then called
Cerro de Pasco. Unfortunately I made $400 profit in about
10 days (a fortune for a high-school boy earning $10 a week).
I say "unfortunately" because the quick profit led me to
believe that I had the animal tamed whereas, in fact, I didn't
even know which end did the kicking.

I was wiped out a few weeks later.

Over the years since then I've put money into most of
the media offered by Wall Street—bonds, convertibles, options, warrants, puts and calls, short selling, hot new issues,
and even commodities. I learned something (if I didn't show
a profit) from all of them. And for the last 22 years, as an
investment column writer for as many as 120 newspapers in
U.S. and abroad, I've collected the experiences of thousands
of readers (via 2,000 to 2,500 letters in some months) who,
often at great length, related their stock market experiences,
their successes, their failures. The net result of a flood of
financial experiences—from rich and poor, from young and
old—added to my own financial history is what I have
attempted to present here as the groundwork for a successful, though sober, philosophy for investing, based on the
conviction that the stock market is no one's private money-
making machine.

SAM SHULSKY

Acknowledgements

Back in the age of the Hollywood spectacular," the phrase with a cast of thousands" was often added to the advertising posters to indicate that no expense was spared in order to really present the scope of the Roman Empire at its historic peak. The last thing I want to be in this book is "spectacular." There are no sure-fire formulas by which anyone can make a million in the stock market or no formula on how to now invest in an infant corporation which will prove to be the General Motors of the 21st century. Nor do I attempt to whet your appetite for Wall Street with those favorite gimmicks of the "you-shoulda" school of financial day dreaming—if you only had bought Haloid pre-Xerox) at .50 per share.

But this book does reflect the experiences of one newspaper man whose duty, for several decades in the middle of this century, was to explain what was going on for the benefit of millions of newspaper readers. In this task he relied on information supplied by scores of professional Wall Streeters involved with mutual funds, with securities underwriters, with brokers, with bankers. An even larger source of information were the investment experiences detailed to me by literally thousands of readers of my daily column which appeared in upwards of a hundred newspapers. These letters, often running to 2,000 to 2,500 a month provided the widest panoramic view anyone could ask for in writing about the average investor in the securities market, and the many dangers as well as opportunities encountered there. The insight gained from the readers' experiences served to broaden my perception of the financial market and how it can best serve the investor.

To that extent and in that sense, this book has a "cast" of thousands. I am conscious of the fact that, in acknowledging those readers, I've listed a lengthy faculty list, but a half-century is a long time and there was much to learn.

Contents

**Financials, Taxes, and Terms:
A Special Appendix by the NYIF Editorial Staff**

1
Introduction

To talk of investing is to call forth images of panelled board rooms where dignified bankers daily move millions of dollars from Machinery Corp. A to Railroad Co. B to Utility Co. C—a true picture, but not a complete one.

Investing, simply defined, means putting money to work, which is exactly what everyone who has a dollar left over at the end of the week MUST do. The question "Shall I invest?" is a popular one, but hardly a meaningful one. If you have surplus funds—of any amount—you MUST invest ... you MUST put them to work in one medium or another: savings accounts in any one of a dozen forms; U.S. savings bonds, Treasury bonds, corporation bonds, tax-exempt bonds, preferred stocks, common stocks ... or rare works of art, antiques, apartment houses, farms, vacant land, gold coins ... in any of the myriad and acceptable forms of storing dollars for present or future use, in hopes of current income or of future gain. Regardless of which medium you select for your surplus dollars, you MUST do something with them! A dollar on hand cannot be ignored—even if it is stored, unemployed, in an old coffee tin at the back of a kitchen shelf. You must deal with it.

This book, then, presents the various methods by which you put money to work: to increase your nest egg for future use ... for home buying, for your children's education, for your own retirement years . . . or to augment your present income.

Preserving dollars and purchasing power for the future and providing more current income are not easy tasks. There are no guarantees. Success is far from assured. But you have no choice. You must make the effort because investable dollars must be invested, put to work. They cannot be ignored.

WHY YOU INVEST

In a capitalistic society such as ours work can be performed by muscle, by brain, or by a combination of both—brains and money.

A man may wield a pickax in a mine, or money may provide a giant drilling machine which works at the touch of a switch. A clerk may enter accounts by hand, or money may provide an electronic machine which automatically scans the accounts and enters them in a data machine. We are no longer a nation which sets out every day at dawn with a hand axe or a quill pen to make a living and further the nation's progress.

Money—accumulated capital—has been used to augment the muscle and brain of workers, has increased their productivity, raised their living standards and still made possible some earnings with which to compensate the providers of that capital. Money, therefore, can work and earn its keep.

If you have accumulated money—no matter in what amounts—or if you can follow a course, a regimen which permits you to accumulate surplus money, that money—invested—can work for you, too.

And so, for your self-interest, you put to work any money you are able to accumulate after meeting your daily, ongoing expenses. We shall discuss later where and how to put that money to work. The "jobs" available for it vary widely. But the purpose of this chapter is to convince you that surplus funds must be invested in one form or another. In fact, you can't avoid investing it—unless of course you hide it under a mattress, or bury it in a tin can in the back yard. Then it becomes jobless money, with all the waste and deterioration idleness implies.

Investing your money, putting it to work, thus serves a two-fold purpose: it works for your profit and it works to advance the nation's productivity by providing more efficient jobs for others. Economists have written library shelves full of books explaining why the national interest requires the saving of money and the investing of that money in increased production of goods and services via more plants and machinery. All of which is true, and patriotic, and good.

But this volume's chief purpose is to concentrate on how this investment will be good for you ... why you should invest for your own self-interest ... how investment can assure your own comfortable present and future and contribute to the well-being of your children and your children's children. In other words, it wants to help answer that old, but vital, question: "What's in it for me?"

ROLE OF SELF-INTEREST

Unless that question can be answered clearly and unequivocally there can be no incentive to accumulate investable capital, because the very act of saving money means denying yourself something you could own and enjoy today in order to help build a better tomorrow. And that, being part of the future, must always remain an "iffy" venture. There is nothing in this volume which will attempt to detract from self-interest. Ancient wise men asked, "If I am not for me, who will be?" This book is "for you." Let others talk to you of your duties to society. This book concentrates on your financial duties to you and yours—present and future—and insofar as it is humanly possible, to better that present and future. If you are going to deny yourself the pleasure of owning "that doggie in the window" your decision should be made on the basis of rational thinking that the money so conserved will help bring you even greater pleasure tomorrow. You will hear on every hand the popular message that our society will require so many billions of dollars in new capital to build the plants and machines which will provide our 21st century standard of living. True. But you have every right to answer that call to provide capital with a question of your own, "And if I help provide that money, what will it do for me?"

Money can work. But if it is your money, it should work for you first and foremost.

What job should your money do for you?

The answer depends upon the particular period of your life in which you plan to benefit.

Money can work in either of two time zones—the future, or the present. The seemingly reverse time order presented here is more logical than it would first appear. An investor, in the normal course of financial events, begins thinking of the future while he is still young, or middle-aged . . . still at work and still interested mainly in building assets.

The investor stressing the present is most often one who has retired and is interested chiefly in getting the most income now out of the money accumulated by self-denial over a working lifetime.

Money put to work building assets for the future has the toughest job, which should come as no surprise to anyone who realizes that peering into the future has never been easy. Will the land bought today ultimately wind up as part of a valuable shopping center? Will an apartment house escape the ravages of "inner city" decay? Will the works of an artist whose paintings you buy now command a high price a quarter century later? Will XYZ Corp., whose shares you buy now, prosper and become a leader in its industry?

The giving of hostages to the future must always remain

a worrisome endeavor. But there is no other method of building assets over a period of time than to exchange dollars today for goods or equities or property which, you hope, will be worth more dollars tomorrow. At least you would hope for enough more dollars to offset the debilitating effect of inflation and still provide sufficient purchasing power for that far-off day.

This is not to say that the mere act of buying a share of stock today is going to guarantee an exact inflation hedge 10, 20 or 40 years off. There can be no such pat assurances because we are not dealing here with an exact science.

RECENT RETURNS

In recent years, common share market values, on average, have barely compensated investors for the deterioration in the dollar's purchasing power. In the ten-year period 1967–76, for example, inflation ran at the average rate of 5.86%. An investor in bonds would have shown a net loss since their average return over that ten-year period was only 5.35%. Common stocks generated an average annual return of only 6.66%—including both market gains and dividends. It was a rough decade. Inflation, at times, reached double-digit levels, while the securities markets were plagued by global unrest, domestic recession, political scandal, and high money rates.

However, a more classic picture is presented in a study covering a fifty-year period which showed an average annual inflation rate of only 2.42%, exceeded by an average bond yield of 4.01% and a combined market gain and dividend return averaging 9.19% annually for common shares.

There are no assurances that either the ten-year or the fifty-year record will be repeated, or that we shall experience something in between. All we can foresee with any certainty is that: 1) with peacetime Federal deficits continuing at record levels, inflation is "here to stay"; 2) the securities markets, as the elder J. P. Morgan once put it, "will fluctuate," and 3) that anyone who wants to increase his or her dollars for the future must take chances by transferring them into some form of fluctuating price tag property.

The distinct advantage which lies with transferring dollars into equity (common share) investments lies in the fact that along with the purchase price paid for the share of stock, for the acquisition of your participation in a company, you also get a share of the management. The price of 10 shares of IBM, or of 50 shares of A.T.&T., covers not only the cost of the small share you thus acquire in the corporation—in its buildings, machinery, inventory, inventions and good will—but also a part of management know-how.

SHOULD YOU INVEST?

- Yes—if you already have surplus funds.
- Yes—if you care enough to accumulate funds to be set aside for your future.
- Yes—if you need income now.
- Yes—if you want to build income-producing capital for your future, to pay for education for your children, to provide retirement income for yourself.

It is only normal to expect that those of modest means should pass over the newspaper's financial pages, convinced that "this is not for me." And when one reads of multi-million dollar transactions in securities and giant corporation takeovers this "not-for-me" attitude would seem to be reasonably based. But the truth is that alongside the multi-million dollar transactions, the financial community provides machinery for the investment of far more modest sums—a few dollars into a savings account, or perhaps $18.75 or $25 a month into additional E bonds, or $25 or $50 a month into a mutual fund.

Wall Street—the trading ground for multi-million dollar deals—is also an all-purpose department store prepared to serve the investment needs of practically anyone who can set aside a few hundred dollars a year.

The question of whether you should invest lies less with the amount of money you now have (or will have) available for investment than with the strength of your desire to build a nest egg toward future financial strength. There is no correlation between amounts of money and investment drive.

WHO IS AN INVESTOR?

Answer: Anyone who has an investable dollar.

Question: What is an investable dollar?

Answer: It is any money left over after your weekly or monthly budget has covered the basic current expense items of food, clothing, housing, medical care, entertainment. It is that money which becomes available only after you have set up, or laid the foundations for a lifetime life insurance program, and after you have protected your home mortgage with life insurance on the wage earner of the family, after you have accumulated at least 3 to 6 months earnings (more, in the case of a large and youthful family) in emergency funds— savings accounts or in E bonds.

2

Life Insurance and Savings Accounts

These prior-to-investment requirements of insurance and savings are not presented here as moral needs. They are not stressed because they are "good"—but because they are part of the foundation required for a sound, long-term investment program.

Life insurance, for example, is an absolute "must" for a young family and often of vital importance for old-age survivors. For the young family, it is the only way a wage earner can create immediate protection for his wife and family with the payment of an initial premium. In old age it often provides the largest portion of a widow's estate. Insurance on a home mortgage often proves a boon by providing a family with a mortgage-free home upon the death of the wage-earner.

However, life insurance is basically a protective device and should be employed only as needed. An unmarried man of 45 may reasonably decide that rather than build a life insurance program (beyond a token amount of protection) he would be far wiser to build an investment portfolio for his own later-life enjoyment. A widow who has seen her children through college and into lifelong professions might well decide that her insurance program should be reduced in order to make more money available for a securities portfolio. In other words, if you have no one to protect, there is no reason to be "insurance poor."

Saving has long been considered a prime virtue. And savings are important—not because thrift is a "good habit" but because a savings account can make the difference between your fiscal independence and your enslavement to every passing emergency or financial crisis—illness, new car expense, or a required trip. The listing of savings before securities purchasing is not a moral judgment but the actuality that you can't call yourself the "captain of your fate" if you have no readily available means to face up to an emergency. So savings of readily available money must be there before you venture into investment in securities, because such investments are not and should not be sufficiently liquid to meet emergencies. And turning to personal credit loans at interest rates which can run as high as 30% a year is not the mark of a prudent money manager. Savings are often maligned as "idle" money, but it should be remembered that "he also serves who only stands and waits."

If you skip building an emergency fund in order to hasten your way into securities ownership, you may find that you may have to sell those securities in an unpropitious market in order to raise cash for needs which can't wait. Never depend upon the stock market to bail you out at a profit in a time of sudden need.

HOW MUCH TO INVEST?

Once you have built these twin foundations of savings and required insurance, your next hurdle is the common misconception that investing requires huge amounts of money. It doesn't. Investable money comes in all amounts—$5 a week, or $50 a month or $3,000 a year—or (if you are that lucky) the $5,000 or $10,000 or half-a-million-dollar windfall you were left by a parent or favorite relative.

Naturally, "rich or poor," it's nice to have a lot of money . . . which brings to mind that philosophical question: "If you found a million dollars on the sidewalk would you return it?" Answer: "Yes, if it belonged to a poor person."

In fact, there are no dollar limits—upper or lower—to what may be considered investable money. (In Japan, just after World War II, investing in corporate shares became so popular that "piggy banks" were designed specifically to accumulate coins toward purchase of stock. And common shares were sold in department stores.)

U.S. department stores do not sell shares of stock. But it may be reasonably argued that Wall Street itself is a giant department store ready to serve a broad spectrum of securities buyers.

The multi-million dollar pools of capital know where to turn. The task here is to convince small investors that there is an investment regimen for literally every purse, even though the small investor is not especially profitable for Wall Street. In fact, a N.Y. Stock Exchange program to provide for monthly or quarterly investments of as little as $40 at a time has been abandoned by practically all of the Street's investment firms because of lack of public interest, no doubt resulting from the unwillingness of the brokerage fraternity to push the program.

However, formal plan or not, you can invest almost any reasonable sum you have available. A few of the larger brokers still welcome modest programs. Many mutual funds will accept $25 or $50 at almost any interval (some, after an initial investment of a few hundred dollars). And in recent years there has been a steady increase in the number of corporations which will allow you to reinvest quarterly dividends (plus additional cash) in shares of the corporation. Several hundred corporations have instituted these reinvestment programs and more join the plan every day. Even more inviting is the fact that some of these firms absorb all the bookkeeping and brokerage costs of this reinvestment. And there are some which even offer the additional shares at a discount of 5% from current market. In fact, it would not be stretching the point too far to remark that many corporations are showing more willingness to attract the small investor than Wall Street itself. But regardless of whether Wall Street is willing or not, the machinery for modest investment programs is there. And if you are prepared to put money aside for your future, you can use that machinery profitably.

WHAT ABOUT THE SMALL INVESTOR?

The excitement that goes with "bet-a-million" trades will be absent. You can't get too excited about a brokerage confirmation slip acknowledging the fact that you've just added 0.467 shares of A.T.&T. common to your holdings. But, then, you're not likely to open the newspaper one day and discover you've been wiped out by a drop in the stock market.

This slow, piecemeal, procedure has other important pluses:

1. it helps establish investing as a long-term, even life-long, procedure (which it should be);
2. it takes advantage of dollar-cost averaging in the acquisition of securities;
3. it tends to discourage in-and-out speculation which generally brings heavy losses;
4. it keeps you investing when public enthusiasm for the market is low (and stock prices fall); it prevents you from plunging with all your money when public enthusiasm and stock prices are high;
5. it helps direct investment funds into quality securities. (If you haven't the ready cash to gamble with 2,500 shares of a $2 stock you might as well settle for that 0.467 shares of A.T.&T. or some other blue chip.)

INVESTOR CHARACTERISTICS

What other factors—even more important than the amount of money available—describe an investor?

There must be a firm dedication to the principle of some self-denial now for the sake of building that nest egg for the future. It is not an easy trait to develop in a consumer-minded society. The ease with which those credit cards slip in and out of plastic sleeves in our wallets makes the job of investing even more difficult.

Our entire economic philosophy seems directed toward spend and enjoy. Of course, that philosophy is clearly "what makes the (industrial, commercial, economic) mare go." Indeed, one feels almost unpatriotic in even suggesting that it might be a good idea to pass up that third television set or an occasional skiing weekend for the sake of planting a few hundred dollars more for future growth.

This volume is not designed to tell you how to live—how much to spend for rent, for food, for jewelry, for entertainment, for automobiles. It can point out only that it is the money you don't spend today which can be put into building your future well-being. The bottom line decision to save $50 or $150 or $500 a month for long-term investment can be made only by you and your family on the basis of temperament, lifestyle, financial background and resources (present and reasonably expected in future).

All that can be stressed here is that the desire to build for the future is far more important an investment factor than the number of dollars available as building blocks. There is absolutely no correlation between the amount of money earned or inherited and the investing process itself—absolutely none. Low income workers with only $500 a year surplus to invest have succeeded in building respectable nest eggs which have assisted them in educating their children and have proven to be a comfort in retirement. On the other hand, earners of high, executive-level salaries have written me of their inability to "save a cent." In fact, one widow lamented that precisely because her late husband had always earned a high salary she found herself with large debts upon his death. She felt, evidently, that the high standard of living justified by the high salary also justified their heavy debt. (All too often the rule that interest on debt is an income tax deduction is allowed to overshadow the fact that the principal must ultimately be repaid—without tax help.)

Investing, therefore, is not governed by the amount of money available but to a far greater degree by the mind-set of the would-be investor. It is governed by your determination to build for the future, no matter at how slow and deliberate a pace. Nothing in this process requires the ability to plunk down a $50,000 check on a brokerage desk.

Almost everyone—and any number—can play.

3

The How and When
of Investing

An old proverb points out that a journey of 10,000 miles starts with but a single step.

A lifetime investment program is begun by making a first investment—no matter how much or how little money is involved, or how often additional investable moneys may thereafter become available. The important points are: get started—as early as possible—and keep at it as long as you can.

These may sound like unsophisticated, almost mechanical approaches to what we all admit is the highly-sophisticated, chancey task of putting our money to work in a still-obscure future. Admittedly, such "mechanical" rules will not guarantee success. But experience has shown that they can certainly provide a sound foundation for success. And in investing—in putting money to work—you need every advantage you can get.

THE ADVANTAGE OF TIME

There are many other factors which go into the making of a successful investment program: seed money, skill in selecting securities, timing, sound broker advice and handling, temperament, luck. All are subject to variation and risk. Only one more important ingredient—Time—is certain, unarguable and unvarying. Time to maximize your financial gains is non-negotiable. Either you have it or you don't. If you do have it—years in which to invest—by all means use it. Begin your investment program as soon as you can. The stock market may decline tomorrow or next week, but there have been few 20-year periods in this century which did not come to a close with the market higher than it was at the start.

Of course, if you are lucky, someone will have begun investing for you long before you become conscious of stocks, bonds, options or convertible debentures.

INVESTING FOR MINORS

Whether it is the understanding of this time advantage or merely the natural affection of grown-ups for children is not clear, nor important, but the fact remains that investment programs for children have enjoyed increasing popularity in recent years. (No doubt, a desire to reduce income taxes via a shift of assets to untaxed minors is also an important consideration.) In any event, investment programs are being set up (usually by doting grandparents) on Day One of babies' lives. Custodial or trust accounts have been established, bank accounts opened, and even stock purchase programs initiated at birth. This might be termed over-enthusiastic by some, although it is hardly on a par with showing up at the lying-in hospital loaded down with footballs, fishing rods and baseball bats.

A share of stock doesn't care who owns it. And if it is a share in a leading, basic industry (or in one you think has a good chance of becoming a leading, basic industry) then it's clear that the potential growth over the next sixty years should prove more rewarding than over a five or ten year period beginning fifty years from now.

Investing for minors has become big business and any broker can supply you with the proper forms for setting up such accounts. Anyone who has money to put aside for the benefit of youngsters can do so easily, regardless of the amount of money involved.

If you were not fortunate enough to have well-heeled grandparents or parents, it is quite likely that you will have arrived at the ripe old age of your first pay check before you get a chance to put money into your future. (Always, of course, after having set up emergency savings accounts and necessary insurance programs.) So you start then. Or, if your 20's find you financially burdened with a growing family and increasing housing costs, you may not be able to start putting money into investments until your 30's or 40's. There is no fixed time for beginning the building of an investment portfolio. You can't invest money you haven't got. The main point is to start as soon as you can—and then stay with it.

There is one special word of warning for "late starters": don't rush to make up for lost time by taking wild chances. The fact that you may not have been able to put a dollar into investments until age fifty is absolutely no excuse for directing your investment course toward the "wild side" of Wall Street. The stock market is no respecter of persons. It has absolutely no sympathy or regard for your need to "make it fast." The same laws of risk and reward apply to an investor whether he is 25 or 55. As a matter of fact, the 55-year old investor can less afford to take risks simply because he has less time in which to try to recoup any losses. So, if you can start early, you're lucky. If you must wait until you are older—act your age.

4

You'll Need a Broker—
And Here's How
To Pick One

A house may be bought and sold either through a real estate agent or directly through friends or relatives, or by merely hanging a "For Sale" sign on the front porch. Some bakeries hang out a sign "Day Old Bread" and sell it directly to whoever comes by. Farmers set up roadside stands at which they sell eggs fresh from the chicken coop and corn from the stalk.

But if we are talking about securities, you might as well forget all these direct contact, or wholesale techniques for investing in stocks and bonds. You invest in securities by using a securities broker. It sounds obvious, but it is mentioned at the very start because too many would-be investors, both novices and "wiseacres," still think there is a sensible way to get around paying brokerage fees.

WHY USE A BROKER?

It is perfectly legal, of course, for you to buy stock from any individual owner without employing the services of a broker.

You might stand on a street corner with a placard reading "I want to buy 50 shares of U.S. Steel" and hope a seller will pass by. You might put an advertisement in the classified section of your newspaper. You might ask at the office, "Got any stock to sell?" You might find someone who wants to sell exactly what you want to buy in the right amount and at a mutually agreeable price. Then all you would have to do is have the seller's signatures guaranteed by a bank, fill out the necessary papers supplied by the bank which serves as the stock transfer agent for that corporation, deliver the stock to the bank, pay a small fee. Of course, you would have to make certain first that the seller is the rightful owner of the shares; that the shares are genuine and not counterfeit, and that the price agreed upon is fair (at least to you).

To repeat: securities may be transferred by individuals without the use of a broker. It's entirely legal—but very, very cumbersome—and it could be risky if there is an unscrupulous seller. As the man said after his obstinate attorney had dragged him through the courts for months fighting a parking ticket, "Please, pay the $5." If you are going to invest in stocks and bonds, do so through a reputable brokerage firm, whether a full service firm charging full commissions, or a discount commission firm which provides no extra services.

CHOOSING THE BROKER FOR YOU

Entire volumes have been written on "Your broker and You." The brokerage relationship is not a subject to be defined in a few sentences. There are no hard and fast rules laid down for picking a broker and then living with him. You must expect a lot of trial and error. The chances of picking a broker with whom you are going to do business for many years are about one in a hundred. Change is no crime. You and your investment temperament will most likely change over the years. The broker, or his firm, may change. The business and economic cycles and the resulting securities markets will certainly change in time. And it is true that brokers function differently in different types of markets. There are aggressive brokers. And there are others who won't call you for three months at a time. Some brokers perform better in bull (up) markets and others better in bear (down) markets. Severe changes in the economic and stock market weather may leave you disenchanted with your broker's performance. In sum, selecting a broker is not easy and you should not expect it to be done as easily as spotting the most convenient newsstand for your morning newspaper.

Many brokers are chosen on the basis of friends' recommendations. And there is nothing wrong with that. It helps, of course, to know what your friend appreciates most in a broker. It will also help if you know what the market climate was during the period when your friend's broker was a "champ." A profitable experience with a broker may often result less from the broker's expertise as counselor or trader than from the fact that during the period of time in question the market engaged in a wild upturn which made successful trading no more difficult than shooting fish in a barrel.

Before you share your friend's enthusiasm for a broker you should make some attempt to understand just what sort of investment policy your friend follows. Is it conservative, long term? Or is he a "hot-shot" in-and-out-trader bent on scalping a few points on quick deals? If you are not of like mind, his broker may be all wrong for you. It goes without saying that the longer this particular broker has handled your friend's account—through up and down markets, through good and bad times for the economy, and so on—the more weight his recommendations should carry.

But in any event there is only one way to select a securities broker—sit down with him or her and talk out whatever program you have in mind. There must be personal contact. (And never—*never*—buy or sell any securities through an unknown broker whose only contact with you is his telephone call.)

It is absolutely imperative that you level with any prospective broker on your very first interview. If you are going to have only $500 or $1,000 a year to invest, by all means reveal it. To conceal that fact, to leave a false impression that your uncle left you independently wealthy and equipped to trade $10,000 blocks of stock on Mondays and Thursdays serves only to invite disillusionment later. There are brokers who do trade $10,000 and larger blocks not only on Mondays and Thursdays but every day and often more than once a day. Don't expect such a broker to welcome your account any more than you would expect Tiffany's to summon the general manager to handle your purchase of a $15 baby spoon. On the other hand, there are many brokerage houses which do a retail business and welcome small investment or trading accounts. These are not necessarily small firms. In fact, they are more likely to be the large houses which operate with the help of sophisticated and costly computer equipment.

The large trader will have no difficulty in signing up with a brokerage firm; the small, occasional investor may have to look a bit longer. It will help if you first accumulate sufficient funds for, say, a $1,000 investment. But even then don't hesitate to point out that future investments may be smaller in size and may be made at infrequent intervals—if that is the best you can hope to manage.

MUTUAL FUND INVESTMENT

You may find that a broker who feels his firm can't handle your small account directly may suggest you buy shares in one of the mutual funds his firm sells. Mutual funds (which will be discussed at far greater length later in this book) are, in truth, convenient vehicles for small investors. But if a brokerage firm suggests one or two funds to you, you may be sure there will be a sales commission running any-where up to 9% of the amount of money actually invested. (The number of mutual funds which do not charge a sales commission is growing. Therefore, these funds have no selling organization. You initiate the investment by approaching the fund—in reply to advertisements—or nothing happens.)

It is not the purpose of this book to argue the pros and cons of sales commissions on mutual funds. A well-managed successful fund will prove to be a desirable long-term investment (mutuals are not designed for short-term trading) whether it charges a sales commission or not. An investment in an unsuccessful non-commission ("no-load") fund will not be salvaged by the fact it does not charge a sales fee. (To repeat: mutual funds will be discussed at length in later chapters of this book. The chief purpose in mentioning them here is to alert you to the fact that a broker who feels the size of your account may not be worth his time will, in many cases, try to interest you in a mutual fund his firm is "pushing." This will assure him a continuing commission credit for as long as you continue buying the fund's shares, even long after he has forgotten you. There is nothing immoral in this. In any event, there is then no reason to accept specifically the fund he suggests and one his firm happens to sell. If you are going to invest in mutual funds then the entire field of hundreds of funds should be wide open to you and should merit your study before you make a selection. With a mutual fund investment you are in a whole new ball game and you must start your investigations anew.)

WHAT DOES YOUR BROKER HAVE TO KNOW?

If the brokerage firm is prepared to take your account, then you must be prepared to identify yourself fully to the broker with all the details his firm requires: resources, age, banking connections, references etc. Baring one's financial "soul" is often resisted by those cherishing their privacy. But it is also true that a dedicated broker can't do a personal job for you if he doesn't have some idea of the goals you are striving for and the risks you can reasonably undertake in achieving those goals. In fact, one could make a good case arguing that the broker who executes a securities purchase order for you *without* first spending some time getting to know you is not being considerate of your privacy. It is merely that he is far more interested in the commission than in you.

It is absolutely essential that you tell any broker with whom you discuss the setting up of an account exactly how active you intend to become. If you plan to buy twenty-five shares of A.T.&T. as an initial investment and then reinvest dividends plus another $200 or so in additional cash quarterly, tell him so. He then won't call you every few days in an attempt to interest you in what he believes is another good investment. And—by the same token—don't you call him every other afternoon and expect him to devote a half-hour or so gossiping with you about a quarter-point change in A.T.&T.'s price. To him time is money and he must expend that time where it will do his pocketbook the most good. There are no hard and fast rules on registered representatives' (customer's men's) compensation. But if you assume that about one-third of the commission winds up in his pay check, you will understand why a once-in-six-months total commission charge of $25 or $30 does not merit a half hour a few times a week with you.

Brokerage firms differ not only in the size but in the types of accounts they handle. Some concentrate on large corporate or bank accounts; others on individual portfolios. If the officer of some austere investment house tells you that he can't handle your account, don't take it personally. You've just wandered into the wrong shop—in the same sense that a company which erects skyscrapers would be the wrong place to shop for a 3-foot board you need as an additional closet shelf. Try another broker.

Once you've found a broker who suits you and is equipped to handle your level of investments, be prepared to "tell all" . . . and sign a lot of papers. You will be expected to give bank references and other financial data and to sign loan agreements, if you plan on using brokerage loans (margin) to finance part of your transactions. However, you are NOT expected to give any broker discretionary powers over your buying and selling. In fact, many brokerage firms discourage that and impose severe management limitations and supervision when permitting such accounts. In other words, the brokerage firm will want a lot of information—and is entitled to it. But that does not include waiving your right to decide what and when you want to buy or sell. The control is entirely yours, unless you borrow so heavily from the brokerage firm that it might have to sell you out to protect its loan in a falling market.

MARGIN LOANS

Loans with which to buy more securities than you can pay for are granted by brokerage firms under regulation by the Federal Reserve. Over the years, the amounts you could borrow have ranged from as high as 90% of the purchase price of the security to as low as zero—the latter at a time when the "Fed" felt market enthusiasm had risen beyond reasonable limits and therefore wanted to impose some restrictions. At a 50% level, regulations would permit you to put up, in your own funds, just half of the market value of your purchase—say, $2,000 for the purchase of 100 shares of stock selling at $40 a share. The broker lends you the other $2,000—and charges you interest for the loan. Margin loans are never cheap, since the broker obviously intends to make a profit on the money he borrows in order to make a margin loan available to you. The interest rate you pay—compounded monthly, incidentally—could be a point or two above the going rate for money. There is nothing automatic about an investor making money by buying securities "on margin." The interest rate he pays on the loan is bound to be more than the interest he can get on a bond or stock bought with borrowed money. And the monthly compounding doesn't help his cause, either.

Margin, however, is a strictly legal institution and, in times of rising markets, helps a speculator acquire more stock than he could pay for in full. As in all cases of borrowing, it helps you win "big" if the market is going with you. But it can induce severe headaches if you owe your broker money in a falling market. Should the price of the stock you bought on borrowed money fall dramatically, your broker is going to call on you for additional funds. (He never intended assuming any market risks when he advanced the money to you.) If you put more money into the account—sufficient to protect his loan—you are still in business. But if you have no funds with which to increase your equity, the broker will sell out your account, redeem his loan and give you whatever is left over—if anything.

If you use margin loans to help finance part of your securities purchases, do so sparingly—at least until you have had a year or so of market experience. And by all means keep your loans well under the permissible limit so that any sudden market decline will not bring you an "or else" telegram—the "or else" being translated into "we will be forced to sell out your account." The investor or speculator who allows market trends to govern his portfolio is asking for trouble.

A margin loan is only one of the factors which will exert influence on your relationship with your broker. Most brokers will adjust to the investment program you present in your first interview. If you make plain that you intend to buy—and hold, long term—a couple of thousand dollars' worth of stock whenever you accumulate that much money, you are not likely to be called every Monday and Thursday with trading suggestions. If, on the other hand, you imply that you have substantial funds which could be employed in more speculative ventures, the broker will try to oblige. It's up to you to set the course. It's your money and no one else has the right to dictate its use. However, it is up to you to be consistent. If you start off buying, and holding, conservative utility stocks and then decide to take a "flier" on a friend's tip in an electronics or oil drilling stock, you can't very well fault your broker for suggesting another, similar venture.

Brokers live by commissions and the vigor with which he or she pursues those fees is not much different from that of any other salesman. Some may push a bit—or enough to make you uncomfortable. When that happens, it may be time to part company and take your business elsewhere.

PARTING WITH YOUR BROKER

Much has been made of the increased incidence of divorce. But it's not likely that marital arrangements will ever be sundered in the same proportion that brokerage accounts are opened, closed or shifted.

There are scores of reasons for saying goodbye to a broker:

1. You've lost money consistently on his suggestions.
2. Your financial situation has changed. For example: you've risen to such a high income tax bracket that short-term trading profits are no longer attractive from an income tax point of view.
3. Your investment objectives have changed. You now want solid, generous, regular income rather than low-income speculations.

4. Your broker has become so successful as a trader with big accounts that he no longer has time to spend helping you make a fifty-share decision.
5. He has moved to another brokerage house which doesn't handle your kind of business.

And so forth—including all the personal factors which can enter into the relationship of any two people even when so touchy a product as money is concerned.

It will also help your relationship if you learn the exact meanings of brokerage terminology before you carelessly use such terms as "stop loss," "short sale," "buying power," "record date," etc. which you many have heard your friends use—often incorrectly. It may seem strange that many broker-client relationships involving thousands of dollars have foundered on the ill-will generated by an investor's misunderstanding of what he had actually asked his broker to do.

The brokerage business is a highly technical one, and the fact that large amounts of money are involved should stress the importance of knowing exactly what you mean when an order for securities is entered. If you don't know, ask. Your broker would prefer to explain what is going to happen before it happens than be faced with clearing up a misunderstanding after a lot of money has been committed. It has been not at all uncommon to find a client angrily leaving a brokerage firm because he felt he was entitled to a dividend which, in truth, wasn't owed to him at all but had to be paid to the previous owner of the stock. Again, the fact that you entered an order to buy fifty shares of General Motors this morning does not mean the stock will arrive tomorrow, or that when it does arrive it will carry the date of the purchase. Or that the broker is trying to put something over if he keeps your stock in his vaults (because you failed to tell him you wanted it delivered). It may seem embarrassing to you not to know the meaning of "free balances" or the effects of a 3-for-1 stock split. But it is far better to ask your broker to explain it than to mistakenly move your account out of an investment house which, in truth, is doing a good job for you.

COMMUNICATIONS

Some brokerage houses will almost flood you with advisory letters both on the general economy and international conditions as well as very specific opinions on the attractiveness of certain stocks. (Somehow Wall Street's letter-writers are very taciturn about stocks they don't like, or no longer like, or securities purchased in error.)

Some firms are "light" on communications, suggestions, advisories. And some—specifically the newer cut-rate commission houses—offer no such information at all. They are there merely to execute your "buy" or "sell" orders. That's why they can afford to cut commissions. Don't expect any hand-holding from them.

MORE THAN ONE BROKER?

A word about having securities accounts in more than one brokerage firm: it's perfectly O.K. But if you, understandably, don't tell one broker what you are doing in the other account, don't expect him to have a complete view of your investment or speculative situation. It will be up to you to see that you don't go overboard in any one direction.

Broker-customer relationships are not made in Heaven. You can move out of one brokerage house into another as simply as you give up one restaurant for another. And the only effort involved is giving your new broker the power to request the transfer of your previous account. You need not make any explanation personally. If the second brokerage firm has your authority to make the transfer, the first broker will get the message.

DISCOUNTERS

In an increasingly consumer-conscious world it was to be expected that the "I-can-get-it-for-you-wholesale" concept would also invade Wall Street. If motorists can save a few cents a gallon pumping gas themselves, if appliance buyers can do better by shopping in a modified warehouse, it follows that if you want to trim your brokerage requirements you should be able to cut costs by employing "bare-bones" brokerage, without frills.

For the first 179 years of its existence—1792 to April 5, 1971—all N. Y. Stock Exchange members observed minimum commission rates, below which they would not do business with the public. During the next four years, under pressure from the Securities and Exchange Commission, these restrictions were watered down, principally for large trades—$300,000, $500,000, etc.—although minimum fees were still fixed on small deals.

On May 1, 1975 (in many Wall Street quarters still referred to as "Mayday" . . . the international distress signal), all commission regulations were abandoned. Clients negotiated charges with brokerage firms according to the amount of business they gave the firm. Discount brokerage houses appeared on the scene and proliferated.

Can you save money using discounters? Absolutely. There are no fixed-rate schedules, of course, for either the old-line traditional brokerage firms or for the new discounters. But it is generally estimated that discount commissions are somewhere between 40 and 70% below "regular" fees.

Should you use discounters? That depends upon what you want in the way of services and "tender, loving, care."

- If you want advice on what stocks to buy or sell;
- If you want a broker to collect some data for you on some obscure company mentioned at a cocktail party;

- If you want your broker to call you at frequent intervals, or if you want to call him at frequent intervals to chat about the market in general or to seek assurance and comfort about some stock which is worrying you—

then you don't want a discount broker.

If you are habitually tardy about paying for your stock purchases, or less than punctual about turning in stock you have sold . . . the discount broker won't want you.

He is in business mainly to execute buy and sell orders . . . period—although some do maintain accounts, extend margin, will collect and disburse dividends for securities left in the account.

However, if you have already decided that you want to buy some A.T.&T. or U.S. Steel—and want no pro or con debate—there's no reason not to use a "discount broker." Of course you must check with him as to his exchange membership, or the exchange firm through which he clears his transactions; his membership in the National Association of Securities Dealers; his protection of your account via the Securities Investor Protection Corp. (SIPC) and—via friends— his record on execution of buy and sell securities orders.

Since savings on commissions is the name of the game, it wouldn't hurt, also, to check around among several discounters to see where you can get the best deal. Although they generally do not maintain as many offices as the old-line brokerage firms, their toll-free "800" telephone numbers make them readily accessible.

5

What Sort of Job for Your Investable Dollar

Every young person starting out on his or her life's work of earning a living is faced with a basic decision:

Do I want to work for someone else—for wages? Or—

Do I want to go into business myself, be prepared to take the good with the bad, hope to hit the jackpot?

You, the investor, must make the same decision about where to put your investable dollars. They can't be ignored. (Remember this old bedroom farce scene? The enraged husband demands of a strange man hiding in his wife's clothes closet, "What are you doing here?" To which comes the timid reply, "Well, everybody has to be somewhere!")

Every dollar you have left over after setting up an insurance program, building a savings account, and meeting your current living expenses, is investable money and you must put it somewhere, even if you do nothing more than hide it in an empty coffee tin, or under your mattress (where it does nothing for you). There is NO way to ignore these investable dollars. But the question still arises: "Where should they be employed, invested . . . for what purpose?"

THE CHOICE IS YOURS

Are you going to lend them out to work for wages?

Are you going to use them to set you up in business—in a corner grocery, in a gas station, or in a small electronics or plastics plant of your own—or as part owner of an already established business, large or small?

These are the two main divisions of investing:

1. lending dollars out to work, in return for payment of interest and for repayment of the original sum at a fixed maturity date; or
2. using them to buy all or part of a business in which you hope for current income and/or eventual capital gain.

If, in lending your dollars out for "wages" you exercise care in selecting a quality borrower-employer; "what you see is what you get." You may lend them as mortgage money to a house buyer (either directly, or indirectly via an account in a savings bank or savings and loan); or to the U.S. Government itself via EE bonds or Treasury bills, notes or bonds; or, for example, to American Telephone & Telegraph or General Motors or to any other corporation via purchase of its bonds and debentures. You are then promised in return 1) a stated amount of interest, and 2) return of your capital at a certain date . . . period.

If, instead, you decide to use these dollars to set up your own business—or to buy a piece of a business already set up by acquiring its stock—you are in a totally different ball game. You are going into business . . . and that could mean results ranging from zero (bankruptcy and the complete, 100%, loss of your investment) all the way to riches beyond the dreams of avarice.

Only you can make the choice between "I don't want

any business headaches. Just pay me my money's wages" and "My money will never work for anyone else."

The first choice, investments in bonds or debentures or savings accounts, requires that you think in terms of dollars. How the borrower fares, and the trend of his profits, are of importance to you only insofar as his hard times may halt the payment of interest or impair his ability to repay your money. Anything above that will not redound to your benefit. The second alternative (common stocks) requires that you forsake dollars entirely and place your hopes for any current income and future gain on the prospering of the property acquired. Some investors favor the former; some the latter. Both may have perfectly sound reasons for their choices.

Neither course is 100% secure, free of risk. There are advantages and disadvantages in putting your money to work at either job because:

- dollars kept as dollars have over the years suffered a decline in buying power which, after all, is what we use dollars for; and
- property value can change daily—up or down—as can its ability to earn income and profit for you.

These problems and hazards are stressed here, and will be stressed time and again in this book because, contrary to the "how-to-double-your-money-overnight" boys, this writer is firmly convinced that there is no one royal road to riches and that every road carries its "traffic" dangers.

So, first: How do you keep your dollars working as dollars?

INVESTING DOLLARS AS DOLLARS

You invest them as dollars. You don't exchange them for property of any kind, be it farm land, rare books, common shares, apartment houses, or diamonds. You invest them as dollars, by lending them as exactly so many dollars.

Example: You turn over $2,000 to a savings bank or savings and loan association. That's investing, even though you don't go near the stock exchange or the commodities or real estate markets. You are saying, in effect, that here is $2,000 for use until I want it back—as $2,000, no more, no less. In the meantime, pay me 5½% interest for its use (or 6½% if you use it for 18 months or 7¾% or 8½% if you use it for 6 years). That's a $2,000 investment at 5½% (or more) ...). period. Assuming the savings institution is a sound one and insured by a Federal agency or a strong state insurance institution you can be quite certain that you'll get back current interest, plus your $2,000—no more, no less—at the end of the contract. You've handed over your money to be put out to any work the savings institution selects: personal loans, or home building advances, or long-term mortgages, or any other business the institution decides is good business. You don't really care which, because all you are interested in is getting the promised interest and your money back at the end of the investment period.

Or you may lend your money to the U.S. Government by buying savings bonds, or Treasury bonds or short-term Treasury bills. Same deal: your dollars are guaranteed by the Government and you earn interest while they are working for the government. There is NO chance ... NO chance whatsoever—that your $2,000 (or $4,000) will become $4,000 (or $16,000). They won't even become $2,001 or $4,001. You are not looking for capital gains. You want the "wages" your money has been promised; and you want your money back when the "deal" ends.

Or you may decide to send your money out to work for your state, or your city, or town government. Or for the county school or water district, or for the state turnpike authority, or the bridge authority. Or you might lend your money to a state or local authority which will use the money to build a factory to be made available, on favorable terms, to a business which the state or town hopes to lure away from some other section of the country. The interest on these bonds, labeled "municipal bonds" as a class, is exempt from Federal income taxes and, in many instances, from state and local income taxes in the issuing state as well. And, if such tax exemption is important to you, you must consider them as another type of job for your money. (They will be discussed in much more detail later.)

Or you can lend your dollars to a corporation, most often in $1,000 denominations. Telephone companies issue bonds (a form of mortgage) to borrow money to install new lines and new equipment. Electric and gas utilities raise money this way to buy new turbines and transmission lines. Railroads borrow to buy new freight and passenger cars. Automobile companies borrow to buy new presses and cylinderboring machinery. Food companies borrow your money this way to build new warehouses. The number of jobs for your money as loans to corporations is virtually limitless. (And these, too, will be discussed later.)

In all these cases, let me repeat, you are lending dollars. If you lend $5,000 to a county school district, you are NOT hoping to get $10,000 in return—and there is no way you will get it. You want your same $5,000 back and you want to collect interest for your working dollars' wages every six months. (Practically all bonds pay interest semi-annually.) And since this money was lent to a state or municipality or local governmental authority, you demand, and get, exemption from Federal income taxes and, in most cases, from whatever income taxes are levied by the issuing state or local governments. In return for this tax shelter you accept lower interest from these "municipal" bonds than you would expect to get from the same quality corporate bonds (which pay interest which is fully taxable). The value of this tax exemption will be discussed fully in later chapters. Suffice it to say here that income tax shelter is not cost-free. Nothing is free in Wall Street.

If you give your dollars a conservative job in any of the above securities—that is, if you restrict your dollars' employment to top quality employers (the U.S. Government and the Treasury are, of course, tops, followed by insured savings, followed by top-rated "municipal" bonds and top quality corporate borrowers) you are making "risk-less" or low-risk dollar investments. Your dollars are secure. Your stated interest is secure. Your chances of getting your dollars back at the end of the contract are good.

So where's the fly in the ointment? Why, then, should you consider any other form of investment? Because—

The dollars you are assured of getting back may not be (in recent history definitely have *not* been) as "good" as the dollars you invested at the beginning of the deal.

You lent $2,000; you will get back $2,000 (assuming, of course, that you restrict your lending to good quality institutions).

But the $2,000 you lent ten or twelve years ago could then have been exchanged for a comfortable automobile. The $2,000 you now get back may not cover half the purchase price of the equivalent model today. And all the while you were receiving $120 a year interest, milk was going from 30 to 50 cents a quart and a head of lettuce from 29 to 89 cents. So even though you had no qualms about the safety of your $2,000, you were paying for that safety. Each interest check bought a little less than the one received six months previously, and the $2,000 you get back at the end of the loan period will undoubtedly buy less than the $2,000 could have bought when you invested it.

Do these facts rule out savings bonds, savings accounts, Treasury, municipal or corporate bonds as places of employment for your dollars ... or for SOME of your dollars? Absolutely not! Certain dollars, like certain people, do their best work at certain tasks, employed by others at fixed wages. All investable dollars, like all individuals, are not the same. They all can't, or shouldn't, go into business for themselves. Later chapters will discuss the precise business employment opportunities for certain dollars, and their owners. For now the important message is that there are many ways of investing dollars. And investing some of them as dollars, for a fixed wage, may be their best employment.

INVESTING DOLLARS AS PROPERTY

The second main avenue of employment for your surplus dollars is NOT as dollars, but as property, as a business. You don't lend your dollars to government units or agencies, or to auto builders or electric utilities. Instead, you send your dollars out into the business world by converting them into property, assets, holdings. You don't lend the $2,000, but convert it into ownership of some antiques, or rare books, or real estate, or into shares of a factory or a railroad, or a supermarket chain, and then take your chances on that property or business prospering. You no longer have a savings passbook or a mortgage bond or debenture with $2,000 stamped on it. You don't have anything with a specific dollar price printed on it.

You may have, instead, title to a vacant lot ... or to a collection of rare stamps, or to a first edition of Walt Whitman's "Leaves of Grass," or to an antique chest of drawers. Or you may have a certificate for fifty shares of a corporation which makes automobiles, or corn flakes, or men's shoes; or of a utility which services a state with electricity, or of a railroad which transports freight across a section of the country. You no longer have the $2,000. You have translated it into ownership of some property—into a portion of a business—which, you hope, will prove a wise investment and return to you, at some future date, not the original $2,000, but $4,000, or $40,000 or whatever dreams of riches you can manage. You may expect some current income from the investment (as dividends from the stock, for example). Or you may be prepared to forego all current income and, moreover, to lay out additional money to insure and safekeep the rare stamps or books or antique chest, hoping that your ultimate reward will not only compensate you for the original investment but for the loss of income from that money over the years you held it.

The point to be kept constantly in mind is that by investing in this property you have cut yourself loose from that $2,000 figure. You're out—you hope—to "break the bank," make a big "score." The property you acquired in exchange for your money has no fixed price tag (even the "par" figure printed on the front of common stock certificates has no meaning). You've sent your $2,000 ship out on the uncharted sea and hope it will return laden with all sorts of riches. You have, in fact, gone into business—either as a manager or as a "boss" ... or even (as in the case of corporate shares) as a silent partner.

6

Putting Your Money
to Work
As Dollars—for Wages

The first of the two employment (investment) alternatives outlined in the previous chapter ... lending out your
dollars on some form of mortgage (and not to acquire equity,
ownership, in a business) is the oldest form of investing. In
fact, it is the subject of Biblical law.

When your grandfather talked of a "gilt-edged investment" he most likely meant bonds—not common shares. He
and his generation, as did generations before him, prized
bonds issued by governments, by leading steel and railroad
and machinery (etc.) corporations. He wanted no part of a
common share which could go up or down on the exchange,
which could raise, or lower, or even omit dividends. No sir,
he wanted the security of a mortgage on a steel plant, or on
some lathes, or locomotives. If any trouble developed, he
could seize the physical property in satisfaction of his loan.
He felt so secure with his investment that he was willing, for
many years, to accept annual returns of 3, 4 and 5% for his
money even though common stocks were yielding half again
as much or more.

That was years ago.

Bonds today remain, of course, the basic ingredient of
many an investment portfolio as well as, in most years, the
fundamental security issued by corporations to raise money

for new plant or equipment or expansion. The same preferred status of the security which endeared it to past investors still attracts many types of investors today even though the higher interest rates now offered can run only neck-and-neck in the race with inflation.

At the end of World War II, corporations with prime (AAA) credit ratings were able to borrow money for 2¾ and 3% annual interest. A decade later they had to pay around 4%. In 1967, when the Bureau of Labor Statistics last readjusted its cost of living index back to a base of 100, top-rated corporations were paying 5% and a shade higher to raise money. But by the time that "1967-equals-100" cost of living index touched 200, in 1978, the same companies were paying around 9½%. The man who had earned $125 a week at the end of WWII was by now demanding, and getting, a wage of better than $300. So the investor who was lending his dollars out on mortgages was demanding and getting twice as much interest. It figures.

Inflation is no longer a strange phenomenon either to workers or to investors. Nor has government indicated any willingness to "bite the bullet" in coming to grips with it. Nevertheless, billions of dollars' worth of corporate, Federal, and state government bonds—all with definite dollar price tags—are issued and grabbed up every year. Why?

Every investment medium has its uses, is needed by someone. Otherwise it would not be offered.

WHY A "DOLLAR" INVESTMENT?

If you were the investment officer of an insurance company which has committed itself to pay out a certain number of dollars to a widow, or a certain number of dollars monthly to annuitants, you could be quite comfortable investing your funds in dollar-fixed bonds and debentures and mortgages. After all, you receive dollars in premiums, you invest dollars and you are obliged to pay out a fixed number of dollars—irrespective of their purchasing power. Why take undue chances with common shares when all you are committed to is the repayment of dollars?

BONDS

Again, you are an elderly retiree living on Social Security, company pension, plus the income from a $50,000 nest egg. If you are the nervous sort, knowing that the loss of any or all of the $50,000 would be irreplaceable, you'd think twice before you passed up a steady, "safe" income of, say, $4,500 a year from a bond, for the sake of a lesser amount from a common stock which offers some future hope of price appreciation you may never live to collect. That's the "A bird in hand is worth *more* than two in the bush" investment formula.

Again, you are a fretful person who is thrown into a tizzy by the thought that your 100 shares of stock may be worth $4,300 one day and only $3,950 three days later. You don't like the stock market, you fear it, you "want no part of it." You are perfectly happy with a high grade $4,000 bond which pays you $160 every six months and whose market price fluctuations you can largely ignore. Is the purchasing power of your semi-annual interest check being hurt by inflation? Yes. But you'd rather pass up a few luxuries than take chances with equities in the hope they will maintain your purchasing power. Statistics advanced by common stock enthusiasts, you admit, are interesting—but you aren't a statistic and you feel you don't want to live by them. So you stay with bonds and peace of mind and trim your budget if and as required. And you may be 100% correct. An investment which does not provide peace of mind along with dollar income is not the "perfect" investment.

Bond prices, of course, do fluctuate . . . but usually within narrow limits. Their price movements are rarely included in the feverish broadcasts which "cover" the common share market. It's pretty difficult to attract any mass interest with the announcement that "XYZ's 8⅞% debentures of 1998 soared a quarter point," or "plummeted ⅜ths."

Bond prices, especially the prices of high quality bonds (and the average small investor has no business even considering a bond rated below the single A level), are most affected by the money market which is the market in which interest rates are set.

If ten-year U.S. Treasury bonds which yielded 8½% a few months ago are now yielding 9.1% you can be sure that other high quality bonds will have to yield about the same or suffer no market demand. Since the amount of interest to be paid on a bond is fixed when the bond is issued—and stays that way until maturity—it is obvious that the only way a bond with an 8% coupon can compete in a 9% interest rate market is to drop to a price which, when divided into 8%, will work out to a return of around 9% on the money invested.

No one is going to pay face value ($1,000) for a bond issued in 1975 and set up to pay $80 a year interest until the year 2005, if that same $1,000 can today buy a bond paying $90 a year interest. So the 8% bond will most likely decline in price to a yield of 8% ($890 per $1,000 certificate) at which level it returns nearly 9% ($80 divided by $890).

Of course, if you had an 8% bond you bought some years ago and interest rates were now to fall to 7%, your old bond would start to climb in value. In a financial climate in which $1,000 earns only $70 a year, a bond pledged to pay $80 a year for, say, the next 19 years is easily worth more than $1,000 . . . perhaps as much as $1,100 or $1,140.

However—and this constitutes the great attraction bonds hold for many non-professional investors—price fluctuations play an extremely small role in bond investing. It's more like a marriage—you stay with it for as long as the benefits live up to the original booking. In other words, if you bought a bond for the $80 or $90 or $95 a year that each $1,000 invested would produce—and the bond continued to deliver that income (which practically all quality bonds would do year after year)—you would stay with it.

Certainly there is little room for the average small investor to trade around in. If a rise in money rates has depressed your bond's market price—not its interest payments—there isn't much point in your selling the bond in order to buy one with a higher coupon because the prices of both bonds will be adjusted to the current interest rate market. It would be like stepping from one of those moving sidewalks to another, going in the same direction and at the same speed. Bonds are not trading vehicles for the small investor. They are bought and held for their income and for the promise that the face value will be paid at maturity—if the corporation doesn't pay them off earlier.

You will find anti- and pro-bond discussions on many levels of expertise. You'll find people who "won't touch 'em" and others who swear by them as the ideal, worry-free investment. As is true of feminine beauty, much lies in the eye of the beholder. In other words, suit yourself. But take time to understand what you are buying and—whenever in doubt—stick to high quality . . . as discussed in the next chapter.

7

How Good is a Bond?

This morning, JKL Corp. is offering to the investing public, through a syndicate of brokers and investment bankers, a $75 million issue of bonds carrying a 9.75% interest coupon and maturing in the year 2010. How good is that mortgage bond, or debenture? If you put down $5,000 for five bonds what are your chances of getting a check for $243.75 every six months and the $5,000 principal back in 2010 (or your heirs' chances of getting it back if you don't live to collect it)?

ABC Corp. is a legal entity and most likely has a perpetual charter. But it is made up of and run by very mortal people who over the next few decades will have to face up to many, many different—and stormy—business climates. Can anyone guarantee that the bond will pay off? Obviously, no. (Only issues of the U.S. Government—the fate of which is "non-negotiable"—can be considered "safe," 100% safe.)

Since you don't know JKL Corp. (you may not even be clear about what business it is in), what help, what guidelines can you depend upon for making a decision to invest your $5,000? One source, of course, is your broker. He may know the company—or his research department does. If his firm is in the underwriting syndicate, or in the retail selling group offering the bonds, one of his partners or bond analysts most likely attended a "due diligence" meeting at which the issuing corporation described its operations and finances and answered Wall Streeters' questions.

RATINGS

But even your broker looks to a higher authority—the rating agencies, the watchdogs of the securities markets who unilaterally assign a quality credit rating to practically every bond offered to the public.

It would be difficult to overestimate the importance of these investment grade ratings. There is nothing in the consumer market to compare with their power. It is said that drama critics can make or break a new play—although stage historians can come up with examples proving the contrary. Many new automobile models are severely criticized in the motor magazines, but sell anyway.

But a bond rating by any (or all) of the three rating agencies—Moody's, Standard & Poor's, Fitch—is rarely disputed effectively. If they announce that a forthcoming bond issue deserves, for example, an "AA" rating, the issuing corporation will have to pay, say, 9¾% interest in order to raise the money. If they judge the issue as worth "AAA" (tops), then the cost may be reduced to 9¼%. If they rate it only "BB," the interest coupon might well have to be 10¾ or 11%.

Ratings start, at the top, with AAA (in the case of Fitch and Standard & Poor's) or Aaa (in the case of Moody's) and then go down to AA (or Aa); A; BBB (or Baa); BB; B; CCC; CC,C; and finally D.

Qualifications among the different agencies may differ slightly, but in all cases, the higher the rating the higher the chances (the rating agencies believe) that you will continue to get your interest for the lifetime of the bond and that you will get your capital back at maturity, if the bond is not retired earlier.

For example, Standard & Poor's says the AAA rating is

assigned to bonds with "an extremely strong capacity to pay interest and repay principal."

AA bonds "have a very strong capacity to pay interest and repay principal and differ from the highest rated issues only in small degree."

A bonds have "a strong capacity to pay interest and repay principal, although they are somewhat more susceptible to the adverse effects of changes in circumstances and economic conditions than bonds in the higher categories."

BBB bonds are regarded as having "an adequate capacity to pay interest and repay principal. Whereas they normally exhibit adequate protection parameters, adverse economic conditions or changing circumstances are more likely to lead to a weakened capacity to pay interest and repay principal."

Ratings of BB, B, CCC and CC are regarded as "predominantly speculative with respect to capacity to pay interest and repay principal" ... BB indicates the lowest degree of speculation (in this group) and CC the highest degree of speculation. "While such bonds will likely have some quality and protective characteristics, these are outweighed by large uncertainties or major risk exposure to adverse conditions."

C rating is reserved for income bonds on which no interest is being paid regularly.

D rated bonds are in default, and payment of interest and/or repayment of principal is in arrears.

In addition to these ten classifications there are variations in each group by the use of a + (plus) or − (minus). As you can see these are extremely fine gradations. And even though such ratings are attempts to judge a corporation's ability to pay off a bond issue 25 or 30 years hence, the rating agencies have an excellent record. In any event, even if you think this system smacks of dictatorship, better pay attention. It's the only guide you have; it's the one guide the general bond market observes; and these classifications are followed by various state banking supervisors in determining which bonds banks may hold and which they may not. As far as the bond market is concerned, this 3-judge "court" is the law, and you ignore its pronouncements at your peril.

8

Bond Yields—
Which One Counts?

A bond is, by nature, a complicated financial instrument. Unlike a common share of XYZ Corp. (which is like every other common share of XYZ Corp.), an XYZ Corp. bond requires precise identification as to its credit rating, its series, coupon rate, maturity, sinking fund, redemption provisions, etc.

And if you want to arrive at just what that bond is yielding you may have to take no less than three different percentages into consideration. (Again, far different from figuring the return on a common share which may pay, for example, the same 75 cents quarterly to every one of the millions of shares of that corporation held by investors.)

The title of a bond will always carry this sort of designation:

"American Telephone & Telegraph 7% debentures due 2/15/2001."

That much would pinpoint the security you hold.

But it fails completely in denoting the return on your investment.

The 7% means only that a $1,000 bond of this series pays $70 a year ($35 every Feb. 15 and August 15). But that 7% is only one interest return designation and, as a matter of fact, is no measure of what the bond is doing for you in today's market. What you want to know is: "What will this bond return me as a percentage of the money I now invest in it?"

What you want to know is: "current yield," and "yield to maturity"—in other words, "what is the bond doing for me now?" and "what will be my total reward at maturity?"

Or, if you want to put the question another way, it would be: "O.K., $70 a year is $70 a year. But what's the yield on the money invested?"

If the bond were to sell exactly at 100% of face value ($1,000) the 7% coupon would mean a 7% current yield and 7% yield to maturity. But bonds don't often sell exactly at 100% of face value (par) and certainly not bonds carrying a 7% coupon at a time when money is earning 9½ and 10%. Let's assume that on the day you go bond shopping this particular A.T.&T. debenture is selling at 81½ which translates into $815 per $1,000 debenture certificate. The 7% coupon ($70 annual interest payment) is not affected by market price. That coupon was attached to the bond when it was issued and will stay with it (unless the issue is redeemed earlier) until Feb. 15, 2001 when the $500 million issue matures and will be paid off.

But the return on your investment IS affected.

When you acquire the right to $70 annual interest for the payment of $815, the return on your investment is NOT 7% but 8.58895705% (which is the number which will show up on your hand computer when you divide 70 by 815). That is the "current" yield on your investment . . . what you are getting NOW for investing $815 or any multiples thereof.

But there is another factor to be figured into the yield formula:

This bond, for which you now pay $815, will be paid off in 2001 (if not before) at $1,000. Even if that redemption doesn't take place until 2001—let's say 21 years hence—you can still figure on a $185 price appreciation, or profit, per $1,000 certificate. So that comes to $8.81 a year, an annual "bonus" in addition to the regular $70 annual income.

The value of that bonus depends in some measure on your income tax bracket since it will be taxable only as a long-term capital gain—which is far less costly to you, tax-wise, than getting it as current, semi-annual interest. But putting aside the wide range of personal income tax brackets, the bond books will tell you that a 7% bond selling at 81½ and due in 21 years provides a total reward, a "yield to maturity" of 8.93%. So—what is that 7% coupon bond yielding you as a "modern day" investment? Not 7%. But approximately 8.59% currently . . . on a cash, NOW, basis; or 8.93% on a total (yield to maturity) reward basis.

The yield to maturity is usually *more* than the current yield and, of course, the coupon rate figure, when a bond is selling *below* 100—the price at which it will be redeemed at maturity.

The yield to maturity is usually *less* than the current yield which is less than the coupon interest rate when a bond sells at a premium; that is, *above* 100. Suppose you were attracted to a bond because it carries a coupon of 10½ ($105 annual interest) due in the year 2004 and selling at 102¾ ($1,027.50 per $1,000 certificate). Your current yield would not be 10½% but 10.22% (105 divided by 1027.50) and your yield to maturity in, say, 25 years when the bond will be paid off at $1,000, would be 10.19—the reduction from 10½% coupon and 10.22% current yield due to the fact that the premium you now pay ($27.50 per $1,000 bond) is going to be lost over the next 25 years.

To sum up:

The coupon rate is stamped on the bond and remains unchanged for its lifetime. A 7% coupon bond pays $70 a year interest for every $1,000 bond . . . period.

The current yield—which is a realistic approach to what the bond brings you in current income—depends upon the market price of the bond, since the yield is obtained by dividing the coupon rate by the market price. This also means that while the coupon rate is fixed, the current yield will change with every market price change. Thus, if you own a 7% coupon bond selling at 81½, your current yield is 8.59%. If the bond rises in price to 90, your yield on that investment declines to 7.78%. If the bond drops in price to 78, your current yield rises to 8.97%. It is, therefore, important to consider the current market price of a bond in addition to its coupon rate when evaluating the job it is doing as a provider of current income. It is not enough to say simply that a bond brings in $70 cash from every $1,000 certificate. To get a true picture of what your money is earning for you, the coupon payment, in dollars, must be divided by the current market price in dollars.

The total reward in bond investing, which includes the yield to maturity, is also a significant figure but not so immediate in its importance for those who turn to bonds for current, semi-annual, income. A high quality bond bought at a discount can be relied on to return face value at maturity, and—in general—to appreciate gradually over the years as that maturity date approaches. But it doesn't become money which can be spent at the supermarket until the bond is sold by you, or paid off by the corporation.

Incidentally, the yield to maturity is a complicated calculation. A rough formula is to add the total discount, divided by the number of years to maturity, to the current yield. Thus, a 7% coupon bond selling at 80 ($800) with 10 years to maturity would have a current yield of 8.75% (70 divided by 800) *plus* the $20 annual price appreciation ($200 discount divided by 10) or 11¼%.

This, it should be stressed, is an approximation because the $800 market price is here used as a constant whereas in the real Wall Street it would rise steadily as maturity day approached. However it will do as an approximation. For the exact figure, to two decimal places, consult any bond guide—which is what the pros do.

The important thing to remember when considering bonds for income (which is about the only reason the average non-professional investor should ever consider bonds) is that to arrive at the true reward for investing in a bond, market price is as important as the coupon price. In fact, in recent years bond market price tables have included current yields based on *that day's* quotation. If we ever again encounter a declining money market (easing interest rates) and you are fortunate to have bought a 7% bond at 75 which is once more selling at 100 you are no longer earning 9.33% on your investment but only 7%. It is on the basis of 7%—not 9.33%—that you will decide whether to stay with the bond, or move on to something else.

Conversely (and more realistically in recent years), if you bought a 7% bond when they were being offered at 100 and find it now selling at 75, you should realize that the bond is returning you 9.33% in current yield on the money now invested and that 9.33, and NOT 7%, is your figure for deciding whether to make a change.

Bonds, it should be repeated, are primarily an income investment. Anger over a decline from your purchase price or elation over a market gain have absolutely nothing to do with whether the bond should be retained in an income portfolio. The question of how well a bond is doing its job in providing current income can be answered only by dividing the annual dividend by the market price of the bond—and comparing that answer with what is being offered elsewhere. And if you are also considering its long-term rewards, you must add in the scheduled price appreciation par at maturity (or subtract any premium paid above par).

9

Discount Bonds—
Are They a Bargain?

At frequent intervals, Wall Street's merchandisers (registered "reps," analysts, researchers, market letter writers) rediscover and exult over "discount bonds." These suddenly become the "only way to go" in almost the same sense that couturiers suddenly rediscover the chic of the pillbox hat or spike heel or, in the case of the male, of the vested suit and the rounded shirt collar.

As with the apparel cycles, the discount bond is nothing new, it has been there all the time. It is not a particular brand of bond. It is not a hidden source of capital gains. It need not be more nor less speculative than any other bond. (Discount bonds are rated all the way from AAA to D.) It is not a bargain basement offering.

It is merely a bond that is trading at less than 100 ... period.

And—as far as the conservative investor is concerned—it is trading at less than 100 because its coupon rate is below current money market interest levels. (There are, of course, many bonds quoted at 22, or 67 or 55 primarily because the issuing corporations are on the brink of bankruptcy ... or have already gone over the edge. Or because they were issued by the Imperial Russian Government or by some other contemporary foreign government which displays no interest in servicing the bond or redeeming it. But there is no way the non-professional bond buyer can get any clues as to their prospects from a book. So we must ignore them.)

The average investor who ventures into discount bonds, as was stressed earlier, would do well to restrict his investments to quality bonds rated BBB or better. Higher risk bonds represent "long shots" which cannot be fully and individually discussed in a general approach to bond investing.

What is more important is that there is no need for the average investor to assume these higher risks. Discount bonds rated AAA or AA are just as plentiful as AAA or AA rated bonds selling at par or better. In fact, they were issued by the same corporations and carry the same backing. To repeat: they are selling at discount prices merely—and only—because their coupon rate, set years ago, is below the levels currently obtainable from newly issued bonds with the same quality rating. Examples:

All American Telephone & Telegraph debentures are rated AAA quality. Back in 1956, when lent money commanded much lower interest rates, the corporation sold a $250 million bond issue, due in 1990, carrying an interest coupon of 3⅞%, which means the company pledged itself to pay $38.75 interest annually on each $1,000 debenture certificate. That was good enough—for 1956. But not for more modern times when investors are demanding and getting anywhere from 9 to 10% a year for lending their money. So, even though the 3⅞ bond continues to carry the AAA rating, it has dropped in price to around 66½, because no one wants to pay 100 ($1,000 face value) for a bond which yields only $38.75 a year income, when that same $1,000 can earn around $950 from a bank certificate, or another high grade A.T.&T. or other bond.

Why would some bond investor now pay 66½ ($665 per $1,000 certificate)? Because he is assured by A.T.&T. of getting the $38.75 annually (bond payouts do NOT change) PLUS $335 in appreciation when the bond is paid off in 1990 at $1,000 face value. These figures translate into a current yield of 5.82% ($38.75 divided by 66½)—low by current standards—but enriched by that $335 cash profit he can count on in 1990, and this capital gain is taxed at much lower income tax levels. The current return of 5.82% plus the $335 capital gain on his investment of $665 works out to a "yield to maturity" of 9.03%. Certainly 9.03% is below what was obtainable elsewhere at the moment, but what is also important is that the $335 will be taxed at lower capital gains tax levels. So—depending upon the investor's individual tax bracket, that ultimate 9.03% reward may be far more profitable than a fully taxable current income of 9½%.

There are other reasons for preferring the discount bond over the Telephone Company's more recently issued bonds yielding 9%.

Let us assume that the investor who buys these 3⅞% bonds is a well-employed person in a high income tax bracket who plans on retiring in 1989. He already has a large portfolio of equities and wants to hedge his "bets" on the future by putting some money into bonds. But he doesn't want 9 or 9½% current income from his money because he is already in a high income tax bracket. All he wants to do is "hide" or "sterilize" his money until he retires, accepting a small, taxable, income now, but locking in a substantial capital of which only 40% will be taxed at what he can now expect will be a much lower overall income tax bracket.

By avoiding his present high tax on income and by assuming his lower tax bracket in retirement, the investor would benefit more from the 9.03% "yield to maturity" of the discount than by accepting 9½% today—subject to full tax.

The discount bond is, therefore, a device for delaying a goodly portion of the total reward of bond investment. The buyer chooses a lower-than-market current return *PLUS* the ultimate price rise to par rather than a current high return, taxable fully as income, with no built-in appreciation to par at maturity.

It is a serious mistake for the non-professional investor to seize upon a discount bond only because, as so many proclaim with "Eureka"-like enthusiasm, it assures him a market price profit. The profit, 'tis true, is there. *But*—it is not "for free." It comes out of your current income. The investor in the A.T.&T. 3⅞% of '90 will get that profit in 1990 because he isn't getting it today. The discount bond *IS* a perfectly sound method for delaying part of one's bond investment rewards. It may even be a profitable method (depending upon when you want your reward and how it is to be taxed). But it is *NOT* a "free lunch." What you get both now and ultimately is figured into today's prices to three decimal places.

It is also a handy device for assuring the cash return of the face value of a bond in almost any year it best suits your book. Bonds issued years ago with much lower than current interest rate coupons come due in every year.

If today you buy a General Motors Acceptance Corp. 4⅞% bond (rated AA) due Dec. 1, 1987 and pay 74½ ($745) for it you can safely count on getting $48.75 interest every year and the face value ($1,000) in cash on Dec. 1, 1987. If you want your money back Nov. 1, 1985 buy the 4½s of 1985; if you'll need the money Oct. 1, 1994, buy the 7¾% issue due then. All sell below par, pay—currently—less than you can get elsewhere, but carry with them a "locked-in" capital gain.

10

Municipal Bonds

The Constitution of the United States set forth in 1789 that the Federal Government may not tax income from bonds issued by states, cities, towns, or their various authorities. And, vice versa, the states, cities, towns may not impose an income tax on bonds issued by the Federal Government. (Interest on Treasury bills, notes, bonds and the popularly held EE and HH bonds—savings bonds—is not subject to any state or local income taxes.)

However, since the Federal income tax is by far the heaviest burden, the widest investor attention is generally directed to bonds sheltered from the IRS. These are called "municipal" bonds or "tax-exempt" bonds and in recent years have soared in popularity.

In fact, it's a safe bet that many modest income folks have allowed their distaste for paying Federal income taxes to result in lower net income merely for the sake of thumbing their noses at tax collectors. The situation is a prime example of the old adage of "cutting off your nose to spite your face." How so?

IS IT WORTH IT?

The tax exemption offered by a municipal bond is *NOT* an unmixed blessing, nor is it free. You pay for it. So the prudent investor—rather than being swayed by his hatred of tax collectors—will first take the time to figure out whether the income taxes he saves by investing in "municipals" compensates for the reduced income he accepts from them. In other words, is he saving $100 in income taxes but losing $125 in net, bottom line, income?

Since—as has been noted here before, and is still true—Wall Street gives away nothing, the benefit of tax exemption must be paid for. And the only one who can determine that cost—and whether it is worthwhile—is you (or your accountant) since your particular tax bracket is the No. 1 factor in deciding whether you should venture into tax-exempt (municipal) bonds.

Suppose you are faced with the prospect of investing $10,000 for income. Your choice lies between a corporation bond paying 9½% (or a U.S. Treasury bond paying 9%) or a tax-exempt municipal bond issued by your state, city or county school district, paying 6½%, and exempt from both Federal and your state's income taxes. Which is the best deal for you—that is, you personally—$950 a year from the corporate bond, subject to Federal, state (and city?) income taxes, or $900 from the Treasury bond, subject only to Federal income taxes, or $650 from the school bond exempt from all taxes?

Obviously, the only way you can pick the best deal is to figure how much will be left to you, net, after you pay all level income taxes on the $950 corporate income; Federal taxes only on the $900 from the Treasury bond. If the resulting figures come out to less than $650, then—obviously—the municipal is the better income buy. But if, for example, the $950 corporate income was reduced by only $100 in total taxes, and the $900 Treasury bond income reduced only by $75 in federal taxes, then there is obviously no sense in your accepting only $650 from the school bond.

The point to be stressed here is that a dollar of taxable income is *NOT* the same to ALL people, thanks to the wide range of income taxes. And tax exemption means one thing to an investor whose income tax bracket runs as high as 50%, and something entirely different to the investor who pays only 14% income taxes, or, perhaps in retirement, doesn't pay any income taxes at all.

If you live in Florida, you aren't likely to need a snow shovel. If you are in a low income tax bracket, immunity from income taxes may prove an expensive luxury. There is no way to determine whether you want tax-free income until you figure out how much of each taxed income dollar you, personally and individually, retain after paying income taxes.

If there is a net saving, if the lower income from a municipal bond is more than the net, after-tax, income from a similar quality taxable security, then consider municipal bonds.

TYPES

There are various types of municipal bonds, differentiated mainly by the government or authority which issues them.

A "general obligation" bond is one backed by the full taxing and revenue-raising power of the state, city or town which issued it. It is generally considered the safest category since the money needed to pay its semi-annual interest, as well as to repay the face amount at maturity, can be raised by all the taxing powers that government has at its command.

Other types of bonds are those issued by a state or local government for a specific purpose. In some cases, the money required to service interest costs and to repay the investor at maturity can come only from fees or special taxes levied to support the specific project built by the proceeds of the bond issue.

For example: a bond issue sold to finance the building of a toll road may be backed by the income from tolls paid by users of that highway or turnpike or thruway. If enough motorists and truckers don't use the road, there may not be enough money coming in to pay the full amount of interest. There have been several examples of special highway bonds unable to meet their debt obligations. In other cases, the bond-issuing government may offer a "moral" commitment to service the bond issue if the project revenues are insufficient. But that "moral" obligation may prove an "iffy" guaranty. Again, some school bonds which are backed by school taxes on real estate may also have an additional defense line in the form of state support should the local county or school district tax not suffice.

In recent years, there has been a steady stream of so-called "industrial" municipal bonds . . . bonds issued by a city or town to raise money to build a plant with which the local government hopes to lure industry from other areas with an offer of low rent or tax concessions. Although the bond is called a "municipal" and its interest enjoys immunity from Federal income taxes and, in most cases, state and local income taxes as well, it is backed ONLY by the rental paid for the plant by the lured industry. If the attracted business doesn't prove successful or if it quits, there may be no income with which to pay bond interest or principal at maturity. Such a revenue "municipal" stands entirely on its own feet and is not backed by the taxing power of the government which issued it.

You may buy an individual, already outstanding, municipal bond through a brokerage firm which either specializes in tax-exempt securities, or, in the case of a large, general securities firm, has a municipal bond "desk" or department. You will pay a commission for the transaction, either in the form of a scheduled buying fee, or in the form of a price "mark-up" by the broker. In other words, he may act as your agent and charge you, say, a $50 or $60 fee to buy the bonds (and this item will appear on your statement) or he may sell you the bonds from his own inventory, marking up his cost by about the same amount. Your bill shows only the price to you. This is no different from the profit you pay a grocer when you buy a pound of coffee from his shelves.

You may buy new municipal bond issues directly from the underwriting banks and brokers on the day of issue advertised in the newspapers. You pay the issue price only; the issuer pays selling expenses.

You may buy shares of a mutual fund which invests and trades solely in tax-exempt bonds, in exactly the same way that most mutual funds invest mainly in aviation stocks, or energy stocks, or general growth stocks, or general income stocks—or combinations of any or all of these. The mutual fund may or may not charge you a buying commission, but does charge an ongoing annual management fee.

You may buy a participation in a municipal bond unit trust fund from a group of brokerage firms which have amassed a large block of municipal bonds and which then offer you participation. You will pay a buying commission at time of purchase, but no further management fees since, once put together, the fund is no longer managed; that is, there is normally no trading in an attempt to take market profits, as is the case with the municipal bond fund.

Your investment in tax-exempts—whether it involves the purchase of a particular bond issued by the school district of Home County, or shares in a mutual fund buying and selling tax-exempt bonds, or in a fixed portfolio unit trust— may be terminated at will and, of course, at the then-current market prices.

You sell any individual bonds through a broker. You get your money out of the municipal mutual by telling the fund you want to redeem your shares. You get your money out of the fixed unit trust by telling the broker through whom you bought the participation. In every case, what you get back may be more or less than what you originally invested, depending upon what has happened to interest rates since you first made the investment. If interest rates have since risen, you can count on sustaining a loss. If interest rates have dropped, your bond, or shares, or participation will most likely return more than you paid originally.

The first instance—where you buy and accept delivery of the actual bond—is the only one which gives you a negotiable security with all the safekeeping requirements that entails. Most municipal bonds are issued in bearer form, which means possession is 10/10ths of the law. It would not be an exaggeration to say that any unscrupulous person who finds your $10,000 municipal bond on the sidewalk, or filches it from your desk drawer would have less problem disposing of it than he would have in passing a $10,000 bill.

Your investment in a municipal bond mutual fund or in a municipal unit trust does not give you any *specific* bonds since your investment represents a pro rata share in all securities held by the mutual or unit trust. You get shares or a certificate registered in your name. While these, too, should be put away safely they are far better protected from theft or loss.

Not only is the interest paid by municipal bonds exempt from income taxes, but, in the case of mutual fund or unit trust investment, you may also protect the money that interest earns. You merely tell the fund or the trust to reinvest the interest payments due you in additional shares or portions of the fund or trust. Example: You own $10,000 worth of county school bonds which pay you $650 a year interest. You collect the interest, deposit it in the savings bank and earn 6% on that money, or $39 a year (and the next year 6% on $689, etc.). That $39 is now reported by the bank to IRS. It is taxable income. But if you tell the fund or trust to reinvest that $650 for you, it is used to accumulate additional tax-exempt investment so that none of the proceeds of that $10,000 investment is subject to income taxes.

If your tax bracket warrants it, municipal bonds are a handy device to thus shelter earnings during all the years you are building a nest egg to meet education costs, to bolster retirement income, or for any other purpose. And since municipal bonds—as do all bonds—have fixed maturity dates, one can buy them precisely to suit one's own specific needs.

Let's assume you are building toward retirement which, you expect, will come in 6 years. You are now in a 45% income tax bracket (plus state income taxes). Tax protection is needed. But you won't need it in retirement when you will want maximum income from whatever money you have accumulated and your tax bracket will be much lower.

Solution: If you buy the individual bond directly, you restrict your shopping to an issue which will be paid off in 6 years. You thus assure yourself of getting back the face amount of the bond in cash just when you may want to turn to high-yielding (even though taxable) securities. Since we're talking here, of course, of high-quality, practically-no-risk-municipals, you now can rest assured that you will have $5,000 or $10,000 or $50,000—exactly—on hand when you retire. And the interest the bonds earned for you in the intervening years was not taxable income at a time your employment put you in a high tax bracket.

If, by any chance, you should now pay less than par for bonds due at retirement, select a bond which will be paid off in the first year you are completely retired—have no taxable income—because the rise in price to par is considered a capital gain and subject to capital gains taxes. (If you now pay a premium for a bond, the loss of that premium when the bond is paid off at face value is *NOT* a tax deduction.)

If you now invest in a municipal bond mutual fund or in a municipal unit trust, you may cash in at any time at the then-current market price.

It should be obvious that with the complex problems of 1) just what and who stands behind the bond, and 2) exactly what and how much income taxes it helps you avoid, the municipal bond—as attractive as it certainly is for those in high income tax brackets—is not a simple, all-purpose investment instrument. Nor is it one that the ordinary investor can analyze by himself. For that matter, you can't even expect every securities broker to be expert in this specific field.

If you feel municipal bonds can be a "plus" in your tax bracket then it will be worth your while to talk to reputable brokerage firms which specialize in this area. Finally, as an investor seeking shelter from income taxes, keep these cardinal points in mind:

- All municipal bonds are free from Federal income taxes.
- A few municipal bonds are exempt from states' and cities' income taxes.
- Most municipal bonds are exempt from state and local income taxes in the state in which they were issued. (Some are not. Be sure to check.)
- Most municipal bonds issued in one state do not provide state and city exemption for residents of another state.
- Tax exemption is *NOT* free.
- And—as is the case with all bonds—there are no bargains.

11

Putting Your Money
to Work
In Common Stocks—Speculation

If you hope to increase your assets, build substantial capital, become a millionaire via securities, most likely you'll have to do it with common shares, or with securities which give you a claim on common shares: convertible debentures, convertible preferreds, options or warrants.

All these offer you a chance of hitting the "jackpot."

All of them involve varying amounts of risk.

There is *no* riskless speculation or investment anywhere in the world. And, the greater the opportunity for gain, the greater the risk.

"Sure thing" speculations or investments exist only in the promotional material offered by securities touts. In the real world of speculation or investment, the "big killings" are won by those who assume the big risks.

Since common shares are perpetual and, theoretically, have no price ceiling, they can offer the most "action."

There are perhaps 50,000 corporations in the U.S. alone with stock in the hands of speculators and investors—negotiable stock which you may sell five minutes after you acquire it, or which you may hold all your lifetime and then pass on to your children and grandchildren. In addition, there are the shares of corporations based in Great Britain, France, Italy, West Germany, Switzerland, Rhodesia, South Africa, Japan and numerous other capitalist countries. All their shares (or American Depositary Receipts for these shares—ADRs) may also be owned by U.S. investors.

There is no shortage of equities for your money, whether you intend to speculate in them for a quick profit, or whether you acquire them for long-term investment.

But before you can make any intelligent decision you must first decide whether the stock you are considering is to be used as a gambling chip, or as a long-term investment for income and/or profit.

"Buying low" and "selling high" is the obvious approach to making money in the stock market, but the time you plan to allot to this profit-making formula is an all-important factor in selecting the stock in the first place. It makes as much difference as there is between playing a slot machine and sculpting in marble.

It is also essential that the investor who considers turning to the stock market make no moral or ethical pre-judgments. He must keep firmly in mind his goal: to make money—by speculation or by conservative long-term investing—but either way at a profit.

Although many of us go through life without ever pulling the handle of a "one-armed bandit," it's a fair guess that the vast majority of those who decide for the first time to put money into stocks find themselves trading for fast, small profits. It figures.

The first-time stock buyer is generally young, optimistic and cocky by definition, earning a modest or better salary, working hard to establish himself in his job and—most important of all—most likely attracted to the stock market initially during a period of booming prices. So he takes a chance with 100 shares of a $25 stock and (it could happen!) sees his stock rise to $30.50 in two weeks ... a net profit—

after buying and selling commissions—of more money than he probably earns in a 40-hour week.

He grabs the profit and urges the broker to go out and do it again. This beats working for a living.

Important questions: Should I sell? Is this stock still cheap at 30½ because of favorable events which occurred since I bought at 25? Is the company and its industry in an upswing which can carry the stock much higher? Is the general market still in the early part of a bull cycle? And so on. But to ask this young novice investor to stop and consider these points would as unrealistic as expecting a five-year-old to put his dime in the bank rather than to invest it in bubble gum cum-baseball-card.

Taking fast—even though small—trading profits is the very essence of stock market euphoria. There is nothing to compare with it except, perhaps, young love. The world suddenly becomes a rosy place and mundane concerns fade away or are blocked out by the new infatuation.

TRADING STOCKS FOR PROFIT

This is, perhaps, a fitting spot to take up the matter of trading stocks for profit. It is, in fact, what the vast majority of people think of when they say "stock market." It is not an unreasonable attitude. After all, millions upon millions of shares are traded daily. Prices fluctuate every day. Why grub for a living at a machine or desk or store counter when a few points' rise could reward you with a week's wages with no more effort involved than one "buy" phone call and, later, one "sell" phone call? Trading is legal. It's even respectable. And it did make millionaires of Ben Smith and Bernard Baruch and Mike Meehan—and many others. The fact that it also ruined millions of less fortunate speculators doesn't necessarily apply to you. You may think.

During three decades of "covering" Wall Street daily—

bankers, brokers, securities exchanges—I kept an informal "poll" going. The poll asked only one question: "How many small, novice, public stock traders ever wind up with a profit? Ever take money home?"

Asking the same question of brokerage firm partners, "registered representatives" ("customers' men"), back-office help, margin clerks, I came away with a consensus of, "Oh, about 1%." And I believe it, despite the fact that my best senior-partner contact in a prestigious Stock Exchange-member firm was hesitant to endorse that figure. He thought, "It's a bit on the high side."

However, I am just as much convinced that 99% of first-time stock buyers are nevertheless tempted to grab small fast profits and becomes short-term, in-and-out traders. And that most of them do trade feverishly until they either 1) lose their money, or 2) learn to curb their greed, and either quit stocks entirely or "retire" to long-term investment programs.

I firmly believe that it is a lesson which must—and should—be learned first hand by the vast majority of those who send their money out to work in common stocks. Some—the fortunate ones—learn it early; others go on for years (or until their money runs out) vainly pursuing Lady Luck in exactly the same fashion that they would at the race track or at the Las Vegas gaming tables. And the ultimate results are often the same, regardless of whether the player was trying for the "big score" or for more modest rewards.

A non-financial newspaper colleague once begged me to take his $100 fortune and use it to pick up a modest daily gain. He argued: "You're constantly watching stocks some of which move 2 and 3 points a day. All I want is $10 profit a day." (We were then working a 50-hour week for $55.) It seemed reasonable enough to him. But I never undertook the chore.

I'm still not quite sure what it does take to become a successful stock market speculator. I'm not even certain that the same requirements would apply in all kinds of stock markets.

But I am quite sure it does require steady nerves, a strong defense against panic, an ability to hold to an unpopular, contrary position, substantial amounts of money, dedication to the game, an independent analytical mind, and a large ego, among other things.

Bernard Baruch, who knew first-hand, once repeated to me: "If a stock speculator is the seventh son of a seventh son, he has a Chinaman's chance."

Speculators are most likely to eschew fundamental corporate and economic factors in favor of short-term clues as to a stock's price direction. Neither must they give much thought to inherent or basic quality of the security. Shares of companies in trouble, or just emerging from bankruptcy, or being gobbled up by other companies, or now undergoing violent managerial changes may all be grist for the speculator's mill. One speculator made it a habit to buy the stocks of companies which had just forced out old management and brought in new. He argued that the new bosses would do everything they could—including doctoring figures—to justify their taking over the reins. Others concentrated on stocks of companies forced to report a large interim loss and, even, omission of dividends. This they labeled "trading on the bad news" on the premise that things couldn't get much worse. (Sometimes they did.)

The speculator is far less concerned with quality than with market-making statistics. He is far more interested in trading volume as correlated with price direction, odd-lot transactions, short-selling, "insider" dealings. In other words, he pays a great deal of attention to what he believes the stock market itself is trying to tell him about a gamble. Every speculator—or even long-term investor, for that matter—will tell you that he or she never ignores what the "stock market is telling us" . . . they will never "fight" the market. But it is quite common to get different interpretations of what the market is telling. And there's the rub. Neither the "story" nor the interpretation thereof is unanimously accepted as meaning the same thing. This is the problem which makes for stock markets just as it does for horse races. If there were no such problem there would be only one horse in a race and only one stock traded on the exchange that day.

You will find library shelves filled, chock-a-block, with books on trading. And if you are venturing into the stock market for the first time, by all means look into them. Some are serious treatises on trading techniques and you may find them fascinating, at least in theory. The long tables of trading volume, price trends (vs. general market movements), industry groupings, etc. are, in fact, scholarly attempts to find the philosopher's stone of speculation—a sure-fire formula for scoring steady, even though small, profits. Some even work for a time, and in certain market climates.

You will unfortunately also find a host of "if you only had" books: "If you had bought ABC at 2 and sold out at 26, and then bought DEF at 6 and sold out at 18, and then put your profits into GHI at 4 and sold out at 39, you would now have X billion dollars." Or—

"If you had only bought insurance (or bowling, or drug, or computer) stocks; or had put your money into convertible debentures. . . ." These books devote entire chapters to history. The figures, of course, are correct, historically correct, but the chances of their happening again in exactly the same order are nil. If you like fiction, read 'em. If you are looking for financial data, ignore 'em.

I grant that "how to" books and articles may have their value in helping to cultivate prize rose-bushes or paper bedrooms or train pets. But whether they will help a so-so tennis player to become a Jimmy Connors or a self-educated fiddler, an Isaac Stern, is extremely doubtful. Genius isn't spawned in books—even this one.

Successful speculation is every bit as much a factor of character, ego, inbred skills, native intelligence as is the ability to star at the Metropolitan Opera, or to come through with a home run in a crucial World Series game. Admittedly, there are many quality levels of opera singing and batting performance at the plate. But I've found over the years that there is little evidence of sustained *modest* success in stock speculation. You either win big, or bust out.

But, to repeat, nothing said here can or should discourage any first-time stock buyer from seeking fast profits. So if you are going into the market for the first time and have the itch, don't be ashamed of it. It's as normal as trying to kiss the girl on your first date.

Nor is it important which "system" you elect to follow. If it works, stick with it—or at least for as long as it returns profits or shows more gains than losses. The important point is to be able to realize the futility of speculating if you are not cut out for it, and to quit while you still have some money left to invest for your future.

12

Putting Your Money to Work in Common Stocks—Investment

Long-term investing—which is where most non-professional stock buyers wind up—is, naturally, a more sedate game. Once the novice stock buyer discovers that even a $5 stock may fall to $2, or that stock splits and increased dividends of higher-priced stocks are no guaranty of profit (in fact, no protection against loss) he is likely to opt for a quieter life. (Rabelais: "The devil was sick, the devil a monk would be.")

He is now far more amenable to the proposition that the stock market is *not* his private money-making machine ... that the beast can bite, and does—that Wall Street may be a one-way street for vehicular traffic but not for stock prices.

He now decides either to sit with his losses in hope of an eventual recovery and a chance to get out "even" (often an erroneous and treacherous financial policy); or

He salvages what cash he can from his initial mistakes and vows to "turn sober." Which, incidentally, is the only intelligent thing he can do.

This means he will now put aside "hot tips," rumors of mergers, stock splits, dividend increases, or takeovers, and concentrate on the fundamentals which are part of the stock market's price-making exercises. In effect, he no longer puts down a $2 bet on a horse and hopes for a favorable result in a few minutes. He is now resigned to taking the longer view; to spending more time studying the fundamentals of a security and measuring the results over months and years.

WHAT KIND OF INVESTMENT FOR YOU?

A long-term approach to investing in common shares also requires that you do a little soul-searching in order to decide just what you want your money to do for you.

A common share investment may provide both current income and hope of long-term price appreciation. It will help you to make a decision if you regard income and growth potential as positioned at opposite ends of a yardstick. At one end, income; at the other, growth. In recent years, most generous income has generally been available from the shares of utility companies in older metropolitan centers. Reason: room for growth is considered limited in some cities which have been losing population. So capital had to be attracted by high dividend payout. Yields of 9% and better have not been uncommon.

At the other end of the yardstick ... growth potential. Dividend yields are generally low (or non-existent) as in the case of newly developing data and word processing companies. Reason: a company enjoying rapid growth of sales and product line will often reinvest all its earnings in research and development, in marketing, in staff expansion, and therefore, will have little left to distribute to shareholders (who are often content to take their ultimate reward in long-term capital gains rather than in current, fully-taxable dividends.

Once you forsake short-term, in-and-out trading speculation for long-term investing, you must take a position somewhere on this income-growth yardstick and decide just how far you will move from one end toward the other to take your investment posture.

If you are a young investor, well-employed and already in a high tax bracket, you might well decide that you'll go all the way to the growth end of the scale, even if it means receiving only low dividends or no dividends at all. You seek out either a small, emerging company which—as far as you can determine—is doing a good job in data processing, or waste management, or drug chemicals, or energy development. Or you admit you can't do the necessary analysis and, therefore, decide to put your money to work with the old established leaders in these and other growth-oriented areas: the IBMs, the Kodaks, the DuPonts, the Exxons, etc.

In between these extremes you will find literally thousands of companies whose shares show some growth and pay modest to higher dividends. Every investor is not only free to pick his own spot on this growth-income scale but, in fact, must decide for himself. Do you want zero dividends with 100% growth potential? Will you be content to accept a dividend return of 4% plus good prospects of growth? Or do you feel you must have a 6% return, even if it means less hope of capital gain over the years? Or do you want a 9% return and even more on your money, even if it means growth potential is very low, or nil? Every stockbroker can help you take the stand which will make you most comfortable.

UTILITIES

If you decide you are going to put your money to work bringing in high-dividend income you may logically turn to utility company shares. Utilities, of course, enjoy monopolies in their areas. But that doesn't mean all utility companies are efficiently run, or—more important—that all areas of the nation are growing in importance, in population, or in industrial power use. Nor does it mean that all state public utility regulatory commissions are equally pro-business in their rate-making attitudes.

RAILROADS

Railroads have for generations enjoyed basic industrial strength, but that doesn't mean all of them are equally successful. In fact, the bankruptcy rate in railroads has been unusually high. So before you put your money to work in rail shares you must decide: (1) is the company plagued by high-cost commuter lines? (2) does it enjoy long-distance freight hauling? (3) is it basically a coal road (and will coal one day take its rightful place in our energy picture?)

PETROLEUM

Petroleum companies have long been successful dividend producers. But will the international companies survive the rampant nationalism abroad? Or would it be best to keep your money at work in a domestic company?

AUTOMOBILE MANUFACTURERS

Will auto company profits (and dividends) be curtailed by the trend toward compacts? Can Detroit successfully counter the rise in imports?

WASTE MANAGEMENT

Waste management looms larger and larger every year. But which companies will prove the General Motors or the A.T.&T. of the industry in 1995, and beyond?

If all this sounds overwhelmingly confusing to a person who must devote his or her working day to efforts far removed from Wall Street, let me assure you that you won't lack help in shifting dollars to common shares. There are scores, hundreds, of advisory services running all the way from tipster sheets to august organizations which counsel banks, mutual funds, religious, educational and charitable funds running into the hundreds of millions of dollars. You may obtain these advisories annually for anywhere from a few dollars to thousands. If you set up an account at any large brokerage house with a reputation for analysis you will be flooded with advice on which industries—and which individual companies in those industries—are most promising, if you only had enough money to follow all these suggestions you wouldn't need any help at all.

Whether you pay a lot of money for advice, or find it stuffed in your mail box by brokerage firms, or glean it from financial publications, it will help if you keep firmly in mind that it was prepared by mortals. And when Alexander Pope wrote, "To err is human...," he predated Wall Street.

There can be no hard and fast rules regarding the value of financial advice other than the common sense approach: If it works, follow it ... follow it as long as it keeps working. When resulting losses exceed gains, turn to another advisor.

LOSSES INEVITABLE

In this connection, it must be said right here that an investment loss is NOT solid evidence of malfeasance on the part of the broker or advisor. No one set out to do you in. Losses are as much a part of investing as rain is of weather. There is no known history of a financial venture or a financier which does not include a record of losses ... large, small, frequent or infrequent ... but always *losses.*

The measure of financial success is not the absence of losses, but the predominance of gains over losses. If you're right 60% of the time you can be proud of your financial acumen. If you are right 75% of the time you may regard yourself as near-genius.

SPREADING THE RISK

There are two schools of thought—diametrically opposed, as it happens—about success in long-term conservative investing.

One holds that diversification reduces the risk of heavy loss. If you spread your money over twenty-five different common stock issues, it is not likely you will suffer a 100% loss of your capital, since bankruptcy of all twenty-five companies is hardly probable. Fair enough. It is also true, of course, that it is unlikely all twenty-five will double in price to give you a 100% gain on your investment. As in most cases in Wall Street, you've made a trade-off—agreeing to temper your profit hopes in exchange for reducing your risk and increasing the comfort which derives from conservatism.

Opponents of the diversification school, however, are quick to point out that if you have to pick twenty-five different issues it is quite likely you will have less than complete knowledge of any of their businesses. Their feeling is that specialization in investment is like specialization in anything else: you must have the ability to make yourself expert in that one field and the time to keep yourself on top of all developments. If you can pass these two tests there is ample evidence that profit opportunities will exceed those resulting from a scattergun approach.

All generalizations made about investing are most likely false—including this one. But for what it's worth, I think Wall Street history will show that more money has been made by individuals with limited portfolios than with investable sums of money spread over three or four dozen different stock issues.

For many years one of my best Wall Street sources—although the most limited in industrial scope—was a quiet gentleman in a small but highly regarded banking house who spent his professional lifetime studying only two industries: oil and railroads. If you asked him what he thought of General

Motors, or A.T.&T., or Eli Lilly he would confess complete ignorance of even the market price of these shares. *But* he had at his fingertips the precise figures describing an oil company's latest well and how much grain a western railroad had carried last month. And when he died, I discovered he had made enough money to endow a small college.

Spreading the risk—within reason—is a sound rule in investing, but one which can become counterproductive if over-utilized. (To add to the confusion on this subject, there is another Wall Street motto: "Put all your eggs in one basket and then watch that basket!") How can a man or woman who works forty hours a week in an office or garage or hospital "watch" a corporation with headquarters 1,800 miles away and with branch offices and operations in fourteen different countries around the globe? How does he analyze quarterly sales and revenues and net profit reports and get behind the highly legalistic footnotes in the annual statement? There is nothing in this book which will prepare you or even promise to prepare you for all that accounting, or give you all the economic, financial and legal knowledge necessary to keep your fingers on the pulse of a giant corporation. And, if it is any comfort to you, there are few volumes which can. In the recent collapse of a giant insurance and finance company, a lone insurance analyst spotted fraud and got his clients out; the rest of Wall Street didn't realize what was going on until their investments in the company had collapsed.

PICKING A STOCK

What can our "average" investor do to solve the ever-present problem of, "How do I pick a stock, or stocks, for my investable money?" "How can I employ my funds for the best results?" What methods are available for the non-professional Wall Streeter, for the investor who makes his money far from the Stock ticker and the securities analyst's reference library?

Method A—

You turn your money over to an advisor—a professional investment counselor or advisory service or the trust department of a bank or a mutual fund. You pay a fee for the service which may or may not prove to be worth the money.

Method B—

You rely on your broker for long-term investment or for trading buy and sell recommendations, which come free of charge and which may or may not turn out to be bargains.

Method C—

You study all the market letters you can get your hands on issued by your broker and by any other firm. You read the financial magazines, try to evaluate the scores of stocks you will find recommended therein. You subscribe to stock market services and try to separate the winners from the losers which must, of necessity, be included in any wideband attempt to forecast the stock market's movement.

Method D—

You study the published statistics on various corporations and make your choices on the basis of whether you feel the corporation is doing better or worse. The problem here, of course, is that the statistics you read in the daily newspapers and in the weekly financial magazines constitute history. They tell you what has happened. And from that you must attempt to chart a future course.

Method E—

You devote hours to charting the market actions of the stock in which you are interested in an attempt to wrest from these figures portents of things to come. This, of course, involves absorbing the many facets of technical charting: price action; volume; relation of the stock to others in its industry; relation of the stock to the market in general; cyclical theory;

visual interpretations of curves and lines formed by the stock's market price action; little or no reference to such fundamentals as earnings, balance sheet, management changes, or operation profit margins. It is not an easy course. I knew one small successful brokerage firm which employed a full-time expert merely to chart the market actions of two dozen stocks in which the "boss" was interested. Evidently, he was worth his keep, because the boss retired a millionaire.

Method F—

You play your own hunches. These can range all the way from deciding that if you buy a sufficiently wide band of solar energy stocks you're bound to hit something, to playing the most active list in the daily stock market reports, to buying only those stocks which appeared among the new highs that day. Or you can restrict yourself to basic industries—steel, rails, oils. How about considering only stocks which begin, for example, with the word "General"? (This last was success-fully used by one investor who later admitted that the basic financial reasoning behind his regimen was the fact that he found it inconvenient to peruse the entire stock market list every morning in a crowded subway car and, therefore, nar-rowed the field by folding his newspaper to the "General" column and concentrating on that.)

Whichever method or methods you decide to adopt, be assured there are no guaranties of success.

One warning cannot be stressed too often: Success in in-vesting cannot be achieved by formula nor even by any one set of rules. The stock market is a complex organism, react-ing to both internal and external influences. Sometimes one set of forces is far more effective than the other. In a time of violent and exciting international affairs the stock market may disregard many domestic influences, including even the technical factors which often rule price activity on the floor of the exchanges. When foreign or domestic economic de-velopments are of minor importance, internal factors play the dominating role in determining stock prices: volume, breadth of the market, odd lot transactions, short positions, interest rates. If you hope to make some profit out of market movements you must be prepared to evaluate all the influences which are factored into the price structure. What's more, you must be able to decide which set of factors has the greatest weight this week.

There is no question that this entire problem of putting money into stocks for investment is highly complex and risky. Anyone who tells you anything different is either coloring the truth or, in many cases, is drawing his inferences from too narrow a base, too brief an encounter with the problems of investing. One swallow doesn't make a summer, and any blowhard at a cocktail party who insists on telling you at great length how he bought A.T.&T. when it was down around the 40s obviously doesn't know enough Wall Street history to realize that Telephone also had many buyers at 75 who "didn't get even," even after fifteen years.

However, the weight of history is on the side of long-term advances in common shares. In his annual stock almanacs, Yale Hirsch, a long-time observer of the stock market, proves quite conclusively that a 25-year portfolio experience—regardless of what year you started the portfolio—would wind up with a plus for the investor . . . a plus large enough, incidentally, to offset inflation. Further, his statistics show that ever since 1870, a span of more than a century, there has been a 72% probability of gain in any five-year investment period, 87% in a ten-year period, 90% in a fifteen-year hold and 90% in a twenty-year length portfolio. These are based on the Dow Jones averages and therefore presuppose investment in "solid" stocks. It does not preclude losses in any one D-J issue or, of course, in any of the thousands of issues of varying quality which are not included in the veteran average. But it does lend weight to the argument that, over the long term, common shares can cope.

13
Preferred Stock

Between the dollar-fixed position of the bond and debenture and the all-out equity common share, which carries no dollar promises whatsoever, stands the corporate preferred share. Disdained by many as a hybrid—as "neither flesh nor fowl nor good red herring," it has been hailed by some as the answer to an investor's prayer. As usual, the truth lies somewhere in between. It's a cinch that there wouldn't be any preferreds around if corporations couldn't use them to diversify their capitalization and if investors didn't want them.

CHARACTERISTICS

The prime characteristics of a preferred:

It is an equity security, representing part ownership of a company's net worth after all bonds, debentures and all other debt are subtracted, but before any consideration is given to the common shares. Preferreds, thus, sit "below" debt at the corporate capital table, but "above" the common.

A preferred's dividend (with only a handful of exemptions) is fixed. For example, it is listed in the stock tables as a

"$4 preferred" which means it will pay $4 annually, usually in four $1 quarterly distributions. Or it may be listed as a 5% (or 7½ or 8% preferred) which means it will pay 5 or 7½ or 8% of its par value in annual dividends. A $50 par 8% preferred share would pay $4 a year in dividends ($1 every quarter). A preferred share's par value *is* important (unlike a common share's, which is merely a bookkeeping figure), because the preferred dividend may be expressed as a percentage of that par value.

A preferred share may be called in (paid off and retired) by the company at certain pre-fixed prices and under certain conditions. So, if you pay more than that call price, you may lose on a redemption. It is not permanent capital in the same sense that common shares are perpetual securities.

The dividend on a preferred may be omitted if the board of directors wishes (which would, of course, also halt dividends on the common stock), but in most cases preferreds issued in recent decades have a "cumulative" provision which requires that any unpaid preferred dividends accumulate as arrears and are a claim against the company which must be satisfied before dividends may be resumed on the common.

Some preferreds acquire voting rights if enough dividends are omitted.

Some preferreds are convertible into common shares at the investor's option. (See Chapter on Convertibles.)

A handful of preferreds, issued many years ago, are "participating" preferreds, which means that in times of high corporate prosperity—prosperity sufficient to raise the common dividend above a certain level—preferred shareholders participate via increased dividends.

Finally, the word "preferred" has only relative significance and should not be taken as a blanket endorsement of any stock's investment value. It is "preferred" to the common, but that doesn't mean that ALL preferreds are "preferred" investments. Company A's preferred shares may represent a far riskier investment than Company B's common. And Company D's preferred may be far superior to Company E's first mortgage bond. There have been preferreds which have failed to pay dividends over a stretch of years. And there are preferreds of some quality companies paying a $5 dividend protected by earnings per share of $125 or more. You can't buy a security merely by its title.

14

Convertibles—
The Two-Lane Road to Riches?

Convertible automobiles have been phased out by Detroit. But convertible securities—long an ingredient of investment portfolios—still enjoy occasionally sudden spurts of public popularity—like discotheques, skate boards, hula hoops and yo-yo tops.

As is the case with most recurring securities fads, much of the temporary excitement over convertibles is generated by a few unusual and rare profits scored in the medium. They are then promptly enlarged upon in one of those "if you only hadda" financial "pop" books which list all the ways you could have made a million: in convertibles, or in insurance stocks, or in bowling stocks or in photo-copy stocks. More often than not these books appear when that particular "craze" has just about run its course . . . when convertibles or insurance stocks have been bid up to far beyond their intrinsic value or potential, or when hurriedly-built bowling alleys are being abandoned, or when the rush to sell options has so narrowed premiums that the income is often not worth the risk or the commissions.

MORAL: if you suddenly become aware of a flood of books pushing convertibles (or options, or computer data stocks, or boating stocks) as a sure-fire avenue to wealth, *be careful!* The cycle which brought them on has most likely run its course. Specifically, the last books I recall which advocated convertibles and life insurance stocks as foolproof came out just as these two types of securities went into a long decline.

Convertibles have been around a long time and interest in them has waxed and waned. Don't let anyone try to convince you that they've just been discovered. They often appear in large numbers during periods of mergers, takeovers and other corporate maneuvers, when they are used as "sweeteners" to put through a deal. ("Instead of cash money, we'll give you a convertible debenture [or a preferred] which you can turn in for stock when we become a huge success.")

They are also popular vehicles for raising money for new, unestablished companies which feel they have to offer more than mere interest to attract senior capital.

FORMS

Convertibles are available mainly in one of two forms—preferreds or debentures (described in Chapters 13 and 7, respectively). They possess all the characteristics of ordinary, or "straight" or non-convertible issues.

The preferred is entitled to a fixed dividend, has a stated par value, may be retired by the company at a predetermined price under certain conditions, may or may not have a vote in corporate affairs, has claims on earnings and on dividends before those held by the common, and must be satisfied before the common in case of a sale of the company, liquidation, or bankruptcy.

But, in addition, the convertible preferred holder has the privilege of converting his investment into a predetermined number of common shares of the company (or, in a few cases, into the shares of a subsidiary or affiliated company) any time he pleases.

The convertible debenture enjoys all the privileges and

is subject to the redemption clauses of a "straight," non-convertible debenture plus, again, the privilege of being exchanged for a certain number of common shares whenever the debenture holder believes it would be to his advantage.

To summarize—a convertible debenture and a convertible preferred have all the advantages of a non-convertible debenture and a non-convertible preferred PLUS the right to be exchanged for common stock. It's a preferred when you want it to be a preferred (and a debenture when you want it to be a debenture) or it's common stock when you want common.

This double life has for years had a special appeal for many investors. In certain stages of the common stock market, preferreds and debentures previously bought at good prices can work out extremely well. At other times they seem to suffer both from their own weaknesses as well as from common stock market troubles. A time of rising interest rates coinciding with a declining common stock market, for example, would (and has) proven especially rough on convertibles because their fixed yields are no longer as attractive as they were when money was cheaper; and—since the common share prices are lower—the privilege of converting to common is far less a price support factor.

Nevertheless, convertibles are among the groups of securities which periodically enjoy a popularity boom, especially among those who think that if you are clever enough you can get something for nothing in Wall Street.

The convertible—preferred or debenture—*does* give you a double play. But its additional privilege is *not* a gift, not a "freebie." You pay for that conversion privilege just as you pay for any other attractive investment characteristic.

Example: If the straight (non-convertible) preferred of Corporation A is priced in the open market at yield 8.8%, it's a safe bet that the same company's convertible security will yield less. In other words, you can't get the conversion (into common) privilege for nothing.

Exactly the same is true of a convertible debenture. If Corporation A straight bonds and debentures are yielding 9¼%, the convertibles will yield less. To put it another way, $5,000 invested in a convertible preferred or a convertible debenture will bring in less income than the same money invested in the same company's non-convertible issues.

The above is true even if the current market price of the common is so far below the conversion price set in the preferred's or debenture's provisions that there is little immediate prospect of a profitable conversion. If that conversion privilege is still good for five to ten or more years, you pay for hope.

And the closer the common stock is to the price at which the senior issue may be converted, the greater will be the difference in income between that yielded by the convertible and that offered by the same company's non-convertible preferred and debentures.

CONVERTIBLES AND NON-CONVERTIBLES COMPARED

Convertibles may be sound, sensible securities for your portfolio—or they may be a form of will o' the wisp. But in either case, they are far more complicated than a corporation's common shares or non-convertible preferreds or debentures. You *must not* buy them by price as though looking for basement bargains. You must take the time to fully understand just what you are getting for your money ... what part of the purchase price is based on current market value and current yield, and what portion represents hope that some future market climate will bail you out of a bad deal.

Example: American Telephone & Telegraph has common,

a convertible preferred and two non-convertible preferreds all traded on the N.Y. Stock Exchange. Each share of convertible preferred may be turned in to the company in exchange for 1.05 shares of A.T.&T. common. On a day when the common shares yielded 7.5% to investors and the straight preferreds 7.9 and 8%, the convertible preferred yield was 6.3%. Now to put these figures into "plain" language:

If you want to be a common share owner of A.T.&T., taking your chances that Bell System profits and dividends will increase over the years (as they have over the past), then you can invest $1,000 of your money for a return of $75 a year, plus a hope of even better days to come.

If you are content to receive a more generous *fixed* dividend from Telephone and forego any chances of increased dividends (a preferred dividend, in practically all cases, is fixed ... forever) you can get $79 or $80 a year income from that invested $1,000 ... period. *But—*

If you want the security and the seniority of owning a preferred (rather than the low-man-on-the-totem-pole common) but you are still interested in sharing any future market gains in the more volatile common resulting from higher earnings and increased dividends, then you put your $1,000 into Telephone's convertible preferred for a return of 6.3%— $63 a year. And there it is, spelled out in actual dollars: $75 from the common stock investment, plus hope; $79 or $80 from one of the preferreds, with senior security but *no hope* of more dividends; or $63 from the convertible preferred, with both seniority *and* hope of a market profit if the common (on which you have a "call") does better. "You pays your money and takes your choice."

The same reckoning is true in discussing convertible debenture bonds vs. straight (non-convertible) debt securities.

Example: American Hospital Supply, a leader in the field of medical and hospital equipment, has common shares outstanding which command the highest quality rating, a rare A plus. The stock is so highly regarded as a growth investment that investors are willing to put their money into it for a dividend return of only 2½%. (This at a time when insured bank accounts could command returns of around 9½%.)

American Hospital also has a straight debenture issue outstanding due in 2007 and carrying a coupon of 7⅞%, a bond which pays $78.75 interest every year per $1,000 face amount certificate. The bond is rated highly—AA. On a day when AA bonds were being issued to yield above 9%, these bonds commanded a market price of only 86 ($860 per $1,000 bond), thus boosting the current yield to 9.16% ($78.75 divided by $860) which was about in line with what was available in the credit market.

American Hospital Supply also has a convertible debenture issue outstanding—the 5¾% debentures due in 1999. On the same day that the straight debenture carrying a coupon of 7⅞% was selling only at 86, to yield 9.16%, investors were paying as high as 102 ($1,020) for the convertible debenture which paid only $57.50 a year in interest, or a current yield of only 5.64%, and rated only a single A quality. How come? Because:

The straight debenture promised the investor only that it would pay him $78.75 every year (actually, one-half that figure every six months) until the year 2007 when it would return his $1,000.

But the convertible debenture, in addition to the $28.75 interest every six months, gave its holder the right to turn in the bond at any time up to its maturity in 1999 and receive in exchange 33.90 shares of common stock, regardless of how high the common rose on the stock market. As of the day the $1,000 convertible debenture sold at $1,020 the common was selling at $27 a share. Now you say: "But 33.90 shares at $27 comes to only $915.30! What's the big deal? Why pay $1,020 for a passel of common shares worth only $915.30? If you want the common go out and buy it, cheaper at $27 a share, not the equivalent of $30 a share ($1,020 divided by 33.90)."

And the answer is that I may not be intrigued by paying $27 for a stock paying out only 68 cents a year in dividends, a yield of 2½% plus a hoped-for market rise, when I can get 5.64% from these debentures and still—whenever I please—turn my bond in for 33.90 shares of common. In other words, if you like American Hospital Supply as an investment, you have these choices:

Draw 9.16% on your money by buying the straight 7⅞% issue of debentures due 2007, secure in the feeling that you will get an interest check every six months and the money back in 2007 . . . period. Or—

You can buy the common at 27, earn 2½% on your money and hope for a market rise in the stock. Or—

You can pay $1,020 for the convertible debenture (which works out to a market price of $30 a share on the stock you may claim whenever you wish), and then hope that American Hospital goes to $35 or $40 a share when your bond will be worth at least 35 or 40 times 33.90.

What does the hope offered by the convertible cost you? The difference between a 9.16% yield you could get on the straight debenture and the 5.64% paid by the convertible. That comes to $35.10 a year on every $1,000 you invest. That's what optimism on American Hospital Supply's future goes for in Wall Street.

COMPLICATIONS

The above data, seemingly complicated, are merely the "bare bones" of the story. Some convertibles are straightforward, as outlined in the preceding paragraphs. Some are far more complicated. The debentures may be convertible into common shares of some other, subsidiary or affiliated, company. The conversion privilege is often subject to change; it may be limited to only several years or might run on to maturity of the debenture. The exchange process may involve additional payment in cash, or in other securities (and when these other securities sell at a discount from par value, you are in for some complicated arithmetic). Both preferred and debenture issues may be retired by the issuing corporation at pre-fixed prices. If your convertible security is selling at a premium (because the underlying common shares have risen) you must sell your convertible on the open market, or exchange for the common *before* the date the company pays you only the par value ($1,000) of the convertible issues. If you can't act in time, you're going to lose money.

To sum up: money has been made in convertible issues . . . and lost. The standard argument is that the fixed dividend on convertible preferreds and the fixed interest payment on the debenture acts as a "floor" under their market prices. Could be. But if interest rates rise to 9 and 10% as they have in recent years, the assurance that you will get 5.6 or 6.3 on your money affords scant "floor" support for a convertible issue which can't be profitably exchanged.

The convertible is a respectable, often worthwhile, two-edged investment. It is *not* (repeat *not*) a royal road to assured riches. If you go shopping for convertibles be very careful that you fully understand what you are buying. They aren't simple securities.

15

Over-the-Counter Stocks—
Second-Class Citizens?

Of the estimated 50,000 incorporated businesses in the U.S. fewer than 10% of the total have their stock listed on the N.Y. Stock Exchange, the American Stock Exchange, or any of the much smaller regional exchanges. The remaining 90% of these companies trade their shares over the counter, in a not-too-well understood market, and one which too often carries with it a vague impression of a slightly substandard, infrequently traded, fringe market.

In fact the counter market is one where all securities not listed on an exchange are traded. It is somewhat like saying that "everything which isn't on land is in the ocean." And to carry the analogy further we should point out that there is a lot more ocean than land.

THE OTC MARKET

The over-the-counter (or simply "counter" or "unlisted") market is a large, rather amorphous institution which, in fact, has no finite geographical market place at all. (Unlike, for example, the N.Y. Stock Exchange, at the corner of Broad and Wall Streets, and the American Stock Exchange at 86 Trinity Place, both in New York City.) The counter market is, in fact, a network of telephone and other communications lines used by thousands of brokers to trade among themselves and for clients. If you order the purchase or sale of 100 shares of U.S. Steel common it's a good bet that the trade will be executed on the floor of the N.Y. Stock Exchange; if you make a trade in Ford of Canada common stock, it will most likely take place at Trinity Place on the American Stock Exchange.

But if you are interested in trading, or acquiring for investment, shares of most bank and insurance companies, or of most small, emerging young companies, or of most corporate and government bonds, your broker will turn to the counter market because these securities are not traded on the listed exchanges.

The counter market is generally thought of as a 3,000-mile-long "trading floor," although the "floor" is really a communications system stretching from coast to coast and tapped into by thousands of brokers. Before February 8, 1971 your broker might have criss-crossed the country by telephone, talking to at least three other brokers trading in the particular stock you wanted in order to get you the best buying or selling price. It proved to be a sometimes cumbersome operation. But in February of that year the market shifted to a computerized operation by acquiring an electronic central nervous system called NASDAQ—pronounced NÁZ DAK—which stands for National Association of Securities Dealers Automated Quotations.

NASDAQ

NASDAQ is a computerized communications system that collects, stores and disseminates up-to-the-second quotations supplied by a nationwide network of counter brokers and dealers. The several thousand stock issues so quoted represent companies with $1 million or more in total assets, $500,000 in net assets; 300 or more shareholders, a minimum of 100,000 shares outstanding and with at least two broker/dealers registered as market-makers and continually quoting the stock. A market-maker is a brokerage firm which stands ready to buy or sell any stock in which "it is making a market."

In addition to those electronically quoted there are about 30,000 issues also traded over the counter—although most of these are classified as "inactive" stocks.

WHAT IS TRADED

Most corporate bonds are traded over the counter (also called "OTC"), although the stock exchanges also list bonds. Also included in OTC are state, municipal and U.S. Government obligations.

A new stock issue will start life on the OTC. And many remain on the counter long after they could have qualified for exchange listing. Some of the nationally known companies which have remained on the counter for many years include Government Employees Insurance, Rank Organization, Anheuser Busch, Combined Insurance, DeBeers Consolidated Mines, Connecticut General Insurance, Rival Manufacturing, Pabst Brewing, as well as most life insurance companies and banks.

In the non-professional investor's mind, the OTC suffers from the fact that its activities are far less publicized than those of the exchanges—principally the N.Y. and American Stock Exchanges. Most daily newspapers which may carry full tables on the two senior exchanges, plus any local exchanges, will give only token space to the counter market. If one asks: "How did the market do today?" he most likely will be answered in terms of the Dow Jones Industrial Average, which is based on the price movement of only 30 old-line war horses on the N.Y. Stock Exchange. Furthermore, the fact that all new issues start on the counter gives that market-place a less-than-seasoned appearance, which is true only of those new issues and has no bearing on the well-seasoned stocks, bonds and, of course, government issues traded OTC.

For what it's worth, the "open-high-low-close-net change" listings of exchange transactions also give many investors a feeling that they have a better check on the market in which they buy or sell a security. The counter market lists only "bid," "asked" and, in some cases, net changes in the bid from the previous day. The "bid" represents the price a market-making broker is prepared to pay for a specific stock. The "ask" is what he is asking if you want to buy from him. Your broker, before executing your buy or sell order will, via his computer, scan the bids and asks of several brokers to see where he can get the best deal.

Some traders will argue that they can get a better deal on an exchange; others prefer the counter. Any such decision based merely on the specific marketplace is bound to be a vague generalization. It used to be true that if you found that your purchase of 100 shares of XYZ on a listed exchange was above the high for the day (or a sale at a price below the low) you could complain to your broker and make a good case for a price adjustment. However, since the national consolidation of the listed exchange price structure, that no longer holds true. Your broker can argue that at the moment of the trade that price existed in the national hookup. Any "bid" and "ask" you read about the morning after on a counter stock you bought the day before has no meaning at all. If your order was executed at 11:15 A.M. or 2:20 P.M. it was done in a market which may have had very little relationship to the finally-reported bid and ask.

It should be obvious that if you intend to scalp points and fractions in any stock—listed or OTC—you had better be on the scene or in constant contact with your broker. If you are buying the stock for long-term investment, you might as well forget the ⅛th or ¼th point variation between what you paid and what you think you should have paid. Your chances of changing the score are about one in twenty-five.

Should you select the OTC or an exchange for investing or speculating? Concentrate on the stock—not the exchange.

16

Mutual Funds—
Are They For You?

A mutual fund is a big pot of money—anywhere from a million dollars or even less to a billion or more. It represents the investment of thousands of persons all of whom want someone else to make their investments for them, in much the same way that a homeowner may ask a gardening service to plant and maintain his yard. Some professional gardeners do a better job than the average homeowner; but most prizes for champion roses seem to be won by "amateurs."

HOW THEY WORK

There are absolutely no hard and fast qualitative rulings which apply to any or all mutual funds. There are no guaranties. You buy into a mutual fund—and as long as you stay with it your money's fate is in the hands of the fund managers. And no one can promise you anything!

Mutuals have been around a long time, more than fifty years, in fact, and have accumulated in that time many billions of dollars of investors' money. Some funds have done well; some have failed miserably. Some have done well in one year, and failed miserably the next; and vice versa. An acceptable long-term performance is one which keeps the fund's progress about in step with broad stock market averages. This means there is virtually no chance that a mutual fund will double your money overnight or even from one year to the next; conversely, there is little chance you will be wiped out.

As is the case with all investing, risk and hoped-for reward are always balancing factors in any mutual fund. Small funds which have latched on to a few "hot" stocks have shown big gains in a short period of time—or big losses, if the stocks have suddenly cooled. Big funds, with dollar investments of hundreds of millions to more than a billion, obviously are stabilized by the very fact that they must spread their investments over a broad field of securities and will not, therefore, be so directly affected by the rise or decline of a single investment.

HISTORY

The attraction of mutual funds for the broad spectrum of investors has varied widely over the years (not too different from the attraction of the stock market itself). Mutual funds launched by entrepreneurs with a reputation for fast stock market profits have attracted hundreds of millions of small investors' dollars in a single day's offering. Other funds have remained small because of their conviction that "smaller is better," that it is easier to successfully maneuver $25 million than $250 million. In some years this philosophy has been rewarding.

During the long stock market drought beginning with the late 60's mutuals as a group didn't do much better than the stock market itself, and for many years investors withdrew more money from mutuals than others were putting in. It was a long "winter" of mutual fund investors' discontent and disinterest. The mutual fund industry countered by setting up funds to serve new, more popular demands, thus attracting new money. If it couldn't show luscious trading profits, the fund industry decided it would offer more of what was becoming popular: tax-exemption (via municipal bonds), bond income funds, money funds which invest mainly in short-term bonds, certificates of deposit and commercial paper. With interest rates rising, their decision proved correct and these high-yield funds were soon greeted with billions of new investment dollars from hundreds of thousands of investors. These new services helped the mutual fund industry continue despite its lackluster performance in its original aim—equity investment for capital gain, plus some income.

The industry as a whole also reduced its charges to the investing public, thus in effect offsetting the broadscale complaint of "Why should I pay you up to 9% or more in buying commissions—plus an annual management fee of ½ to 1% of total assets—if you can't do any better in the market than I can?"

"LOAD" AND "NO-LOAD" FUNDS

Mutual funds were first sold by agents, or brokers, who were compensated for their effort by a generous commission—called the "load." The industry proclaimed a ceiling of 8½% in buying commissions (there are generally no fees when you redeem your shares and take your money out). But that 8½% was charged on the entire amount you paid in to the fund. So if you invested $1,000, $85 was taken out for commissions, leaving only $915 actually invested in your account. If you divide 85 by 915 you discover that the rate charged you to invest $915 was 9.2896% and not 8½%.

If the fund did well, you didn't begrudge it 8½ or

9.2896%. (And you were never conscious of the annual management fee, which was taken right out of the pot before you got yours.) But if year after year your investment went "nowhere" you began to wonder about paying 9¼% to obtain a service which wasn't—for many years—doing as well as a savings bank account.

A result was the appearance and steady increase in the number of mutual funds which did not charge a buying commission—the "no loads." (They do, of course, recompense management with a continuing annual fee.) And these were joined by funds which had originally charged investors a buying commission but were now eliminating that fee in order to attract more investors.

One of the most popular misconceptions about the mutual fund field is fostered by agents who make a living selling "load" funds and who want to justify that charge. Asking the question: "Do you know anyone who will work for nothing?" they imply that a "load" fund has more effort expended in its portfolio management than a "no-load" and that, therefore, the no-load investor is somehow short-changed. There is no truth whatsoever to this argument.

The selling commission charged by a "load" fund is used only to pay its sales force. None of that fee compensates the investment management staff which, as already reported, receives its wages from the management fee, an on-going annual levy of about ½ to 1% of total assets. Thus, any mutual fund (load or no-load) with, for example, $5 million in assets charges its shareholder investors a total of $25,000 to $50,000 a year to cover research, investment advice, etc.

How does the "no-load" fund manage to get along without paying a sales force? Simple. It has NO sales force! It's a form of self-service industry in the same sense as savings bank life insurance. You walk into a savings bank and ask the officer in charge to sell you some. If you want service at a fancy boutique, you expect to pay for it. If, instead, you want to cut costs, you go into an outlet-type store and pick the clothing off the rack yourself. If you want to invest in a no-load mutual fund you must first approach the fund by replying to any of their advertisements in newspapers or magazines or broadcast over radio or television. Or you request a list of funds, their addresses and other data from the No-Load Mutual Fund Association at Valley Forge, Pa., 19481.

You will also find various directories listing both load and no-load mutuals on most libraries' financial book shelves. As with most popular investment media, you can get all the statistics you can handle, and probably more, both in these record books and in the brochures and prospectuses any fund will be glad to send you at the drop of a postcard.

These data are scrupulously honest. You can depend upon their accuracy to a penny per share and to 3 decimal places on yields or capital gains, etc. Whether they will assure you of picking a winner is an entirely different matter.

Investing in mutual funds, like investing in anything else in hope of profit, is an exercise in looking into the future. Without a crystal ball you're back to taking your chances: "You pays your money and takes your choice."

PATIENCE ESSENTIAL

Whether that "choice" will prove profitable for you only time can tell. And by "time" here is meant, literally, years. Do not expect "action" from a mutual. If you put your money into such a venture you can be sure you won't have any boasting material at the next social affair . . . never a chance of declaring: "I bought XYZ at 21 three weeks ago and sold out yesterday at 37." It is not that kind of animal. Any gains, if they come at all, are likely to come slowly and unspectacularly. But there are certain advantages to the mutual fund route. And its obvious appeal has kept hundreds of thousands of investors' names on the industry's shareholder lists. What are these advantages?

CONVENIENCE

Once you sign up to invest in a mutual fund, the entire investment process becomes automatic and worry-free. You mail your check into the bank acting as agent and you automatically acquire the exact number of shares in the fund that amount of money will cover on that day—figured to 3 decimal places. You get a receipt for the payment and the shares are kept safely for you by the bank trustee. If you choose, any dividends and/or capital gains declared by the fund may be automatically reinvested in more shares.

You have no safekeeping problem with your share certificates. Danger of loss by fire or theft is non-existent.

With every payment you get an exact figure of the number of shares thus acquired, plus the total number of shares to your account.

If you want to redeem part or all of your shares at the current price, a letter to the bank trustee is all that is required.

HABIT-FORMING

For a large number of people, building a nest egg— whether in cash savings or in securities—is best done by habit. (That is the reason for the great success of the payroll deduction program for the acquisition of U.S. savings bonds.) If you set up a mutual fund program for investing $25 or $50 or $150 a month it's a safe bet that you will accumulate far more over the years than if you put aside $500 one month and then didn't save another cent for months or a year or two. The monthly reminder received from a mutual fund investment account is perhaps the strongest point in favor of mutuals.

MANAGEMENT

As has been noted, some mutual funds do better than others; some do very well; some don't do well at all. Exactly the same thing can be said about individual investors with the advantage obviously with those who have some knowledge or expertise in investing. Mutual funds' money (the money you and thousands of other individuals put into the pot) is invested by professionals. Granting that none of them has found the royal road to stock market riches (there is none) we must assume that, on average, the knowledgable investor, the professional, can do better than the novice. (At least, if he loses money, he does so for the right reason.)

To those disgruntled mutual fund investors—and their number is legion—who complain that they have nothing to show, and, perhaps, even losses, for the decade since the late 1960s, I can only reply: "You ought to see the losses rolled up by the majority of small investors who tried Wall Street on their own!" Bad news is relative and while a mutual fund investor is entirely within his rights in complaining: "I could have done better putting my money into the bank," he is making this statement with the advantage of 20/20 hindsight. Let's face it: it was a bad period for the broad-scale equities market, for most mutual funds, for many, many individual investors. As the bartender put it: "name your poison."

This chapter is neither an endorsement nor an all-out attack on the mutual funds industry. It is an attempt to put funds in their proper perspective—an industry, professionally run, offering to oversee the investment of billions of dollars put up generally by small investors who feel they dare not venture into Wall Street on their own.

CHOOSING THE FUND FOR YOU

If you decide that is the way for your dollars to go, then your first and most important task is to select the specific fund which is to serve as the vehicle.

It's a tough task because there are literally hundreds of funds out there, all willing and eager to take your money. There are funds which invest in bonds for income; in short-term money obligations (Treasury bills, certificates of deposit, commercial paper); in long-term obligations; in municipal bonds (for exemption from Federal and, in many cases, state and local income taxes); in common stocks and bonds (for balance); in common stocks for high income; in common stocks for appreciation; in common stocks for speculation; in foreign stocks; in energy stocks; in gold mining stocks, etc.

You must first decide to eliminate those you don't need or don't want. And then you must start looking at the scores which compete in the specific fields which attract you. It's not easy—but there's no rush, either.

Don't *ever, ever, ever* allow anyone to tell you that you must buy a mutual *today* or lose the *big chance*. That is typical salesman pressure and utter nonsense. Mutuals don't work that way. They move slowly (up or down) and, in general, are about as exciting an investment as a piggy bank.

There is a great deal of information available on mutuals, on all levels from the Wiesenberger reports—the bible of the industry—to The Mutual Fund Almanac, from the statistics in the monthly Standard & Poor's stock guide to more sensational and less factual forms of "tipster" sheets which will try to tell you that you can make a fortune by trading mutual fund shares. These last you can safely ignore.

Fortunately, there is not too much difference among the many funds now dedicated to yielding high income. Some may restrict their portfolio to "A" rated, or higher bonds; some may dip down into the Bs—in order to show a higher yield. But in general it is a straight income situation adjusted for risk and that's all you should expect. The same applies to the recently popular "money" funds which concentrate on high-yielding short-term investments—90-day bank deposits, commercial paper, Treasury bills, etc. The municipal bond mutual funds do go in for trading and the relative expertise of their managers may make a slight difference. A few minutes spent looking over their track record may help you decide.

It is in the field of equities—and especially common stocks aimed at growth—that the choice becomes difficult. Information is plentiful and readily available. A postcard or a phone call to any mutual fund will bring you a prospectus and record of past performances as well as literature on goals, operating costs, etc. (and in the case of a "load" fund, a salesman).

Since the future is veiled, all you have to go on is past records. If a fund's management has missed one stock market boom after another, you may safely assume you can pass it up today. If it has risen and fallen with the general stock market, you may assume it will continue to do so. But watch if it scored sensational gains at one point or another; then you must do more research before accepting that gain as gospel. Was the fund small at the time, so that a big gain in an individual stock commitment resulted in an inordinate overall advance? Did it rightfully interpret the bowling boom years ago but did little since? Was its recent success due to a flurry in the data communication stocks only?

In general, don't expect a fund with a billion or more in assets to put on as stellar a performance as one with $750,000 total investments. The doubling in market price of a lucky $200,000 commitment won't budge the big fund but will make the smaller fund look like a winner.

If you are a young investor and rightfully feel you should take outside chances, go with the smaller fund. If you are older, nearing retirement and nervous about the nest egg you've been building for thirty years, you might sleep better with the bigger fund. As Shakespeare put it: "To thine ownself be true."

The mutual fund has its advantages: diversification of investment; professional management; safekeeping of securities; easy and habit-forming acquisition; ease of redemption; emphasis on long-term investing. Balance these with the fact that they could be dull, and be assured that they will not likely furnish you with boasting material at your next college reunion.

17

Formula Investing

One of the most popular topics you will find in a survey of investment decisions is that of timing. There are some Wall Streeters—both veterans and novices—who will even argue that selecting the best time to buy stocks is fully as important as deciding on what stock to buy. Cyclical factors are held in high regard by many students of the stock market. There are 50-year cycles, 49-month cycles, 9-year cycles—all affecting the trend of equity prices. There are popular slogans claiming to help you buy soft-drink stocks, air conditioner stocks, leisure industry stocks. There used to be strong following for a formula which said that it is best to sell stocks on the eve of Yom Kippur, the Jewish Day of Atonement, and to buy them back after Rosh Hashonah, which marks the New Year of the Jewish calendar, although I have never found any satisfactory explanation of what that 10-day period of religious soul-searching and penitence had to do with stock market quotations.

There are, in addition, theories as to the probability of pre-Christmas rallies, of January trends predicting the course for the entire year and of how the market of even the first five days of January will provide clues for the balance of the entire year.

Statisticians delight in these charts, pictures, formulas . . .

as they do in running down every clue to future stock market prices. Prophecy is as attractive a Wall Street endeavor as ever it was in ancient Greece. The more the future beclouds man's fate, the more he is fascinated by it. If only some *crystal ball could give us tomorrow's closing stock prices!!!*

Lacking such mystic powers, large numbers of investors ignore timing entirely. These march to the beat of an entirely different drummer. Their technique might best be described as regular, periodic investment in a stock, or stocks, with absolutely no regard for market price at the moment or, for that matter, with no regard as to whether a Democrat or a Republican is in the White House, or whether revolution is rampant or quiescent in Africa or the Far East.

These are the long-term investors who practice "dollar cost averaging," or subscribe to what has more recently become popularly known as "dividend reinvestment."

Naturally these formulas also have their strong adherents and opponents and, as with any other financial regimen, have resulted in profits or losses.

All that one can say about them with any conviction is that once the investment stock is selected, the investor puts aside all fretting about *when* to buy, at what price to buy and in what dollar amounts. In this respect, these formulas are counterparts of the most popular methods for acquiring U.S. savings bonds (by regular deductions from pay envelopes); life insurance (by regular monthly or quarterly or semi-annual premium payments); savings accounts or credit union accounts (by regular weekly or bi-weekly deposits); investment club participation (by monthly "dues"); mutual fund shares (by reinvestment of dividends plus monthly or quarterly contributions).

HABIT

In nearly a quarter-century of listening to other folks' financial and investment problems, I feel it is difficult to overestimate the importance of *habit* in building a financial nest egg—whether it is in a savings account, in savings bonds or in securities. Marshall McLuhan wrote that "the medium is the message." I firmly agree. The way people save and invest actually becomes as important a factor in building an estate as the savings or investment itself. The "slow and steady" financial runner will not win every race. But it isn't likely that he will be wiped out, either.

"DOLLAR COST AVERAGING"

One popular formula is "dollar cost averaging." It is based on the premise that many of us aren't in a position to call a broker and order the purchase of $10,000 worth of U.S. Steel or Ford Motor or Union Pacific RR. shares. We can't generate $10,000 of investable cash every Monday and Thursday, or even every first of the month. And even if we have accumulated that $10,000 over a period of years, how do we know that May 1 is the best day to put it all into the stock market? Answer: We don't.

So the "averagers" believe that the simplest way to acquire the shares we want is through small, periodic, regular purchases which are attuned to our ability to develop investable cash, and which ignore market action.

Several years back, the N.Y. Stock Exchange community came around to this realization and announced that its member firms would henceforth set up accounts for the little people, accepting payments of $50, $100 or so, monthly or at other regular intervals. The money, after modest commissions, would be applied to the purchase of exactly as many shares of the stock of your choice as $50 or $100 etc. (minus commissions) could cover . . . right out to 3 decimal places.

It seemed like the answer to the "little man's" prayer. He no longer had to scrounge around "in the pits," shopping only for $3 stocks because $100 wouldn't buy many shares of Union Oil of California. He wouldn't have to watch—and try to predict—the stock market. He'd merely send in his money every month or second month, or quarterly, and leave all the rest to the brokerage firm's computer department. It was a great plan to bring Wall Street to Main Street.

But it received little promotion and sales effort by the Exchange's member firms who, despite the Exchange's slogan "Own Your Share of American Business," preferred active, large-commission-paying traders of 500 and 1,000 and 10,000 shares to the $4 and $5 fees provided by those who added 1.875 shares of a stock once a month or quarterly. As a result the program withered and died on the vine—except for less than a handful (one, to be exact) of large brokerage firms who possessed the electronic capability to carry on with a "little man" program.

However, "averaging"—within certain limits and above certain minimal dollar amounts—is still possible for the small investor in individual stocks and, in fact, remains a basic ingredient of mutual fund acquisition. It goes like this.

Let's assume you are interested in the long-term acquisition of a stock selling in the $20–$30 area. Having already established a life insurance program and amassed a comfortable savings account, you are now in a position to put $500 every three months into this stock. You could, of course, save this money for two years and then buy, in one transaction, 150 to 200 shares of the stock. If the stock were at $20 you would acquire 200 shares; if at $30, approximately 135 shares. You would then sit back and hope you were right, that you had bought at the right time. Or—

You could buy $500 worth of the stock (to 3 decimal places if you found a broker who would set up a dollar averaging account for you, or to the nearest whole share if you couldn't). Three months later you would buy another $500 worth. And so on. One law is fairly well established in Wall Street: "The market will fluctuate." If we were to assume that your stock moved back and forth, or even in one direction between 20 and 30, a little bit of arithmetic would prove to you that $500 worth bought at 8 quarterly intervals would give you an average cost per share below the arithmetical average price of the stock over the two years. Example: let us assume that the price of the stock over the eight quarterly buying dates moves thus: $20 per share, $22, $25, $28, $27, $25, $23, $27. If you bought $500 worth at these eight quarterly intervals you would acquire (putting aside commissions): 25 shares, 22.73, 20, 17.86, 18.52, 20, 21.74, 18.52 at each purchase. A total of about 164 shares for the $4,000 two-year outlay. This works out to an average cost of $24.39 per share even though the mathematical average of the eight prices listed above is $24.625. Extended over a period of years—and of wider price fluctuations—the average cost per share would benefit even more from the averaging. Even more, the investor would eliminate the very real danger that if he had put his $4,000 into the market on a single day, he would have been moved to do so on a day when the market was "boiling" and the price of his stock in the higher 20s, rather than in the lower.

Mutual fund investing is in most cases carried on in this fashion. After an initial payment of $100 or so, the investor may send in a monthly (or less frequent) check for $25 or $50 which is used to buy exactly as many shares as that sum will cover (minus commissions, where they exist), using the asset value of the day as the buying price. In addition, quarterly dividends and annual capital gains distributions are most often left with the fund to acquire still more shares.

If this all sounds quite dull . . . it is. Completely absent is the excitement which goes with watching your 100 shares of stock bought only last Wednesday, climbing steadily, eighth by eighth, until you are a couple of hundred dollars ahead in a few weeks. Under dollar cost averaging investing, there is no chance to double your money on an average twenty-five-share purchase and there would be little profit left over if you did. Dollar averaging in securities is far more akin to regular savings bond acquisition or to building a savings account than it is to Wall Street speculation. However, it does afford a comfortable, let-you-sleep method of slowly and steadily acquiring a portfolio of stocks during a working lifetime. Except for those who automatically fall into the "dollar averaging" system of buying mutual fund shares, first-time investors do not normally favor this method. It is most often adopted as a haven for those who have first tried 2-point scalping and frantic trading . . . and have, most often, failed.

18

Options
For More Income

The option is an old, long-recognized financial instrument. It is a right, or privilege, granted by one person to another in exchange for payment of a sum of money generally called "the premium." Perhaps one of the oldest, and best known, uses of an option relates to the right to purchase real estate. The owner of a piece of property—home, farm, apartment house—grants an interested buyer a six-months' option to buy the property for $100,000. The would-be buyer pays the owner, say, $2,000 for that privilege because the option gives him time to raise the money for the deal without fear that the price will go up in the interim. Also, because he is a real estate trader, he wants to lock up his right to buy the property for $100,000 while he scouts around to find a third party who will pay him $125,000.

The present owner of the property grants the option, in return for $2,000 cash in hand now, because he is quite prepared to sell the property for $100,000 and the $2,000 premium is merely a bonus. And if the buyer doesn't go through with the deal the owner keeps the $2,000 and, of course, his property.

Options have been bought and sold on stocks for many, many years—usually a one-to-one deal between a particular seller and a particular buyer and handled by an options dealer called a "put" and "call" broker. In recent years, this arrangement has been drastically changed by the setting up of The Chicago Board Options Exchange, as well as by similar options markets on already established stock exchanges. The main thrust of these new option markets has been to make the option a highly negotiable instrument. The options are no longer set up between specific buyers and sellers but are traded on the exchanges in exactly the same way as securities. In other words, Mr. Smith no longer sells an option to Mr. Jones. He merely sells an option on the market ... period. And the man who buys it can easily re-sell it five minutes after the purchase, if he regrets the deal.

The option thus becomes a form of security in itself—bought and sold, traded and exchanged on a marketplace with no specific ties between buyer and seller.

This highly increased liquidity has, naturally, increased many times over the trading in options since there is always a ready market. And that's good.

It has also increased many times over the number of non-professional investors who think they have discovered a 100% surefire gold mine. And that's bad.

And yet, options may be used advantageously, and conservatively, by any investor who takes the time to learn what he is doing.

"COVERED" OPTIONS

Perhaps the simplest (and most limited risk) option deal is the selling of an option on stock you already own. For example: You own 100 shares of Eastman Kodak. (Options are always traded in lots of 100.) You decide that in addition to the $2 annual cash dividend you would like to earn some extra income by selling an option to buy the stock good for anywhere from three to nine months off. You so inform your broker; now you must make a decision:

Kodak, on the day you decide to act, is selling at 59¾—$59.75 a share. You may sell an option (a) giving the buyer of that option the right to claim your stock at $60 a share over the next five months in return for his paying you, now, a premium of $325. Or you may sell the right (b) to claim your stock at $70 a share over the next two months for a payment (premium) of only $25; or an option (c) at $70 good for 5 months at $200; or (d) good—at the same price—for 8 months for $350.

It is readily apparent that the "premium" amount is a factor of time and hope.

Option buyer (a) thinks Kodak is going up in price over the next five months but he doesn't want to lay out $5,975 for 100 shares, (or part of $5,975—the remainder borrowed on margin from his broker) to "get aboard" the stock. He'd much rather make a $325 bet on Kodak even though he realizes that while Kodak common is a perpetual investment, the option must prove profitable in only five months. After that it is worthless. So he hands over the $325 in exchange for the right to claim the stock upon payment of $6,000 additional (only $25 more than it would cost today). The most he can lose is the $325. Potential profit is, theoretically, unlimited. More, he doesn't even have to pay out $6,000 to acquire the stock if it goes up in price because his $325 option will rise in price, too, as Kodak common goes up. And he can always take his profit by selling the option. True, it's more than a $2 bet on a horse, but we're talking big figures here.

Option buyer (b) is willing to make a long odds bet of $25 that Kodak will go well above $70 a share during the next two months. If it does, he can claim 100 shares at that price—even if it is then selling at $75, $85, or whatever. If it doesn't surpass $70, all he has lost is $25. Option buyer (c) feels the same way about Kodak's prospects, i.e., that it will climb above $70 a share, but he is willing to lay out $200 now to give him more time (five months) during which, he hopes, Kodak will top $70. Option buyer (d) wants still more time to reach that price and is willing to bet $350 now for an eight-months' play.

These are the reasons the buyers *bought* these options. You *sold* any of these privileges simply because you want the premium money now and feel that only two things can happen to you: (1) Kodak won't rise in price above any of the "striking" prices named in the options—or may even decline. In this case you will remain a Kodak investor just as you have been right along; or (2) Kodak will rise in price and you will be forced to either deliver the stock at the agreed-upon price, anywhere from $25 to several hundred dollars above the current level, or buy back the option you sold (most likely at a loss) and thus cancel out your original option sale.

In essence, the seller of an option against stock he owns (a "covered" option) accepts a premium now in exchange for pledging to sell his stock at some agreed-upon price during future months.

The best that can happen to him is to have the pledged stock "go nowhere" in the market. If Kodak in the above examples hangs around the 59¾–60 (or lower) area for the next two to eight months, you, the option seller, continue to hold your Kodak stock but have anywhere from $25 to $350 of cash money you didn't have before. Of course if Kodak were to dip to 55 or 52 you would—to be most conservative— feel compelled to hold the shares in order to have the stock to deliver should it suddenly turn around and climb past 60 or 70 by the date of option termination. Or you might decide to take your profit by buying back the option before then because it might be selling for less than you received when you sold it.

The "worst" that could happen to you would be a sensational climb in Kodak price during the option period. The option buyer then, most certainly, would claim his stock at the agreed-upon price, which means your effective selling price—including the premium money already received—would be around $6,000 to $6,350 for stock then worth $7,000 or $8,000 or whatever price was attained on the open market.

The "covered" option seller is essentially a non-speculator who sells the right to someone who is willing to place a "bet" on the future market action of the stock in question. The seller gets (and keeps) the "premium" money in return for offering a claim on his stock; the buyer is limiting his speculation to the amount of the premium he pays for that privilege.

These are merely the bare bones of the matter, however.

"NAKED" OPTIONS

By putting up sufficient collateral, anyone may sell a call on 100 shares of stock even if he doesn't own the stock. If Kodak is selling at $60 a share today and you feel it won't go higher over the next several months, you may sell a call option (a *"naked" option* because you have no stock to cover it) on 100 shares of the stock for, say, $300 or $350 or whatever the going market may be. You get the money now and wait. If Kodak does, in fact, "go nowhere," you most likely do nothing. If Kodak begins to climb, you become more nervous with every point rise because you have agreed to supply 100 shares at a pre-determined price. You may cancel out your agreement by buying back an option similar to the one you sold. If Kodak has risen you might, naturally, have to pay out more than you originally received. But it would be one method of taking your licking early, rather than sitting tight, and, fearfully, having to pay a still higher price at the maturity of the option in order to satisfy the buyer.

"Naked" options are straight bets between seller and buyer in diametrically opposed positions.

"CALL" OPTION

The "call" option discussed thus far is an option, a right, to "call" a stock from its owner, to buy it. It is bought by those who expect, or are willing to bet, that a stock will rise in market price during the option period, and that they will then be in a position to "call" the stock at a previously agreed upon, lower, price.

"PUT" OPTION

A "put" option is also a bet on the future market movement of a stock. But it gives the buyer the right to "put," sell, stock to the option seller. If you sell a "put" option on Kodak at 60, good for several months, you agree to buy the stock back at 60 at any time during that period the "put" option buyer wishes to sell it to you, at 60—even if it has fallen to 59 or 55, or lower.

Your ("put" option-seller's) risk: you've agreed over a period of months to buy 100 shares of Kodak at a price determined today which may be higher than the open market price on the day the option buyer decides to "put" the stock to you.

The option buyer's risk: he today hands over the "premium" money to you and then must hope for Kodak to decline sufficiently so that he may pick up 100 shares in the open market and force you to take it at the higher price you both agreed upon when you sold the option. If Kodak doesn't go down, the option buyer tears up his ticket. After all, he isn't about to pay, say, 75 for the stock in order to make you buy it from him at 60. If Kodak goes down to 52 (from a current "striking" (agreed upon) price of 60, you may feel bad about paying 60 for a stock you could then buy at 52, but you would have the premium money of a few hundred dollars to actually mark down your price. (And you had intended to buy some Kodak anyway.)

"STRADDLE" OPTIONS

And then there are "straddle" options—the simultaneous buying (or selling) of both a "put" and a "call" on the same stock with the same exercise (striking) price and expiration date. The buyer of such a combination option expects a substantial price movement in the stock, but wants protection in either direction—for a price. Let's say that with Kodak at 60 he buys a "call" for $400, good for the next five months and, at the same time, buys a "put" option for $300. So he has bought protection and profit potential in both directions. The arithmetic works out in this fashion: total invested, $700 ($400 plus $300). If the stock rises above $67, he exercises his "call" option, at a profit; if it falls below $53, he exercises his "put" option, at a profit. If the stock remains at $60, he loses the entire $700, since neither option is exercisable at a profit. At any other price between $53 and $67 he can exercise one of the other of his options and thus reduce his total loss.

These are the basics. As one would expect, experts have discovered countless variations and combinations of "puts" and "calls" and "straddles." Complicating the entire picture is the fact that an option need not remain in force until its maturity date. Since the options are traded almost as quickly as stocks themselves there is plenty of room for exercising one's judgment or gambling spirit. You may have sold a "call" option for $300 good for five months, but then you discover one morning that owing to a drop in the price of the underlying stock, the option is now selling at only $200. You may then buy back your option for $200, pocket the $100 profit (commissions are ignored for the sake of these examples) and look for new fields to conquer. Or you may have sold a "put" for $300 which drops to $150 because the stock has risen, and not declined. So you cancel out by buying in the option for $150 and then turn your hand to some other issue.

Or the seller of a $500 "put"—which committed him to buy stock at, say, 75—finds the "put" price has fallen because the stock is now around 80 or 85 and no "put" option holder in his right mind is going to force him to buy it at 75. Figuring a bird in the hand is better than two in the bush (the stock could turn around and fall to 70 during the remainder of the option period) he buys back his "put" at the now lower price and comforts himself with the profit.

WHAT ARE THE DANGERS?

It should be obvious—and ignore it at your peril—that these modifications in the employment of "calls" and "puts" (that is, deciding to buy back the option before maturity) and, for that matter, the selling of the option in the first place, require judgment. If you set your limits at the moment you enter the agreement you at least know where you stand . . . how much you will get (a "call") for your stock, or how much you stand to pay for a stock (in the case of a "put").

But if you decide midway in the deal to take your profit (or your licking) early, you are engaged in playing the market, albeit with risks severely circumscribed.

However, face the fact that you can lose your shirt taking a steady stream of $300 or $250 option losses in the same time that it takes 100 shares of a $50 stock to fall to $40. To put it another way, you can play an evening of bridge and wind up losing $4.25 or winning $3.50. Or you can decide to perk up things by jumping to 10 cents a point.

Options may be sold as conservative, limited instruments for picking up extra "premiums" on stocks already owned—"covered" options; or they may be bought as a bet on the market movement of a stock over the next few months.

But once you decide to try to outwit the market by trading options, you are in the market neck-deep and there are no limits on what you can lose.

Options have become big business with the brokerage fraternity. They certainly have their place in the average investor's book as a source of income, as "price insurance" on stocks already in the portfolio and for many other staid reasons. But don't let anyone tell you that they are loss-proof. If you hedge them so closely that "heads-you-win, tails-you-can't-lose," you may find yourself fattening the broker's commission account without ever giving you much of a chance for a "big score."

Don't ever lose sight of the fact that 99.44% of the time there is a guy just as smart on the other side of the deal. Option dealing has expanded considerably, but it is still a sophisticated endeavor.

Options—as is true of every offering by Wall Street—have their proper usage. They are not risk-proof.

They may serve as a source of extra income in common shares you already own.

They may prove a profitable vehicle for participating in a market rise—or decline—all the while limiting your money risk to the "premium" money paid for the option, or to the "striking" price at which you are pledged to provide stock. As is true in all financial deals, the money risk is in exact proportion to the opportunities for gain. No one gives anything away in Wall Street.

If you decide to engage in option selling or buying, make certain that the brokerage firm through which you intend to trade options specializes in this area. And make sure that whoever is handling your purchases and sales is not only an expert in options but will take the time to explain to you just what you are undertaking.

Try it—you may like it. But know when to cut your losses.

19

It Isn't Immoral to Sell Short— But It Could be Dangerous!

Somehow the practice of selling a security "short" has become associated in the minds of many non-professional investors with immorality, underhandedness, a desire to tear apart the fabric of American business and the economy. Undoubtedly, the fact that the short-seller is playing for a decline in prices is an important factor in this opprobrium. It's not "nice" to talk of falling prices. "Up" is good. Even professional traders will term an eight-point rise in the Dow Jones Industrial average as a "good" market, whereas an eight-point decline session is described as a "bad" or "rough" day on the Street. The "pro" has his reasons for employing this nomenclature. After all, if your living depended upon trading commissions you'd want more, not fewer, people trading stocks. And in the stock market, it is certainly true that you can attract more people with "sugar" (sweet price rises) than you can with "vinegar" (bitter losses).

But more dispassionate observers will admit to you that change is at the heart of the financial system. Just as April showers are needed to provide May flowers, 52 straight weeks of rising prices would bring on so many excesses as to practically destroy the system.

The short-seller, therefore, is a realist and willing to take chances to make his point.

In essence, he is proclaiming that "bulls" should not exert the only price-making influence on stock prices. Why, he asks, should the price of XYZ stock be influenced only by the investor who wants to buy? What about the investor, or trader, who has reason to believe that XYZ is over-priced? Shouldn't he have the right to express his feelings? If he wants to risk X thousands of dollars on his judgment, why shouldn't he have his say in the marketplace?

Through short-selling, he has his "say"—although a much more limited influence on market trends than "bears" had on a stock in the less regulated pre-SEC days. Then, market raiders could throw thousands of shares on the market driving down prices ruthlessly and ruining thousands of other traders as well as many, many more investors. Today, this "raiding" is severely curtailed by SEC requirements that "short" sales be barred at steadily declining prices.

HOW DOES IT WORK?

But the philosophy (far tamer than the robber-baron thinking of days past) still remains basic to the practice of short-selling. This is: "I believe XYZ at 42½ is far too high. I'll sell stock at 42½ (even though I don't own any) and buy some back later at (I'm convinced) lower prices and deliver that stock to the buyer who pays me 42½ today."

The short-seller thus provides stock on the sell side of the market which was not there before. He is increasing the amount of stock available for sale, thus tending to keep prices from rising and hoping it will, in fact, depress prices so he can buy back later at a lower cost.

The investor who bought the stock at 42½ is saying: "I think XYZ is a good buy." The short-seller says: "You're wrong and I'm putting my money where my mouth is."

In a democratic economy, that's only fair and is not too much different from what goes on all the time in many fields of business endeavor.

Examples: A monthly magazine sells you a two-year sub-scription for $24. You will pay $1 a copy for the next 24 months—promised you by a publisher who is just now work-ing on only next month's issue and hasn't the slightest idea of what it will cost him to send you the magazine 18 or 24 months from now. He is, in effect, "going short" 24 maga-zines at $1 a copy and hoping that costs don't rise so sharply during the next two years that he will be wiped out.

You sign a contract with a developer to build you a home for $75,000—firm. The day you sign there isn't even a hole in the ground where your new home is to stand. The builder has "gone short" one house at $75,000.

You plunk down $750 for some furniture, not yet built, but promised you in 3 months.

DANGERS

Much of our economy is predicated upon future de-livery of a product which, the deliverer hopes, he will be able to buy for less than today's selling price.

So—short-selling of stock is not only well-established but reasonably based. But it can be very dangerous. Much more dangerous for the short-seller than for the trader or investor who buys the stock. All he has done is buy 100 shares of XYZ at 42½ because he likes the stock. His total commitment is $4,250 (plus commissions) . . . period. If the company were to go bust, he couldn't lose any more than that $4,250.

But the short-seller is in a far different bind. He has com-mitted himself to deliver 100 shares of XYZ to his broker to replace the 100 shares the broker borrowed in order to deliver the "short" stock to the buyer. (The buyer knows nothing of the short sale. He bought stock. He wants his stock. He gets stock.)

The stock delivered to the buyer was lent either by the

short-seller's broker, or by another broker who may have thousands of shares of XYZ in his own or customers' "street name" accounts, and who is perfectly willing to lend out a hundred for the free use of the $4,250 which he holds until his stock loan is repaid. So far, everyone is happy. The short-seller has sold stock at 42½ and is hoping for a price decline so he can buy back cheaper. The buyer got the stock he wanted. The lending broker has $4,250 on hand for which he pays no interest. (And if XYZ stock becomes tight, that is, if there isn't enough around to lend, he may even charge an additional daily "rental" fee for the stock lent.)

If XYZ shortly falls, say, to $35 a share, the short-seller is happy. He buys in 100 shares at 35, his broker turns the shares over the lending broker, satisfying that debt, and our short-seller has a gross profit (before commissions) of $4,250 minus $3,500, or $750 for having taken the risk. Not bad. But—

If XYZ rises in price, Mr. Short-Seller begins to feel distinctly uneasy. Every point XYZ climbs means a loss of $100 in replacing the borrowed stock. All this leads to the shattering risk in short-selling . . .

There is NO limit to the short-seller's potential loss.

The man who bought the 100 shares originally could possibly lose all his $4,250, but that only if XYZ is wiped out with nothing remaining for the shareholders.

BUT the short-seller is out $100 for every point rise in price. And since there is no limit to how far the shares can rise, Mr. Short-Seller's headache grows worse and worse with every point climb. He may yell "uncle" when the stock gets to $49. OR, insisting that his original analysis is still right, he may dig in his heels, declare "they can't do this to me," and refuse to buy in the stock at 55 or 62½ or 75 or 103.

Of course, his mulishness requires more than mere stubbornness. It requires additional money. No broker in his right mind is going to allow Mr. Short-Seller to remain in debt for stock now selling at $75 or $95 a share for which he has collateral of only $42.50 a share. So the short-seller will have to put up more cash—or securities—to the level which makes the lending broker comfortable.

Worse. XYZ Corp. pays a quarterly dividend of 75 cents a share. But NOT to the man who loaned the short-seller stock at $42.50 a share. Reason: XYZ doesn't even know he exists. He's no longer on the company's shareholder lists. So—guess who has to pay that dividend to the stock lender who, after all, wants his dividend? Right! Mr. Short-Seller pays it, right out of his pocket. And he pays for anything else XYZ distributes on its shares—extra dividend, split stock, etc.

Short-selling represents a relatively small portion of stock market activity. But it has been responsible for some major financial headaches. There have been instances where unfavorable reports or predictions of a company's future have brought in a flood of short-selling, sometimes to the level where the total of stock sold short represented a sub-stantial portion of the outstanding issue. In some cases, "in-siders" who owned large blocks of the stock made it readily available for lending out to short-sellers, knowing that a sen-sational recovery of the company's prospects was nearby. When the good news came out, the lenders stopped lending stock, market prices soared and the short-sellers were caught and often wiped out in a "squeeze" which could only be duplicated in novels or movies.

To sum up: short-selling is not illegal, immoral or fat-tening. But it can be dangerous to your bank or brokerage statement.

If you are "bearish" on a company, if you feel the stock is over-priced, you have a perfect right to "short" the stock. But before you do, make sure you understand exactly what you are letting yourself in for in terms of dividend obligations, possible rental fees, etc. One thing you can be sure of: you will be shown no mercy if the market goes against you. Dividends will be taken out of your account, and if the stock price rises sufficiently to even approach the point where your original investment does not represent sufficient collateral to protect the lending broker you will be called on for more collateral. And if you don't come up with it, you will be bought in . . . pronto! That lending broker isn't in business to back up your "bearish" whims.

There have been rare instances in Wall Street history or legend of "short sales" being made for "investment" purposes. The reasoning: a successful company's share of its market had reached the saturation point; its stock had gone as high as could be expected. So, short-sellers sold the stock, taking the position that it had no place to go but down. The stock may have been investment grade, but the risk proved to be just as great as though it had been a wild speculation. The company diversified and its stock went still higher.

There is an old bit of doggerel in Wall Street:

> "He who sells what isn't his'n
> "Must buy it back or go to pris'n."

There are no recorded instances of short-sellers going to prison. But many have been wiped out, financially.

So, be careful!

20

Keeping Records—
Just What Do You Own?

There used to be old-time brokers whose highest praise, when "pitching" a security to a potential investor, was: "You can put it away and forget about it!" That implied that the security was so sound that it would take care of itself (and you) without any effort on your part. Now it's quite true that if you today buy a six-months' Treasury bill there isn't much point in doing anything with it except leaving it on "bookkeeping entry" at the bank, and making a note of the due date on your calendar.

But it certainly doesn't follow that that is all you have to do to keep track of municipal bonds, or corporate bonds and debentures, or preferred and common shares. These must be more closely watched, for many and diverse reasons, most important of which is to preserve the data you need to answer the reasonable question, "How am I doing?" Examples of such data:

- Cost data, including commissions and date of purchase, in case you decide to sell; dividends and interest received—to make sure some checks haven't gone astray (generally you can count on quarterly dividend checks each year from stocks and two semi-annual interest checks from bonds and debentures);

- Stock splits, certificate numbers, including the corporation's number, the CUSIP (securities industry) number; amount of shares or par value of bonds, date of issue.

You should have all this data on hand even if your securities are kept in a bank vault. Safety deposit boxes rarely carry any insurance. If the vaults are broken into, you have only your word about what you had in that box, and your chances of recovery are far better if you can show, black on white, just what assets were kept there.

You will find record books for securities in any business stationery shop. Many are excellent but expensive. Suit yourself. There is no reason you can't set up your own records with the help of any 5 x 8 or 8 x 12-inch looseleaf notebook.

WHAT TO RECORD

At the top of each page should be a complete description of the security. A bond page, for example, should carry the name of the issuer (U.S. government, state, city, or corporation), the coupon rate (that is, the stated interest rate), the semi-annual dates on which interest is paid, maturity date when the bond must be redeemed (if the company doesn't choose to pay it off before maturity), the number of your particular bond and, of course, the amount of the bond. If instead of a single certificate your $5,000 investment brought you five $1,000 bonds, the individual numbers of each bond should be listed.

Following this data should be the figures which apply directly to your particular investment:

- Price paid, when purchased, through what firm;
- Any accrued interest you paid to the previous owner who owned the bond from the time of the last interest payment until the day you became the owner.

(Bond interest is computed on a daily basis. If the last semi-annual interest payment was March 1 and you acquired the bond March 15, your cost of acquisition will be increased by the amount of fifteen days' interest to which the previous investor-owner of the bond is entitled. Keep a record of this interest because it becomes a tax deduction for you as "interest expenses" on your income tax report in the year you acquired the bond.);

- Commission costs and total amount paid. All these data are necessary to determine taxable gain, or tax-deductible loss if and when you sell the bond.

If the bond is registered in your name, which means you will receive the semi-annual interest by check (instead of clipping coupons, as in the case of a bearer-type, unregistered bond) you should leave room on the page to make note of the receipt of such semi-annual interest, just as protection against the possibility of a check lost in the mail. (If that should happen, immediately notify the company [generally a bank] which is the paying agent for the corporation, and is so named on the bond itself.)

If you own a debenture bond which is convertible into common shares, the conversion data should be listed also (including any date on which the conversion privilege is adjusted or terminated). From time to time you should check the price of the common stock of the corporation. It might reach a price, or a dividend level, which you would consider attractive for conversion of bond to stock.

Keeping records on common shares requires less data since there is generally only one issue of a company's common. Your shares are no different from any other investor's common holdings. However, here, too, the data should begin with the name of the corporation, the number of shares held, when and through whom acquired, and total cost of acquisition (including buying commissions, which, for tax purposes, become part of the initial cost). If and when you sell, it is the total figure on your confirmation slip (plus any transfer taxes charged) which is used to determine whether you have a taxable capital gain, or a tax-deductible capital loss. Also include the corporation's certificate number, date of issue and CUSIP number.

Most commons pay dividends four times a year. Leave room to note these payments as received, just so that you can spot any gap caused by mail loss and also keep record of your taxable income from this source.

Common share holdings may be increased by stock splits, or by a dividend paid in the form of additional shares, or by the exercise of rights which will involve additional cash layout on your part. All these increases in shares held must be listed exactly because they all affect the total cost of your investment—both in actual cash figures and for income tax purposes. For example:

If your original 100 shares holding has been increased to 200 by a 2-for-1 split, the original cost of the 100 shares now becomes the tax cost for the 200 shares. If you paid $40 a share, or $4,000 total, your total cost for the 200 shares remains $4,000, bringing the tax basis cost of any or all shares you now sell down to $20 a share.

If your original 100 shares holding was increased to 125 by the payment of a 25% stock dividend (or a 5 for 4 "split"), your cost per share for any and all of your shares now held is reduced to $32 a share (4,000 divided by 125).

If you add cash to your original $4,000 investment in order to acquire more shares by the exercise of any "rights," that additional cash should be added to the $4,000 to arrive at a cost per share of your now increased holdings.

IMPORTANCE OF RECORD KEEPING

Record keeping is important not only to have data at hand with which to check dividend or interest receipts, but also to help you review your portfolio from time to time and to determine whether individual securities deserve retention. It is great help in overcoming sentiment: "Grandpa left me those 100 shares, and they've been paying a dividend ever since. I'm not going to touch them."

It's all well and good to cherish Grandpa's memory, but it doesn't follow that his shares of Buggy Whip, Inc. are as potent an investment for you as they were for him.

Again: has your convertible debenture risen to the point where it no longer yields income in step with current interest rates? You may have bought a 5% debenture at a discount when it was yielding 7%, but if it has since risen in price (thanks to the rise in the underlying common shares for which it may be exchanged) where the yield is now less than 4.2% (and you need or are interested in generous income), then perhaps it is time to make a change. Either sell the debenture and employ the money elsewhere, or—if the common pays a generous dividend—switch to that common.

Or perhaps you hold a common stock on which the dividend has not kept pace with the market price advance.

Record keeping techniques will vary widely. Some investors are naturally tidy and like to keep a close check on their holdings. An excellent idea, although care should be taken to avoid translating close attention into over-trading. If you also keep records of market price movements, don't let a 1½ rise in one week, or a ¾ point drop the next day exert any undue influence on your decision to hold on to or sell what was originally intended as a long-term investment.

If you are a long-term investor . . . interested in long-term capital gains, or long-term income . . . you should keep records as an ongoing picture of what you own and how it is performing. Day-to-day traders can keep most of their records in their hats.

21

Focal Points of Investor-Broker Infection

In the course of a long investment lifetime you will, without fail, encounter many reasons for becoming angry with your broker—especially if you choose the route of the "hot-shot" trader who tries to "beat the market" by fast and furious, in-and-out dealings. Often, the trouble is nothing more complicated than a common back-office clerical error, a dividend not credited, an error in balances, failure to send out a dividend check, etc.

But it will help alleviate these sore points if you take the time to learn the exact meaning of some of the important but all-too-often loosely used Wall Street terms. When misunderstood, these terms can lead to serious accusations which can destroy the sensitive relationship between you and your broker. For example:

"EX-DIVIDEND" DATE

There is no fury which quite compares with that of an investor who bought stock before a dividend was distributed but failed to get it; or (worse yet) if he did get it was told by his broker that he had to return it . . . that it didn't belong to him.

The confusion and anger derive directly from failure to understand that there are at least four different dates which apply to the payment of a dividend: the day the corporation's Board of Directors declares the dividend; the record date set by the directors which determines the list of shareholders entitled to the dividend; the "ex-dividend" date on which the stock is no longer entitled to that quarterly dividend; and finally, the date on which the dividend check is mailed out to the investor. They are all different dates and the crucial one, which determines whether you are entitled to the dividend, is the "ex-dividend" date.

If it so happens that you don't receive the dividend, make sure you learn the "score" before you yell "Stop, thief!"

You read in the daily financial section of your newspaper that "Directors of XYZ Corp. today (let's say, January 18) have declared a quarterly dividend of 50 cents a share payable February 15 to shareholders of record February 1."

A crucial date missing from the announcement is the "ex-dividend" date ("ex" meaning "without")—in other words, the date the stock is no longer entitled to this dividend.

The reason the corporation just doesn't vote the dividend today and send out the checks immediately is that XYZ shares are being traded every day on the exchanges, or over-the-counter, and some cut-off date must be fixed in order to separate those investors entitled to receive that check from those who are not entitled to it.

You have at least two chances of yelling "we wuz robbed":

1. You own 100 shares and, feeling that you have earned the $50 in dividends, can now move your money elsewhere; you sell the stock; or
2. You like the idea of getting that $50 dividend and make a note on your desk pad to buy the stock February 14 and receive the dividend check "for free" on the next day. Wrong—both ways.

Because it takes time to transfer shares to any new owner's name, on the books of the corporation, the directors arbitrarily set a "record date," a cut-off date. If your name is listed as a shareholder of record February 1 you will receive this quarterly dividend on the 15th. That's fair enough. It wouldn't do to have shareholders fighting over a dividend check at the Post Office. But—in addition:

It takes about five days to record a transfer of a stock from one owner to another in a market transaction. The seller must deliver his stock to his broker, who gives it to the buyer's broker, who must send it to the bank which acts as transfer agent for the corporation. The bank cancels the old certificate (which carried the name of the seller) and issues a new certificate with the buyer's name on it, and then sends the new certificate to the new investor or his broker. This all takes time, and to avoid any confusion during the days when this certificate is in the transfer machinery, the financial community establishes an "ex-dividend" date ahead of the record date—a date when the dividend "goes off" the stock. And that is the most important date in our story.

The date the dividend was declared means nothing. The date it is finally mailed means nothing—unless you're desperate for the money. The record date is an official, legal date and is important, but rarely meaningful to the investor since weekends and legal holidays can ball up the day count.

The date you must pay attention to is the "ex-dividend" date. Let's say it is, in this case, January 26. If you presently own XYZ stock and sell it any time before the closing of the stock market on January 25, you are selling the stock *with the dividend attached.* When that check is mailed out February 15 it will not come to you (and if it does you will have to return it). Anyone who buys the stock from you before the closing bell of the stock exchange on January 25 collects the dividend. The only way you can get that dividend is to still own the stock at the closing of the stock exchange on January 26. If you sell it on the 26th or later you keep that quarterly dividend, because shares sold on the "ex-dividend" date (or thereafter) are sold "ex"—without—the dividend.

So, if that upcoming quarterly dividend is important to you, be sure to check the "ex-divided" date of the current quarterly dividend. If you are not now a shareholder and want to collect the payment, be sure your "buy" order is executed before the exchange closes on the day *before* the stock goes "ex-dividend." If you own the stock and intend to sell, do not sell it before the day the stock goes "ex-dividend" if you want that dividend. Your broker can tell you exactly when the stock goes "ex."

Incidentally, there is little point in buying a stock just to get the dividend, or conversely delaying sale of a stock until it has gone "ex" to assure yourself of the right to the dividend. Reason: All other factors being equal, the market price of a stock is adjusted to the payment of the dividend. If a stock pays a quarterly dividend of fifty cents you will generally find that if it closed at 25 on the day before the "ex-dividend" date, it will sell at 24½ on the morning of the "ex-dividend" day—when the dividend is no longer attached to the stock. Incidentally, the 24½ price will be tagged as "unchanged" rather than as a market drop of ½ point.

There are no free lunches in Wall Street.

PAR VALUE

Evidently, there is no shock which quite compares with that experienced by a novice investor who pays 32⅞ for a common stock, plus commissions, and who sees his certificate clearly marked "$1 par value."

Relax. Par value in the case of a common share is merely a bookkeeping term, a dollar amount fixed in the company's charter, but of no significance to the investor. In fact, "no par" common shares have become popular in recent years. "Par value" has no bearing on a common share's market value, dividend, liquidation value or anything else. It is a meaningless term (for the investor) left over from ancient times when it was supposed to indicate the value of the original investment.

However—par value in the case of a preferred stock or a bond *is* important, because it may determine the amount of the dividend (in the case of a preferred) and will fix the amount of interest you receive (in the case of a bond).

A preferred share may be designated as a "$4.25 preferred" which means the annual dividend is $4.25 (or $1.06¼ quarterly). Or it may be called the "8% preferred" which, in a way, is meaningless unless you also know the par value on which this 8% dividend payout is based. If the par value is $50, the dividend will be 8% of that or $4 a year; if it is a $100 par value stock, the annual dividend comes to $8.

Bonds are generally issued in $1,000 par amounts (although $500 and even $100 par bonds are not unknown). The interest is figured on the par value. And furthermore, bonds are traded in percentages of that par value. If you are talking of the vast majority of bonds, a bond market quote of 85½ means 85½% of $1,000 or $850 per $1,000 par value certificate. If the bond is listed as an 8% bond, it will pay $80 a year interest per $1,000 par value certificate irrespective of its market price. That $80 payment is fixed when the bond is issued and does *NOT* vary according to market price. However, the current return yield does vary since $80 annual interest on a bond selling for $850 represents a current yield of 9.41% on the money invested. And if you want to look ahead to maturity, when the bond will be paid off at $1,000, you can add a $150 per bond long-term profit to that 9.41% yield to get the total reward from your investment.

So—par value in a common share ... ignore it. In the case of a preferred or bond ... very important.

"STOP LOSS" ORDERS

This is, perhaps, one of the most misunderstood and most loosely used stock market trading techniques. Never does it fail to cause an argument when the result is wide of what was intended.

In the first place, it is generally labeled incorrectly. It is not a "stop loss," but a "stop order." It may be used in an attempt to limit a loss or to sell out at a profit.

The chief problem is that those who place such an order without really knowing what it does feel mistakenly that it will guarantee a fixed price for a sale or purchase. Not so.

A "stop order" becomes an open market order whenever the stock sells at, or goes through, the stop price.

If you are losing money on a stock (bought at 32, and now selling at 27) and you decide to cut your loss at 25½, you tell your broker to place a sell order at 25½, "stop." If the stock recedes further to 25½ or lower, your broker will sell your stock on the open market at the best price then prevailing. A selling price of 25½ for your stock is *not* guaranteed since the first transaction at 25½ did not involve your stock but was set by someone else and merely served to put your stock up for sale, immediately, at whatever price appeared next. You might bet 25½, or may have to take 25¼ or 25⅛ if the decline in the stock is rapid . . . or 25¾ if the stock were to rebound a fraction.

The "stop order" may also be used to protect a profit: you bought a stock at $40 a share and watched it rise to $55, and have now thought of taking your profits. But first you want to give the stock a chance to go even higher, if it wants to. Why sell at 55 if it may subsequently rise to 60? But, also, you don't want to let your greed mislead you (or you may be planning a vacation and will be unable to watch the stock). You tell your broker to put in a selling order at 50, "stop." In other words, you're prepared to see the stock decline 5 points and cut your gross profit to $10 a share in exchange for taking the chance of seeing the stock climb further to 60. If your stock continues to rise, your order is held in abeyance until cancelled. If the stock should decline to 50, your sell order becomes a market order and your broker immediately offers it at the best price he can get . . . which may be 50, or either side of it.

"Stop orders" have their purpose, but offer no guarantees.

A "QUOTE"

You call your broker to express your interest in owning JKL common stock. You ask him: "What's the market on JKL?" He will punch a few buttons on his information machine and come back with "28½–29" and may even add "2 by 5." Translation: buyers for 200 shares are bidding $28.50 a share; sellers of 500 shares are asking $29 a share.

Since the stock market is a two-way auction (bidders may raise their price and sellers may lower theirs) it is quite likely the next deal will be somewhere in the 28½–29 range. "Likely"—but not necessarily so. If you want the stock and you say: "Buy me 100 (or 200, or 400) at the market," you may discover—even in an active stock—that you've paid 28⅝ or 28¾ or 28⅛ or 28⅜ or 29⅛ . . . or more, or less. How come?

The "quote"—the "bid and asked" and the "market size" your broker reported to you—was true *as of that moment.* When he asked his trader on the floor of the exchange for the quote, the trader went into the "crowd" trading JKL and called out: "How's JKL?" and received the information he passed on to your broker either from members of the crowd or from the specialist whose business it is to make an "orderly" market in JKL common.

That was the picture at that moment.

It took several moments to transmit that information to the office. It took several more moments to transmit your "buy" instructions back to the trading floor, and several more moments for your firm's trader to get back over to the post where JKL is traded.

In that few minute interval, it is quite possible that a broker, acting for some investor half a continent away, grabbed the 500 shares being offered at the asking price of 29, leaving no stock for immediate sale below a price of 29¼. And when your market order reached the floor, that's what you paid ... because you didn't specify any limit on your purchase order.

Or the reverse could have happened: the bid for 200 shares at 28½ may have been withdrawn and the closest bid then became 28. So those—or some of those—who had offered 500 shares at 29 thought better of it and decided to take 28⅜, which is what you got the stock for.

Quotes are true ... as of the moment they are given, and transactions taking place at the time of the quotation are generally executed within the limits of the quotation. But don't expect that price is going to be around very long while you are making up your mind. A "market" order is executed at the market—and no one can assure you what that price will be five minutes from now.

By the same token, if you play it too cozy—insist you won't pay a penny more than 28⅜ or 28½ for the stock (which is your right)—you may not get the stock at all. There is a middle ground on penny pinching in buying or selling stocks, and only long, and often sad, experience can tell you exactly where that is. A good maxim to remember is: "No one ever got the top eighth-of-a-point in selling, or got the lowest eighth in buying." (Someone did, of course, or else the price wouldn't have been established. But generally it's no one you and I know.)

"THE OPENING"

The first trade in a stock after the 10 A.M. opening bell at the stock exchange may be a casual affair at just about the same price which had prevailed when the market closed the previous afternoon—or it may reflect any number or magnitude of price influences: a drastic overnight change in the corporation's affairs, a "hot tip" over the evening airwaves or in the morning newspaper.

The point to remember is that whether the first trade is only an eighth of a point away from the previous closing, or 4 points higher or 5 points lower, *all* "market" orders given brokers between the time of the closing and opening bells are executed at the *same price. Example:* XYZ stock closed Wednesday afternoon at 35, and was either touted by some experts or was treated favorably in the corporate news Wednesday evening. You told your broker at 9:30 Thursday morning to buy some "at the market." You can be sure you got your stock on the first trade after 10 A.M. Thursday at whatever opening price was arrived at on the floor: $35\frac{1}{8}$ or $37\frac{3}{4}$, or whatever. If you had fixed your buying price at 35, your order was not included in the opening execution. If you told your broker to pay up to 38 for it, you paid only what everyone else paid on that first "clean-up" transaction.

Allowing yourself to become enthusiastic over a "tip" after the market has closed can often lead to paying much more than you had expected when the stock opens the next morning. Be sure your broker understands any price limits you have in mind, because your "at the market" order will be lumped with everyone else's on that first trade. Years ago, a Sunday news broadcaster tipped an oil company stock which brought a flood of buying to the American Stock Exchange. After long official consultation with the specialist in the stock, who responded magnificently to the insane demand for the stock by personally going short, the opening trade satisfied all the buyers at a price only a point or two above the previous close. That higher price was never seen again. (Who was left to bid the stock higher after all the speculators got all the stock they wanted on the very first trade?) And the specialist was able to cover his short position and come out with a $75,000 profit on his high risk effort.

Orders to buy at the market can be dangerous if they are put in at any interval up to the 18 hours per day that the exchange is closed. You can never tell what you'll pay in the morning.

WHERE'S MY STOCK?

Anyone handing over $150 or $1,500 to a clothing store for an overcoat expects, naturally, to be handed the coat—either immediately or right after alterations have been completed. Twisting the meaning of the old adage, you're supposed to get what you pay for. But too often first-time or inexperienced investors get themselves into a tizzy when their stock certificate doesn't appear in the next mail. It's unnecessary grief.

If you today order 100 shares of XYZ common and the order is executed, you are expected to pay for the stock within five business days. But then, you complain, you wait two or three weeks before you get the stock certificate. T'ain't fair . . . and to some non-professional investors, even a bit suspicious.

My answer to all this is: relax. I've owned stocks for three and four decades and have never seen the certificates. I've been content to leave them with the broker—let him worry about safekeeping, collecting the dividends, and crediting them to my account, furnishing me with tax data at the end of the year, going into his own vaults to pick up the stock and deliver it if and when I decide to sell.

But even if you want physical possession of the certificate—and that is certainly your privilege—you can't expect to be handed the stock over the counter as if it were a pound of coffee taken off the shelf. After you've paid for the stock, your broker collects it from the seller and then sends it off to the corporation transfer office to have that certificate cancelled and another issued in your name. Then it must be sent out to you—*if* you specifically tell the broker you want possession. In some cases this may take a couple of weeks, or even a month or so. And, of course, if you never tell the broker you want the stock, he assumes you want it held in his bank vault with your ownership attested to only by your brokerage account statement. With brokerage insurance now running up to $300,000 and beyond for each individual account, more and more investors are leaving securities with their brokers. Suit yourself. But before you become angry, make sure you've told your broker exactly what you want done with the stock or bond you've just bought.

"STOCK AHEAD" AND "MATCHED AND LOST"

You ask your broker to sell your XYZ common at 28. The next morning's stock market listing shows XYZ had a trading range of between 27¼ and 28, but the day's mail brings no sales confirmation. When you call the broker, he tells you: "Your stock wasn't sold." And you are angry. How come someone sold stock at 28, but you didn't get in on it? Because, you are told, there was "stock ahead" on the specialist's book. Stock was entered on the specialist's book ahead of yours and, therefore, was sold when the 28 bid first appeared. Thereafter the bid dropped to, for example, 27⅞ or 27¾ and never touched 28 again for the rest of the session. So your stock remains unsold. Or—

Your broker's floor trader rushed to the XYZ trading post, offered your stock for sale at 28 at the same instant as another broker's representative who made the identical offer. The potential buyer, at 28, then waited until the two offering brokers flipped a coin to see who was to make the sale. Your broker lost the call. Sounds primitive, but who has time during a hectic trading day on the floor to make a federal case of a single transaction?

WHY DOESN'T HE CALL ME?

The phrase "damned if he does, damned if he doesn't" applies directly to the "registered representative" (or, to use a more comfortable appellation, "customer's man").

One type of broker is criticized because he's on the phone every day, urging you to buy X and sell Y. And you get the distinct feeling he's only after your commissions.

Another doesn't call you for months at a time. And you get the distinct impression that he doesn't value your business at all and, in fact, wishes you would go away.

Both impressions may be true; both can result from misunderstandings.

Let's face it—a broker lives by his commissions. Even if the firm boasts that it pays salaries, and not commissions, to its registered "reps," the fact remains that the salary is very definitely related to the amount of commissions generated. "High producers" are valued in Wall Street as well as anywhere else.

So all a broker has to offer is his services. Time is literally money to him.

If you are an active trader, you will have no difficulty getting your broker on the phone or in having him call you daily or even more frequently.

If he calls you three times a day for a week and gets no response in the form of trading, he will reasonably assume that you don't want to trade—which is certainly your decision to make. So he'll stop calling you that frequently and, perhaps, check in with you only once every three months.

The other side of the coin: If you buy 50 shares of Telephone, take it home, and then do nothing more in securities for nine months, don't expect that he will welcome calls from you three times a day wherein you ask for a fresh quote on A.T.&T., or seek his opinion of the Federal budget or the advisibility of your sending money to a Swiss bank account. He's got to "make hay" between 10 A.M. and 4 P.M.

and making hay does not include long economic discussions or comments on personal trivia.

An elderly woman whose portfolio consisted of 75 shares of International Harvester once complained bitterly to me that her broker did not voluntarily call and explain to her why Harvester was climbing in a "down" market. Another expressed her disappointment in the broker who purchased for her $10,000 worth of AAA quality utility bonds but never followed it up with quarterly telephone discussions about the company's progress . . . an exercise about as purposeful as reassessing the value of her table silver every three months.

A broker is a professional who works for a living. As in the case of a physician or lawyer, time is an important factor and an investor should not impose upon it.

(In the same context, it should be obvious—although the question is often raised—that a broker who is doing a good job for you is NOT to be rewarded with gratuities . . . tips. A frequent question: "Am I supposed to tip the broker if I make money on his suggestions?" The answer: *No.* It is not only demeaning but in violation of many brokerage firm rules.)

WHY CAN'T I GET A NEW ISSUE?

Commissions on securities transactions have gone up . . what hasn't? If you are a frequent trader, they represent a sizable obstacle to scalping small and frequent profits. If you are a long-term investor, they are relatively unimportant.

But either way no one likes to pay them . . . all of which leads to fascination with the "new issue" which you can buy at net price, that is, without paying a commission to the broker.

A "new issue" may be common shares, preferreds, bonds, debentures offered on the market for the first time either by a brand new company or by a long-established one.

XYZ Corp. may have three million common shares out-standing, as well as two million preferred, and $50 million worth of bonds and debentures already in the hands of investors. But if it offers additional common shares or pre-ferreds or new bond or debenture issues, and the new se-curities are offered to the public through underwriting bankers and brokers, the purchasing investor pays no commission to the sellers because they, the sellers, are reimbursed for their effort by the issuing corporation. If the morning paper, then, carries an advertisement offering a new issue of 1,500,000 common shares to the public today by the "undersigned" bankers and brokers at $32 a share, all you pay is the $32 or $3,200 for 100 shares, and not approximately $55 additional in brokerage commissions.

The 1.7% savings is nothing to sneer at and if you liked XYZ common or wanted some of its bonds, you feel you've been neglected if you call your broker on the day you read the "ad" in the newspaper and are told: "Sorry, they're all gone." If that happens you have no one but yourself to blame. You were perhaps a week late. Although a broker may not sell a new issue before the formal offering date—the date on which the advertisement appears in the press—he can ac-cept "indications of interest" long before that date. And that's what you should have given him days and even weeks before. How could you know a new issue was on the way? By watching the financial news items which list filings of new issues with the Securities and Exchange Commission (at least 3 weeks before the public offering date). Or by informing your broker that in general you are interested in new issues of stocks or preferreds or bonds which might be coming along. If a new issue is desirable, it will be oversubscribed via "indications of interest" long before the offering date. If a lot of the issue is still unsold on the offering date, maybe you don't want any, either.

It all boils down to maintaining an open line of com-munications with your broker, in exactly the same sense that you make sure he understands what you want when you give him a limit order, or any other extraordinary set of instructions.

There is another method of obtaining new common shares without paying a commission, and that is via the exercise of rights sometimes granted by a corporation to existing shareholders. The "right," for example, will give the shareholder the privilege of subscribing to additional shares in proportion to the amount of stock he or she already owns. For example: XYZ Corp. has one million shares of stock outstanding, trading on the market at, say, 20⅞ ($20.875) a share. The company announces it will offer 250,000 new shares, giving present shareowners first privilege (called preemptive rights) to subscribe at $20 per share—one new share for each four already held. That means that if you already own 100 shares of XYZ, you will receive 100 "rights," and every four rights plus $20 in cash will bring you a share of the new stock. If you exercised all your 100 rights, you would be entitled to buy twenty-five of the new shares for a total $500 payment (25 X $20). Again, no commissions.

Sounds like a bargain—and it might be. If you like the stock and want twenty-five more shares, it's a good way of acquiring them. If you don't want more XYZ common, then you tell the bank acting as agent for the corporation to sell your rights and send you the proceeds. In the above example, the rights would have a cash value of nearly twenty cents each, since four of them are required to buy, for $20, a stock that is selling on the open market at just under $21.

The one thing you *do not* do is ignore the rights you receive in the mail; usually they have a short life ... perhaps a couple of weeks, after which they become *worthless*. So you either exercise them, or sell them *before* termination date. Your choices are clearly indicated on the computer card you receive from the corporation. (Your broker is in no way involved.) And don't throw the notice away just because it isn't a check.

Many small investors, or unsophisticated investors, make a "big deal" of getting stocks and bonds commission-free in the form of new issues; they also become very much excited over rights to buy new stock, again commission-free, via "rights." There's nothing wrong with it. In fact, I'd rather have investors excited about their investments than neglectful of them.

But, I think a long-span survey of the new issues market or of new offerings via "rights" will show that on average the commissions savings may well be illusory . . . at least in terms of on-the-spot savings. Reason:

Unless you are in the middle of a runaway bull market, the sudden single-day availability of 250,000 additional common shares (or an additional $75 million of bonds) will obviously go a long way toward dulling the appetite for XYZ common, or bonds.

Any investor who had been building up a desire to own XYZ common would obviously order it, commission-free, on the day of formal offering. Ditto, the bond buyer. If no less than $5 million is put into the stock (or $75 million into the bonds) on a single day, you can assume that XYZ fans have had their fill of that security and won't be around in the succeeding days and weeks with bids to buy more. It is not at all unusual—given a somewhat-less-than-dynamic market—to see XYZ common, which sold at 20⅞ on the market on the day of the offering and which was priced at 20 for the new issue, drop back to 19 or 19⅛, or some such under-20 quotation in subsequent sessions. This occurs when non-commission faddists find that buying at a net price did not guarantee a profit and that perhaps their original 100 shares of the stock was enough.

Moral: By all means save on commissions where and when you can, but don't invest in something merely because there is no purchase fee.

DISCOUNT COMMISSIONS

In recent years, as exchange commissions have risen sharply, a new type of broker has emerged—the discount broker who will execute orders to buy or sell stock for you (and furnish no other services) at a substantial discount from traditional brokerage firms' commission schedules. If all you want is the execution of your order to buy or sell, by all means consider using them. But first make sure of their brokerage industry affiliations, of their insurance coverage, and their standing in the industry. Also make sure you don't want analyses, opinions or hand-holding.

22

An Annuity—
What It Can, and Cannot,
Do for You

An annuity is *not* an investment by which you hope to "make money." It is a *contract* to provide income ... predetermined, guaranteed, unwavering, fixed-dollar income, for life, if not longer. It offers NO chance of a profit. What you buy at the outset is what you get ... period.

However, since income is one of the primary goals of all investing, the annuity deserves a place in the investment listings and a discussion of just what it can and cannot do for those seeking income.

But, first, there are some basic differences between an annuity and any other place you might put your money in the hope of obtaining income:

An annuity is not a security. It may not be traded. Once it begins producing income, it generally remains in force for the buyer's lifetime, or longer. As a matter of fact, once purchased, you no longer have a capital asset, any form of property. What you hold is a contract—fixed and non-negotiable. To obtain that contract you have "kissed your money goodbye."

OPTIONS

Again, whereas a 9½% bond produces $95 annual interest for every investor who owns it, an annuity payout depends upon the sex of the buyer and the age at which he or she begins to receive income. It is also affected importantly by various options selected at the time of purchase:

1. Whether the income will be forthcoming only during the lifetime of the beneficiary, or whether the contract will leave an estate if he or she does not live long enough to collect all the money paid in;
2. whether it covers a man or a woman or a couple;
3. whether the survivor is to receive the same amount of income as the two received, or a reduced amount, etc.

HOW IT WORKS

Annuity income is determined basically by actuarial tables which are the life expectancy tables used by life insurance companies—as well as by charitable, religious, and educational institutions—when they decide how much they will pay out to an annuitant of a certain age and sex. A man of 74, it is assumed, will be around for fewer years than a man of 69, so the 69-year-old will receive less per year (or per month) from each $1,000 paid into the contract than will the 74-year-old. Again, women—statistically—live longer than men, so a 69-year-old woman will receive less annual income per $1,000 paid into the annuity contract than will a man of the same age. Reason: the annuity seller figures the man will die sooner and therefore won't collect as much total income.

The respective ages of the annuitants also have some effect in determining the amount of each annuity payment which is to be considered a return of the annuitant's capital—and, therefore, exempt from income taxes.

It should be obvious, then, that although annuities are based on impersonal, cold, statistical tables, the individual annuity you consider should be shaped to your particular needs. Above all it must be compared with what current money market conditions indicate you could receive in the way of income from other sources—stocks, bonds, bank accounts, commercial paper, etc. etc., which do not consume assets, as does an annuity.

But before any attention is given to actuarial formulas or to going interest rates for money in the general investment market, the first questions anyone considering an annuity must ask himself or herself are:

Must I leave an estate . . . or do I want to leave an estate?

Am I prepared to accept the fact that this $10,000 or $50,000 I put into this lifetime annuity is *gone* as far as my heirs are concerned?

WHAT IT OFFERS

The annuity has one unmatched virtue: the buyer, the annuitant, will never run out of income for as long as they, or he or she live. And, while the income will not be increased, neither can it be decreased. No other investment can boast that assurance. On a lifetime income basis, the annuity is the closest one can come to activating the "bird in hand" theory in finance. In return for your agreeing today to accept $200 or $500, or whatever sum, monthly for life, you rid yourself of any doubts about receiving that money for the remainder of your lifetime. Finance offers no other such guarantee.

As is to be expected, peace of mind costs money. Not only do you hand over the money for the contract but you agree that the set $200 or $500 sum is *all* you are going to get, regardless of whether bread goes to $2 a loaf at the supermarket and heating oil to $3 a gallon. With inflation on the front pages daily the annuity's fixed payout represents an obstacle that cannot be lightly ignored. In fact, it pretty much indicates that annuities—as comforting as they may be from the standpoint of safety and stability—are perhaps only part of the total picture for providing later years income. (Stability can be carried too far, as exemplified by the over-enthusiastic barfly who insisted that the more he drank the "steadier" he got. He finally became so steady that he had to be carried out.)

Nevertheless, the security that steady income can provide for the elderly is not to be dismissed in offhanded fashion. The annuity deserves serious consideration for at least part of the income-seeker's funds, with increasingly more funds as a buyer's advanced age minimizes the problem of long-time inflation.

There are, fundamentally, two types of annuity:

TYPES

1. Lifetime . . . that is, for the lifetime of the purchaser or purchasers. At death, the money is gone;
2. Refund or "years certain" contracts which *may* leave an estate *if* the purchaser or purchasers do not live long enough to collect all the principal paid in.

Since there are no "free lunches" in finance, the first type of annuity yields more income to the purchaser.

HOW TO BUY

Annuities also may be acquired in different ways:

By payment of insurance premiums over a period of years;

By a lump sum payment when the buyer wants to begin receiving monthly income;

By transfer ("roll over") of IRA funds.

The last is a relatively new procedure which requires individual consultation with both the annuity seller and the buyer's tax adviser.

The first is a form of insurance acquisition. Insurance is, of course, important... often "non-negotiable." But from the annuity-only point of view the installment purchase over a long period of years seems undesirable since it extends the inflation hazard over many, many years. The inroads of inflation during the years the annuitant is receiving a fixed income are dangerous enough, without increasing the inherent risks in beginning with a contract twenty, thirty, or forty years before income payments are to start.

Which brings us to the second, the lump sum payment... in effect, the most direct form of purchase and one which reduces the inflation risk to only the buyer's remaining years.

For the sake of these examples, let's deal in terms of $10,000 paid in a lump sum for an annuity designed to begin immediately and to provide a lifetime monthly income.

Although the monthly income is based primarily on the sex of the buyer and his/her age, there is good reason to do some shopping—even though, for added safety purposes, only those companies which are licensed to do business in your state should be considered. (Insurance company failures are uncommon, but if it should happen and the company is licensed to do business in your state, your State Commissioner or Superintendent of Insurance can intervene in your behalf.)

A man of 65, going shopping with $10,000 for an annuity which will provide a monthly check for the remainder of his lifetime, will find a fairly wide range of income benefits... all the way from around $76.50 a month to as high as $92 a month. State taxes in certain instances may account for some of the difference. You should check on this before signing. If the male shopper is aged 75, his benefits, naturally, will increase substantially—all the way from around $105 to $120 a month.

A woman of 65 going shopping for lifetime income with $10,000 can expect to get approximately $70 to $80 a month. If she is 75 when she buys, her income would range from $98 to as much as $105 a month.

Income provided by joint (husband and wife) lifetime annuities will vary widely according to the ages of both and particularly the age of the wife who, all other things being equal, is expected to be the survivor. Another factor, of course, is the amount the contract is pledged to provide for the survivor. In some cases, joint contracts provide for the continuation of the same amount monthly to the survivor. In others, the benefit is reduced to two-thirds or some other formula. All these terms can be negotiated at time of purchase.

One of the most powerful mental blocks to annuities is, naturally, the recognition of mortality: "Why should I hand over $10,000 for an annuity to receive $100 a month, only to lose it all if I should die in, say, 3 months or even 3 years?" There can be no answer to this argument, mortality being hidden behind an impenetrable veil.

The answer for those who feel the insurance company will wind up a big winner is the "refund," or five- ten- or fifteen years "certain" form of annuity.

These are nothing more nor less than a way to "hedge your bets." Instead of playing "all or nothing" with the insurance company selling you the annuity, you word the agreement so that the annuity will either:

1. pay into your estate whatever portion of the $10,000 initial purchase price you do not live long enough to collect in monthly benefits; or
2. if you do not live five, ten or fifteen years (you decide which) after beginning to receive monthly income checks, your heirs will get the balance of those monthly payments.

The first is called a "refund" type annuity; the second, a five (or ten or fifteen) year "certain" contract.

It should be clearly understood, however that *neither* contract guarantees that your heirs will ever see any of this annuity money. If you live long enough to collect the $10,000 you paid in, there will be no remainder for your heirs.

If you live long enough to collect monthly checks for five (or ten or fifteen) years, your heirs will receive nothing.

With both annuities you (actually your heirs) can win ONLY if you die "too soon." If this would be a comfort to you, consider one of these "refund" types. Naturally, you must be prepared to give up a bit of income for the better "odds."

A man of 65 who would receive $86.15 a month for life from one leading insurance company upon payment of $10,000 would receive only $80.19 per month under the "refund" contract and $80.39 a month if he wanted a ten-year "certain" deal. In other words, if he wants to make sure that the insurance company doesn't profit by his early death, he can do so by settling for about $6 a month less income during his lifetime.

A woman of 65 who would receive $76.62 from $10,000 paid for a lifetime plan would receive only $73.54 from the same company if she wanted a "refund" plan, and $74.04 under a ten-year "certain" program.

This data—and much, much more readily available to any annuity buyer—come straight from the life insurance industry's most recent tables. They are, in every case, figured out to the penny and are not negotiable.

But what they don't answer is whether an annuity is a logical purchase for you in the first place, for in addition to the question of age (are you too young to get a good return?), there is also the all-important question of "how much income could you get for your $10,000 elsewhere?" And that question opens up an entirely new area of income buying.

We have established that a man of 65 can receive, say, $86.15 a month for life from a $10,000 annuity. That comes to $1,033.80 a year for his lifetime. After that—nothing. But at the same time that this annuity table was issued, $10,000 worth of AAA-rated corporate bonds were offering approximately $950 a year, with capital pretty much intact and "perpetual." Should a man of 65 "kiss" his $10,000 good-bye for the sake of an extra $83.80 a year from the annuity? Hardly seems worthwhile, even when one admits that the $1,033.80 is fixed and the $950 is subject to the vagaries of the money market. And what about a 65-year-old woman receiving $76.62 a month, or $919.44 a year, from the same company when the same bond would pay her $950 and not extinguish her $10,000!

Of course, it was not ever thus. Back in the days when corporate bonds were yielding 4 and 5%, the insurance company offer looked much better.

So not only is shopping among licensed-in-your-state insurance companies necessary, but the annuity shopper must also weigh the annuity's income advantages against what is obtainable elsewhere in the world of corporate securities, U.S. Treasury offerings and insured savings accounts. The rewards are not exactly identical but the differences are mostly human in impact (life expectancy, desire to enrich heirs, etc.) and can be handled, therefore, without resort to statistics alone. (Not to overlook the insurance companies' claims that folks living on annuity income live, on the average, two years longer than those who don't have this income source.)

One further footnote which may help you make up your mind:

Annuities are also sold by religious, charitable and educational institutions. In many cases, the benefits paid are slightly less than those offered by insurance companies. After all, the idea is to leave some of your money to continue the good work. But, these institutions also offer you the opportunity to pay for your annuity with appreciated securities. This means that a share of stock for which you paid

$50 and which is now selling for $70 may be turned in at the $70 figure, and you escape any tax on the capital gain. These institutions also may be able to offer some income tax (gift) concessions. If you hold appreciated securities and if income taxes are a consideration, it might pay you to investigate what your church, alma mater or favorite charity is offering in the way of annuities before you sign up with a commercial life insurance company. But make sure the institutions are licensed by your state insurance department.

23

"Hot Tips"

It would be ridiculous to assert that there is no such thing as a good "tip." After all, some well-touted horses *do* come in first.

But 99.44% of the time the "hot" stock market tip must prove to be self-defeating in the long run. (Again, as in the case of horse races, if the "tip" is too widely spread around, the parimutuel odds must come down.)

There are two problems always present in a stock tip:

1. its accuracy—which can range from 100% down to zero;
2. how many people have heard it, and already acted on it, before it reached you.

As to the first:

You'd think that Wall Street, an institution which includes giant corporations and giant banks and is often considered the citadel of dignity and conservatism, would not go in for sheer gossip. But the truth is that gossip is part of its basic fare and can, and often does, play an important role in the securities industry. As a reporter walking daily around the financial district and stopping in to see contacts in dozens of banking, brokerage firms and the exchanges, I've seen first hand how rumors work; in fact, more than once I have been in the middle of it. Example: Ask one brokerage firm office at 10:15 A.M. "Have you heard anything about Paramount increasing its dividend?" and by 12:15 P.M. you may be told by a contact: "I hear Paramount is going to boost the dividend next month." It didn't happen, but that doesn't mean the stock didn't rise on the story.

Even assuming the story proved correct, only an expert trader watching the particular stock closely hour by hour, day by day, analyzing trading volume and price movement, and with sources of information on where the buying (or selling) was coming from, could guess how old the tip was, how many speculators had already heard it, and acted on it.

You are told—honest Injun—that XYZ Corp. is going to make a tender offer at $20 a share for JKL stock now selling at $16.125 a share. And, sure enough, JKL appears actively on the tape in unusually large volume, moving up in price. You decide to go with the story and buy 100 at the market. This is no time to quibble about whether you should pay 16¼ or ⅜ or ⅝. You want to get aboard, and do—at 16½. At 17, you're elated; at 18¼ you're ecstatic; at 18¾ you're thinking of quitting your job. But then, at 18⅞, with volume of trading still heavy, the upward price movement stalls. There's nothing quite as discouraging to a market speculator as the sudden halt in a rising price accompanied by still-active trading. Something's wrong—as when a car's roaring engine still makes for no forward motion. Was the story a fake? No. It turns out (and shows up in the next morning's newspapers) that XYZ IS making a tender offer of $20 a share for 200,000 of JKL's 3,470,000 outstanding common shares. It's fact— not rumor. But those who got the story first loaded up on the stock at 14¾ to 15⅛ and decided, reasonably enough, that a fast 3-to-4-point profit in hand made far more sense than gambling that their shares would be included in the 200,000 accepted by XYZ at $20 a share. Experience told them, unequivocally, that if they didn't get in on the tender offer at

$20, that if they were left holding the shares after the tender had been terminated, the stock would probably back down overnight to around 15 or 16 where it had been selling for the last nine months prior to the tender offer.

Exactly the same situation prevails in regard to reports (all of which may prove correct) that XYZ is going to split its stock 3-for-1; that XYZ is going to raise its dividend; that XYZ earnings in the latest quarter spurted from 35 cents a share to $1.05. "Someone always knows something first." Or second or third or—in any event—before it becomes popular rumor... and most certainly before it appears in your morning newspaper.

And if enough of those who got the news before you did are speculators or active in-and-out traders you can be sure that the bloom is off the rose long before you pick it. In fact, since one of the basic laws of Wall Street teaches speculators to "sell on the good news" you can well expect that the official announcement of the stock split or the increased dividend or better earnings will bring liquidation by those who had the story a few days or a week ago. If you rush in to buy on the announcement, who—do you think—is selling you stock?

But how, you ask, did those lucky traders get the news before I did?

I hereby impugn the honor or actions of no one. But I believe that only in a very few cases can corporate action of a price-setting nature be kept 100% secret. The moment the action is decided upon in the board room, it must go through the hands of secretaries, mimeographers or copiers in the public relations department, messenger boys, newspaper editors, typesetters and compositors.

A few exceptions come to mind. A.T.&T.'s 3-for-1 split in April 1959 burst on Wall Street like a bombshell. A leading financial editor who was having lunch with some members of the giant company's board, had to learn of the split from the newswire. General Motors, for example, sent out its earnings report in a sealed envelope which was not dropped on the financial news desks until the stock market had closed. And U.S. Steel zealously guarded its earnings reports and dividend actions in its own offices, to which reporters were summoned and forced to wait until the closing bell on the exchange.

And there are others. But that still leaves 40,000 corporations where reports and market traders can find "leaks." I once approached a director of a large manufacturing corporation with: "What if I write a piece about a boost in your dividend?" To which he replied: "I won't holler." That's all I needed.

Nor should you expect that corporate activities will remain 100% secret. Let's face the hard facts of the trading floor of the stock exchanges. XYZ Corp. is going to double its dividend and will announce that fact at 3:15 this afternoon. Down on the floor of the exchange, XYZ's specialist is busily making an "orderly market" in the stock, which is what he is charged to do by the exchange. That means he is buying stock for his own account if there are no "nearby" bids to buy offered stock, and selling from his own holdings (or going "short") if there are no sellers available to meet demand at normal price changes. Any corporation with any respect for its financial image, any corporation which wants its shares considered something more than horse race tickets or gambling chips prefers an orderly market in its stock. Doesn't it seem reasonable that if the specialist contacts the company with reports of Street rumors, or asks about any possible reason for suddenly increasing trading activity, that the corporation will at least intimate that something is in the wind about the dividend? After all, it wants the specialist on its side, not against it. It wants him to maintain an orderly market and certainly that would mean warning him against going far out on a limb by selling short a half-hour before the dividend is doubled. Specialists, of course, have lost lots of money in price downdrafts brought on by any number of corporate, domestic economy or international incidents. But it seems only reasonable that a corporation would not want to double-cross its specialist on its own announcements.

So the next time you get a "tip" you must ask yourself:

1. what are the chances it is a fake?
2. how many know this already?
3. what has the stock already done on the basis of this tip?
4. how much more profit is left in the picture, even if the story is true?

As for jumping into a stock seeking a quick profit on the published formal announcement (often the next day) of any "good news"—forget it. That boat has sailed, and you may have to "take a bath" if you still try to catch it. Strange as it may seem, newsmen develop considerable respect for the integrity of a corporation whose affairs and plans are rarely "leaked" ahead of time in Wall Street circles.

24

Those Beautiful
First Losses

Fortunate indeed is the stock market dabbler, trader, investor who gets smacked with a walloping loss on his very first effort. Now he knows! And he's not likely to forget, because he learned his lesson in dollars—a far better scoring medium than a B minus or a 62 on an economics exam.

Unfortunately—at least for a time—my first effort was a mind-boggling success for a 16-year-old high school junior who was making an extra $10 a week telephoning "open-high-low-close-net change" stock market quotations on a few hundred stocks from a brokerage office to the financial editor of the local newspaper. (An "extra" $10 because he was already on the payroll for $1.67 earned as a 6 P.M. Saturday night to 2 A.M. Sunday morning copy boy.)

One day, not long after I took up my 3 P.M. daily and noon Saturday quotation duties, one of the "customer's men" at the brokerage firm called out: "Hey, kid, why don't you buy some stock?" When I mumbled something about "got no money" he waved aside that shortcoming and said "Whaddya like?" With at least three weeks of financial expertise under my belt, and with all the brashness of youth I came right back with "Cerro de Pasco," a popular copper stock of the day. He replied: "You got a hundred." Cerro at that time was selling at $40 a share. If you point out that:

1. I didn't have $4,000 or even the 5 or 10% which served as "margin" in those days, and that
2. I was a minor and therefore not of legal age to own securities ... you're quibbling.

And the mid-Twenties stock market was no time to quibble about either margin or legalities. Over the next ten days or so I watched Cerro climb to 44 the way a four-year-old watches a toy in the store window. I wanted it to be mine but was afraid to ask for fear that customer's man was merely pulling my leg. (It was the age when new copy boys were asked to watch out for "type lice" in the composing room and young plumber's apprentices were sent for a "bucket of steam.")

But one afternoon, when I walked in a few minutes before the 3 P.M. closing, the broker yelled: "Hey, Sam, what do you want to do with your Cerro?" I yelled: "Sell it, sell it!" and within a few minutes I had a $400 gross profit—on paper. "O.K. what now?" he asked, commission-hungry right up to the closing bell. And just as quickly I came back: "Manhattan Electric Supply," a "hot" stock with the ticker symbol MSY (and therefore aptly nicknamed "Misery" on the exchange floor). It lived up to its name. In about three days I was wiped out, losing not only my Cerro profits but about $75 additional from a meager long-time savings account.

I thereupon pulled back out of the reach of the lion's cage and didn't venture into stocks until nearly a year later when I was handed an "inside tip" on the approaching merger of a Buffalo power company with a new utility holding company and made about $50 profit on a "sure thing." I've owned stocks ever since—have made money and lost money—but I've never forgotten that fast wipe-out in MSY. I urge all novice traders not to sweep losses under the rug, but to trust them as expensive, meaningful lessons that have lifelong values.

25

The E Bond—
Friend or Enemy
of the Little People?

In the decades since they were first offered, U.S. savings bonds worth more than $276 billion have been bought by millions of Americans. At least one in three households still holds them—a national total of more than $75 billion—and more than sixteen million people still buy them annually.

Yet the savings bond remains one of the least understood media of investment and certainly one of the most maligned. For years ultrasophisticated economists, financial writers, and purveyors of "doom and gloom" have assailed the popular E bond as:

A "rip-off" of the poor people;

Vulnerable to inflation (what isn't?);

A low-return investment (although 1978–when yields from Treasury, corporate bonds and savings reached all-time highs—saw bond sales topping $8 billion, the highest annual figure since World War II);

A device for increasing the funds government has available for pork barrel ventures (as though the government couldn't get all the money it wants to spend from other sources).

What its critics have failed to understand is that the savings bond has provided the average worker and saver with a government-backed investment, available in modest denominations and purchasable on a regular, systematic, habit-forming basis for expenditures as low as under $5 a week. Moreover, the accrued interest is sheltered from Federal income taxes for as long as the bond is held.

Without question, the popularity of the E bond, which accrues interest at the current rate of 6 to 7% a year, average, is due primarily to the popularity of the payroll deduction program which takes the money out of the pay envelope of about ten million workers a year BEFORE they get it. Over the years, the success of this plan has demonstrated the truth of the old adage: "The money you don't get is the money you can't spend." And the habit it has reinforced bears out the value of McLuhan's "the medium is the message." This near-automatic system of "painless" payroll deduction, subscribed to by about ten million workers in approximately 40,000 companies and organizations, has in fact become another term for describing a savings program. And it is in failing to appreciate this habit-forming regimen that critics of the bond program fall down. Preoccupied with interest rates figured to three decimal places, they completely overlook the fact that millions of average workers are not preoccupied with whether 8.765 is more than 8.250 but with the more fundamental question of "How can I manage to put a few thousand bucks aside?" And the payroll deduction plan has given them a positive answer.

And so, despite the scorn of the ultrasophisticates, it makes sense for the average small investor to consider the purchase and holding of EE bonds for a PART of his investment program because of several advantages: they may be bought in small amounts at no price disadvantage; they are protected from loss by theft or fire; they impose no income tax burden during the years they are being acquired and accruing interest; they are Government-backed; they are quickly converted to cash by the owner; they are non-negotiable—

Too many savings bond critics fall wide of the mark because their evaluation of an investment is almost always based on pure computer math. And no computer sees children's college tuition expenses or retirement day approaching, with nothing a-building in the way of family assets with which to meet those expenses.

"Set up a plan that will *force* us to save" is *not* the type of plea addressed to a computer, but I received them every week in sufficient number to convince me that it would be fallacious to underestimate the American's ability to earn money but equally as dangerous to overestimate his knowledge or willpower to do anything constructive with it. For example, a letter from a new, young widow . . . "My husband died three weeks ago. Because he was a well paid executive he left me with a lot of debts." That man (and his widow) could have profited from any payroll deduction plan, or any forced savings program.

thus eliminating danger of loss or theft and restricting their value to the owner only; they may be converted into income-producing HH bonds still deferring the tax liability incurred during the original EE bond's acquisition and growth.

Perhaps the EE bond's greatest value lies in its role of an emergency savings fund which is always immediately available as a cash fund but does not cost anything in Federal income taxes until it is used. Savers who put $5 to $10 a week into their savings accounts for years and who may fall back on this money only once in ten years can realize the value of the tax deferment which accompanies the EE bond. The interest accrues year after year with nothing being drawn out to pay the Federal tax collector. And if bond holdings remain untouched into retirement, they may either be cashed in then at lower income tax rates or, if transferred into income producing HH bonds, can continue to work "full strength" with the continued deferment of unpaid income taxes on past EE bond interest for as long as the HH bonds are held.

The important point to be considered in determining whether one should or should not acquire EE bonds is NOT whether one can "double his money" with greater dispatch elsewhere but whether the EE bond offers a safer, simpler, more convenient method of building and maintaining an emergency fund than is obtainable elsewhere.

In recent years, various mutual fund organizations have offered new types of "money" funds which may also serve as depositaries for funds to be kept available at short notice. In most cases, the funds are invested in Treasury bills, bankers' acceptances, certificates of deposit and other short-term paper. Yields have risen and fallen in step with the general interest rate market. Proceeds—in the form of dividends on shares in the mutual fund—are, of course, taxable in the year received, as are any capital gains. They have proven their worth as current income but cannot offer the tax shelter provided by an EE bond accumulation program.

Under the Treasury's most recent revision of the savings bond program, money invested in a new EE bond will double in value in eleven years and nine months, with no payment of Federal income taxes on that appreciation during that period. The tax deferment continues for as long as the investor holds the bond, or the new HH income bond for which the EEs may be exchanged.

To sum up: the principal pluses of a savings bond program are primarily encouragement of a habit-forming savings program, and tax shelter during the years when an investor is likely to be in his highest tax brackets. Add to these the safety of principal, immediate availability in case of emergency, freedom from worry about loss through fire or theft, acquisition via modest investment funds, flexibility of usage once the investor turns to his savings bond portfolio for income.

If a 50-year-old employee tells his employer today to take as little as $25 bi-weekly out of his pay envelope and apply it to the purchase of EE bonds, his bond account at age 65 will amount to $16,514.36.

If the 50-year-old begins a $25 weekly deduction program the EE-Bond nest egg at age 60 will be $17,886.58 and at age 65 $32,978.88.

Now we come to the day when you turn to this money and, in effect, ask: "O.K. what can you do for me now?"

Suppose, as an example, that you had acquired a $50 E

bond (then costing $37.50) every month over the last fifteen years. The money you put into the program now totals $6,750. Interest accumulated comes to $3,960.72, making a total current value of $10,710.72 for your holdings.

What are the various ways in which this investment could be put to work for you? You have these choices:

a. You could take the entire bundle of bonds into your bank and ask that they be redeemed for the $10,710.72 current value. Let's assume that your income tax bracket in retirement goes as high as 25%. (Obviously, if at all possible, you would defer redemption of the bonds until your tax bracket declined to retirement levels.) That means the $3,960.72 of accrued interest (on which you paid no income taxes while you were accumulating the bonds) would now become subject to income taxes, or a Federal tax payment of $990.18. (Any state or local income taxes do *not* apply to interest earned on U.S. Government bonds. Furthermore, the Federal tax applies only to the $3,960.72 interest and *not* to the total stake of $10,710.72 ... as far too many E bond investors mistakenly believe.)

After you paid your $990.18 income taxes, you would be left with $9,720.54 cash which you could use to defray the expense of a retirement home or any other retirement need, or could reinvest in savings, stocks or corporate or Treasury bonds for current income. Or—

b. You could bring the entire $10,710.72 bundle of E bonds into your banker, add just under $290 of new money and ask him to exchange the $11,000 total for that amount of HH bonds which pay interest by check every six months. (HH bonds are sold in multiples of $500—hence the extra cash to round out your investment to $11,000.)

The H bonds provide average income over their first ten-year period of 6% and a flat 6% thereafter, so that you could count on your investment yielding $660 a year, again subject to only Federal income taxes. Important: the tax-sheltered status of the $3,960.72 interest accumulated on your original EE bonds would continue in effect. You would pay no tax on that past interest when you exchange the EE bonds for HH bonds (as you did when you redeemed the EE bonds for cash—Plan A). The tax liability is stamped on the face of the HH bonds you receive in exchange for your EEs and may remain unpaid for as long as you keep the HH bonds. If you hold them for life, you can let your heirs settle that deferred tax liability out of the redemption value of the bonds. Or—

c. Instead of redeeming all the EE bonds (Plan A) or exchanging all of them for HH bonds (Plan B) you could elect to redeem only a portion of your EE bonds every year . . . a portion sufficient to yield about 6% of the current value of your present EE bond investment. You would thus realize about $660 a year of spendable income and still retain your EE bond stake, with the remaining bonds growing by 6% each year and thus keeping your investment value undiminished.

The advantage of this plan over the total exchange of all EE bonds for HH bonds is that only the accrued interest portion included in the value of the EE bonds cashed annually is subject to Federal income taxes, whereas all the HH bond interest is considered taxable income. The disadvantage: you have to go through the EE bond cashing process periodically instead of receiving an interest check in the mail. Or—

d. A "wasting" program which would exhaust your EE bond investment in, say, twenty years. Suppose you had $15,000 invested in bonds and were concerned only with maximizing your income for the next twenty years, not with leaving any EE bond money in your estate.

For the first ten years you could cash in increasing amounts of bonds—from $1,008 to $1,715.90. For the last ten years you could redeem $1,820.40 worth every year. Total money coming out of your $15,000 investment would be $31,545.64, leaving a zero balance. Again, only the accrued interest included in the bonds cashed each year would be subject to Federal income taxes.

There are a multitude of programs for building retirement income. Most have their virtues and drawbacks, and the EE bond is no exception. But none can surpass it for worry-free investing and for assured income when you want it.

SAVINGS BONDS

Mainly for administrative and record-keeping purposes, the Treasury Department announced early in 1979 the first changes in savings bond format in nearly 40 years, taking effect at the start of 1980. Because the old E (and H) bonds had been so taken for granted, the announcement proved disconcerting to many savings bonds holders who, because of the safety inherent in the bonds, had really never given much thought to that particular investment. However, the changes proved more surface than fundamental.

To distinguish them from the bonds which had been issued as far back as May 1941, the new bonds are labeled EE and HH. But except for some technicalities, the investment is fundamentally unchanged.

The most important consequence of the introduction of the new program, in fact, is the setting up of final maturities for the old savings bonds, E and H, which many small investors had been acquiring as a "permanent" investment ... that is, with little or no thought to a maturity date. Final maturities, however, are now a factor with which savings bond investors must cope.

If you have been acquiring savings bonds over the years and ignoring them, secure in the belief that since they were government-guaranteed and since they did not fluctuate in price they required little, if any, attention, you still have no reason to fret over the new factors. The bonds remain backed by the full faith and credit of the U.S. Government, are still not negotiable and, therefore, continue to appreciate at a fixed rate regardless of stock or bond market conditions or the state of the national or world economies. But—

They now do have a final maturity date. So if you have been accumulating these bonds over the years, it behooves you to make a note of approaching maturities. Any bond—government or corporate—held beyond maturity does *not* continue to earn interest. If you want your invested funds to continue earning their keep, you should therefore make note of these final maturities over the years ahead.

Series E savings bonds which bear issue dates from May 1941 through April 1952 will reach final maturity in 40 years ... from May 1981 through April 1992. Thus, bonds issued in 1942, 1943, etc. will come due, respectively, in 1982, 1983, etc;

E bonds issued May 1952 through January 1957 will reach final maturity in 39 years and 8 months, thus coming due between January 1992 and September 1996;

E bonds issued February 1957 through May 1959 will come due in 38 years, 11 months—that is, between January 1996 through April 1998;

E bonds bearing issue dates June 1959 through November 1965 will have a lifetime of 37 years, 9 months, coming due between March 1997 and August 2003;

Bonds sold from December 1965 through May 1969 will earn interest for 27 years, coming due between December 1992 and May 1996;

E bonds issued from June 1969 through November 1973 will come due in 25 years, 10 months, or from April 1995 through September 1999, and bonds sold from December 1973 through December 1979 (when issuance of E bonds ended) will mature in 25 years ... that is from December 1995 through December 2004.

And so millions of small investors who had come to regard their savings bonds as a "permanent" investment have been put on notice that, as is the case with all bonds, there is now a termination date for their E bonds. However, there are alternatives to any forced redemption.

An E bond reaching its final maturity (beyond which it will not earn interest) may be redeemed for cash, or exchanged for HH bonds which will send you an interest check every six months.

If you redeem for cash, the accrued interest over the years (assuming you, like most E bond buyers, did not report that interest on your annual income tax forms) becomes subject to Federal income taxes. For example, if you bought a $25 bond for $18.75 in May 1941, you will receive $89.49 for it in May 1981 (or at any maturity at the end of 40 years' life). The difference—$70.74—will be taxable at regular income tax rates.

If you want to further postpone the payment of income taxes on that $70.74 accumulated interest, you may (instead of asking for your money) exchange your E bond for one of the new HH type income bonds which sends you an interest check every six months subject to Federal income taxes but not state or local taxes. The past E bond tax liability ($70.74) will then be stamped on the face of the new HH bond, but no tax payment will be due on that amount until the HH bond matures or is cashed in. In other words, the entire $89.49, undiminished by any tax payments, will continue to work for you bringing in semi-annual income. (An important word in this alternative plan is "exchange." *Do not* cash in your Es with the intention of then putting the money into HH bonds. Once you cash an E bond, you have created a tax liability regardless of where you next go with the money. Don't cash, but *exchange*.)

Now the question arises: "Do I turn in my E bonds for cash? Or would it be best to turn them in, *exchange* them, for HH bonds?"

Only you can decide what you want this money to do for

you and then perform a little tax arithmetic to find the best way to do it.

If you are still employed, and already in a high tax bracket, you may not want additional taxable income from the HH bonds. But neither would you welcome the tax on all that past interest which would come due now if you redeem the Es.

If a substantial amount in E bonds is involved, it might be better to turn in all which are facing immediate nearby maturity in exchange for HH bonds. Reasoning is that it would be far better for the next few years, until your tax bracket drops in retirement, to pay the Federal tax on only the 6% annual interest income from the HHs than it would be to pay a tax now on forty years of accrued E bond interest which could easily approach 80% of the total amount you receive for your E bonds. Take the HH bonds in exchange for your old Es, have your accrued interest tax liability stamped on the HH bond and hold it until you are in a much lower (retirement) income tax bracket and *then* cash it in.

If you are already retired and in a lower income tax bracket, it might pay you to take cash for your maturing E bonds and put the net proceeds (after you pay your tax on the accrued interest) into much higher-yielding corporate or Treasury securities.

You can see that a convenient rule of thumb for deciding between cash for maturing E bonds or an exchange for HH bonds involves the investor's income tax bracket, the difference in yield between HH bonds (most recently 6%) and the going rate of interest on corporate and other Treasury bonds which could be 50% higher. In other words, if your income tax bracket would result in reducing the proceeds of your bonds by more than a third, you could be further ahead—on a current income basis—by switching Es into HH bonds. If the tax bite on a redemption is minimal, take the cash and reinvest elsewhere.

In any event, don't allow yourself to be stampeded into redemption for fear of losing interest on your old E bonds. The oldest bonds have a forty-year life. Only those issued as early as May 1941—when Es were first sold—will mature in May 1981. Subsequent issues will not reach final maturity until they have been outstanding for forty years. The end of the line for all the old Es will not be reached until the end of 2004.

The new EE savings bonds which went on sale January 2, 1980 will be sold at 50% of face amount (instead of 75% as was the case with the old E bonds) and will mature in eleven years (versus five-year-maturity with ten-year extensions in the case of the original Es). Tax status, registration, non-negotiability remain the same.

Savings bonds are held by millions of investors in every state. And the confusion surrounding their terms, yields, registration, redemption is just as widespread. Self-appointed financial experts, even bank officers, have been guilty of offering misleading advice. If you are now the owner of E or H, or EE or HH bonds and in the dark about some facet of this most popular investment in all financial history, don't rely on hearsay or friends' advice. For general information, including "Tables of Redemption Values" (which tell you what your bonds are worth as of this moment) write to

THE COMMISSIONER
BUREAU OF PUBLIC DEBT
Department of the Treasury
1435 G Street, N.W.
Washington, D.C. 20226.

26

How to Read the
Financial Pages
or
What is Your
Portfolio Worth?

There used to be a school of investment which advised: Buy only stocks you can put away and forget!

This implied a state of euphoria and complacency which was never justified . . . in any financial or economic climate. Common shares you "forget" are very likely to forget you. Corporate fortunes can change drastically from one year to the next; managements may change in a matter of weeks or days. Or your company may be swallowed up by a conglomerate or by some "take-over" artist and the money you thought you had invested in the manufacture of men's clothing is now employed mostly in gambling resort hotels or snack-food shops.

If you want your money to work loyally for you, it won't hurt to look in on it from time to time. Don't forget it.

Of course, the diametrically opposed school of investment is exemplified by the nervous owner of 100 shares of XYZ Gas & Electric who lines up at the newsstand every afternoon to grab the "closing market" edition in order to find out whether his stock closed at 35⅛ or 35⅜—down an eighth or up an eighth on the day.

Let me explain right now that for about forty years I was involved with getting the closing stock market newspaper edition on the street with the least possible delay. For at least twenty-five of those years that closing stock market table was my responsibility, among other duties. Even years ago it cost at least a million dollars a year for a big city paper and engaged the efforts of about twenty-five printers and editorial clerks. And left me near exhaustion five afternoons a week. And I will declare on a stack of Bibles that the whole endeavor was an empty egg, a kowtowing to an "ancient" fetish, a meaningless bit of malarkey (except, of course, to brokerage house margin clerks who had to use the closing quotes as the basis for sending out telegrams demanding more margin money and, of course, to the hapless speculator who received those telegrams).

Those closing quotations!!! They have driven some speculators to jump out windows and have hallucinated others into spending their imaginary paper profits on a big night on the town . . . "profits" which all too often were wiped out by the following day's closing quotes. Not to mention the chaos they brought about in newspaper composing and press rooms at 3, 3:30 or 4 P.M. every afternoon.

Listen in on three small speculators, each holding fifty to 100 shares of a $12 stock, as they wait for the 5:12 P.M. bus to Homeacres, and you can bet that the first query will be: "What did it close at?" If the last trade was at 12¼ . . . jubilation. If it was 11⅞ . . . despair.

All utter nonsense!

What is a "closing" quotation? It is merely the last price at which the stock traded during that six-hour stock market session. The trade could have been made at 10:05 A.M., just five minutes after the opening bell, or at 12:22 P.M. or at 2:32, or at 3:59½, just one half-minute before the closing bell. So the words "close" and "last" have as much definitive meaning as "let's have lunch some day."

If the Yankees are leading 3 to 2 in their half of the fourth inning you can't collect any bets on the game. And even if you have the final score of the third game you still can't collect any bets on the outcome of the World "Serious" (as old-time sports writers liked to call it). A closing stock quote is just one of many way stations on the road to ultimate profit or loss—and only a flag stop at that. If stock markets were open 24 hours a day—as are some supermarkets—what would happen to the "closing" quote?

Having said all this, I must admit that, since most non-professional investors and speculators generally do their portfolio-bookkeeping at the end of the day, it's only natural that they should hang their hat on that closing quote even though it is just another price. Let's just say that is just one handy figure, even though far removed from gospel.

Financial tables ... and the data they offer ... vary widely. The old-time newsboy greeted his customers with "Wha d'ya read?" which indicated they had a choice. However, in these days of often only one or two newspapers in a town or city, the investor must make do with whatever financial information is provided by his local daily newspaper. Of course if he is sufficiently involved he should take the time to add one of the big financial center dailies or the Wall Street Journal or some other special, detailed financial publication to his reading schedule. (No consideration will be given here to the amateur speculator who spends six hours a day glued to the Translux or quote board in a brokerage firm's "customer's room." That way lies madness— all too often panic, snap decisions and ultimate loss.)

Whatever paper or financial publication you read, you should make an effort to understand what the tabular material is trying to tell you.

The most widely-published ... and studied ... financial table is the 5-times-a-week record of issues traded daily on the N.Y. Stock Exchange. It is the most representative index of the equity market. The "Big Board" trades close to 2,000 different issues, including most of the country's leading industrial, utility and railroad companies and is the scene of 85 to 90% of all daily transactions.

The transactions on the American Stock Exchange, second largest and also in New York City, are the second most widely circulated, although its volume will normally run to only about 10% of the Big Board's total trading. Accounting for smaller percentages of total trading are other regional exchanges such as the Pacific, Midwest, Boston, Cincinnati, Philadelphia, Intermountain, Montreal, Spokane, Toronto, Vancouver. Then, too, there is the over-the-counter market with more issues traded nationwide than all the exchanges put together. You can expect to find quotations of regional exchanges in the cities where they are located. The over-the-counter quotes may number as many as a few thousand in some publications but only a handful (mostly local companies) in others. Except for the more popular "counter" issues an investor in such issues will most likely have to call his broker for a "quote."

Open any newspaper's financial section and, if it carries any stock price table at all, it will most likely refer to transactions on the N.Y. Stock Exchange. The list may run all the way from a brief sampling of the day's trading to a full report. Newsprint today has become an extremely costly commodity and you can't expect the Smalltown Eagle to devote pages to expensive tabular matter if its publisher is convinced that his readers are far more interested in the makeup of the church dinner committee. Such papers may disregard Wall Street altogether, or may merely print a list of twenty-five widely-held issues (including those of any company which may have a plant in the vicinity). It may give the name of the company and a price identified only as "latest"—thus

American Telephone............. 58½
General Motors.................. 55¼
Hometown Elect................. 26½
Republic Steel.................. 26¼
Smith's Machinery Works 18½
  and so on down to
U.S. Steel...................... 22

If you hold any of these stocks as long-term investments, these bare quotations are most likely sufficient to keep you au courant ... to keep you in the "ball park."

Another newspaper might add a "plus" or "minus" figure—

General Motors.................. 55¼ +⅛

which would indicate that the latest quotation available when this newspaper went to press was a price of 55¼ ($55.25 a share) which was ⅛th point or 12½ cents a share above the quotation at the close of the previous day's stock market trading.

Or—Gen. Motors ..... 55¼–⅛ which indicates that the latest available price was ⅛th point below the previous day's final trade.

Or—55¼ ..... "n.c." or "no change."

These price changes ... plus, or minus, or none ... are *always* reckoned from the previous day's quotations at the same hour. They do not indicate any change from the previous transaction, or from the day's opening trade, or from any other base. No matter when the latest transaction took place, any price change indicated is always the variation from the previous day.

From these somewhat elementary reports, the stock market tables can and do expand, all the way to the detailed data carried by those appearing in *The Wall Street Journal*, various big-city daily newspapers and other financial publications.

A detailed table will show all this information:

30¼ .. 21⅛   U.S. Steel   1.60   7.4   5   571   21¾   21½   21⅝–⅛

Translation:

1. During the last 52 weeks, U.S. Steel common shares sold as high as 30¼ ($30.25) and as low as 21⅛ ($21.125) per share.
2. Currently it is paying, annually, a dividend of $1.60 per share.
3. That $1.60 dividend, divided by the day's closing price, 21⅝, works out to a current return (yield) of 7.4% on the money invested at that price. Since the quote changes every day, that same $1.60 dividend will represent a different return every day. On the day U.S. Steel sells for 23, for example, the $1.60 dividend generates a return of only 6.9%. If the stock were to fall to 20, the $1.60 dividend would represent a yield of 8%. (This should be a warning to those smug investors who boast about the 15% return they are getting on a stock—now paying a $5 dividend and selling at $75—which they originally purchased ten years ago at $30 a share. Their investment is now yielding them 6⅔%—as the stock table will indicate—and NOT 15%.)
4. Next comes the price/earnings ratio. In this case "5," which indicates that on this day U.S. Steel common sold at roughly five times the last twelve months earnings per share. That is, a market price of $21.625 is equivalent to about five times the annual earnings per share of roughly $4. This price/earnings (or p/e) ratio is a valuable investment index . . . one of many,

but valuable. It is discussed in more detail in Appendix A (pages 237–238).

5. Next comes the figure "571." Add two zeros to it and you arrive at 57,100 which is the number of shares which changed hands during the day's market session—the number of shares "sold." It is also the number of shares "bought" since every share sold had to find a buyer. But ignore the buy side. If a real-estate broker says he sold three houses last week we assume he also found three buyers.

6. Then come the price figures.

Years ago, many tables began this section with the first or "opening" transaction of the day. Now, because of the other more important items included in the listings, the opening price is generally omitted.

The first price given, 21¾, represents the highest level at which Steel sold that day . . . $21.75 a share. Next, the lowest price, 21½, and last the latest available (or the final price of the day) 21⅝, followed by, in this case, "—⅛." This shows that 21⅝, the latest or closing price, represents a decline of ⅛ from the closing price of the previous day which was, obviously, 21¾.

While I have argued that the final price, 21⅝, has no special significance and should not be the basis for either despair or elation, all the figures in this long line of statistics *ARE* important to the serious student of the stock market and to any investor who wants to have a "feel" of how his particular stock is doing.

It is not my intention here to analyze the investment virtues of U.S. Steel common at $21.625 a share. It is no secret that Big Steel stock has been no ball of fire in recent years. As a cyclical stock its earnings have gone up and down like a yo-yo. Ditto its market price. Dividends, though, have been paid continuously since 1940 and its Standard & Poor's rating of B+ carries the definition "average."

On any market day you will find investors buying Big Steel and other investors selling it. You will find hundreds of thousands of its shares in the portfolio of large investment trusts. And you will find equally respectable investors who declare they wouldn't "touch it with a 10-foot pole." Such a difference of opinion is to be expected and one which, in fact, should be encouraged since it makes both horse races and stock markets possible. I can imagine no greater Wall Street disaster than a "unanimous" rush to buy or sell a stock, or even a particular group of stocks.

So what can you learn from this line of figures, all relating to one day's market in U.S. Steel common shares?

Some of the data is "absolute" and some mostly comparative.

For example: the closing price of 21⅝ is only a half-point above the lowest price at which the stock sold during the previous months (to late July, 1979). And if you do a little more research in the standard stock guides you will discover that the 21⅝ is only the same half-point above the lowest price reached in all 1978. And, to go back further over the 1966–77 period, only five points above the lowest price of that eleven-year period, but 47 points below the 68⅞ high reached in the years since 1966. Clearly U.S. Steel, as is true of most steels, has not enjoyed popular favor for years.

If you own Steel (and want to remain a shareholder) this day's statistics are pretty much a yawn . . . no news. You could get some corroborating evidence from other leading steel issues' action that same day. Bethlehem, for example, was up only one-quarter point that day, yielding 6.6% and selling at only three times annual per share earnings. Republic Steel yielded 7%, with its price unchanged and selling also at only three times earnings. Trading volume in all three issues, about "average." Obviously Wall Street that day had no news affecting the steel industry in general, or steel stocks in particular.

If it's any comfort to you, you could note that Big Steel commanded a market price of five times per share earnings, whereas Bethelem and Republic Steel sold at only three times earnings. You could argue, from this, that investors felt Big Steel was worth a higher p/e ratio, offered more price appreciation potential. Again, if the general market, as measured by the Dow Jones Industrials or the Standard & Poor's Index or the N.Y. Stock Exchange average, had fallen sharply you could draw some comfort from the fact that your stock had proved immune to the overall selling pressure. At least, it wasn't driven down to a new low.

If you place some weight on statistical chart data (and many experts do) you might keep a daily record of the volume of trading in your stock (on this day 57,100 shares) as well as the closing price and price change. This would help you determine whether volume picks up when the stock's price is rising, or when it is falling. Technical chartists place great store on this statistic, among many others. If trading volume expands when the stock's price is firm, or rising, you have reason to believe that there is more demand for the stock than there is pressure to sell it. In the stock market, as in any other market, every sale must be matched by a purchase (and vice versa) so it is not enough to merely note that 100 shares of U.S. Steel changed hands. What is important is the answer to the question of whether the buyer was eager enough to pay a higher (than the previous) price for the stock, or whether the seller was so eager to sell that he accepted a lower price just to get rid of his shares.

This does not indicate necessarily that the buyer knew more than the seller. It does indicate that some buyer wanted the stock badly enough to pay an eighth- or quarter-point more than the previous closing sale to get the stock. And for those who believe—with considerable justification—that the stock market is an independent phenomenon which tells its own story, regardless of many external factors, the relative strength of demand versus the urgency to sell are what makes the market, whether in Steel or some "hot shot" electronics issue.

For the experienced reader, the financial pages can provide many interesting and exciting stories.

Mystery stories, for example. How come XYZ Corp. common, which has been dragging its heels at around 24 for months, suddenly shows a net change of "plus 2" and on much higher-than-normal volume? The next day there may be another big plus, again on big volume. On the third day the story breaks. JKL Conglomerate has made a formal public offer of $32 a share for two million shares of XYZ's three-and-one-half million shares. (Someone always knows something first.)

Now the story is out, but you still have some decisions to make on your 200 shares of XYZ you bought two years ago at 20½. Should you tender your stock to the conglomerate's buying agent in the hopes that your shares will be accepted among the two million shares to be bought at $32? Did JKL reserve the right to buy no stock at all if it doesn't get the full two million shares? May it buy more than two million shares? Is that $32 buying price merely its first offer? Will it subsequently go higher? Or will another conglomerate or take-over artist enter the fray with bids of $33, $35 or more? If no deal goes through, or if your particular shares don't get in under the wire, will the open market price fall back to $24 for another two years? In which case, would it be better to sell out now on the open market, accepting a certain $27 or $28, minus commissions, instead of gambling for $32? Or more? All the exciting "wheeling and dealing" doesn't take place in the sports section!

While the answers to these questions are difficult, you can get some clues—at least to the pros' betting—from the subsequent days' market trading. If the stock rises steadily and holds steady as a rock at $32, you can assume that the experts feel JKL is going to take all the stock offered at $32, or that it may even offer more to get all the XYZ stock it can. Or that another buying group is in the wings and preparing to compete for XYZ stock.

If the stock shoots up on the take-over announcement but then settles to $2 or $3 a share below JKL's bid price, you can assume that there is considerable doubt that JKL will buy more than it announced it would buy, and that the amount of stock already turned in has pretty much satisfied the demand. Moreover, it would seem that XYZ stock would not continue near $30 a share in the open market after the supporting bid by JKL expires.

Take-overs are always chancy maneuvers and there is many a slip betwixt the cup and the lip. But a careful following of trading action in a stock will provide some clues.

If you are sufficiently interested in the course of the stock market or of particular stocks, you should be prepared to spend some time with the financial pages and, in addition, to seek out some answers (to sudden price moves) from your broker or from direct contact with the company's officers. You may not always be successful. In fact, you are more likely than not to find yourself up a blind alley. But you can try. If you can determine that a sharp drop in your company's earnings (and a subsequent market drop in the price of its stock) resulted from some nonrecurring problem or from a raw material shortage which has been corrected, you won't be in such a hurry to dump your stock at a loss. Leave that loss to others who will grab the phone and yell "sell" just because the morning newspaper reported the most recent quarterly earnings per share at 85 cents versus $1.05 a year ago, and because the stock fell 1½ points. If you don't already own shares, knowing the underlying reasons may guide you in buying some on the price decline which resulted from publication of the lower earnings.

There aren't too many "golden rules" in Wall Street, but one is certainly: "Buy 'em when nobody else wants 'em." One of the founding Rothschilds explained that he made his fortune by being accommodating. "When people wanted stock, I sold it to them; when they wanted to sell, I bought it from them."

The rule of "contrary opinion" is still well observed in Wall Street. The unanimous, or popular, opinion is to be regarded with suspicion. The crowd reaction to a bit of news may prove right for a day or two but will often prove costly to follow for any length of time—primarily because mob buying tends to drive a stock too far above its inherent value, or above the price which can be sustained. Conversely, panic mob selling will drive a stock's price to below its inherent or maintainable price.

Example: XYZ, which has been a market favorite for several months, and therefore has been bid up to a "rich" price, suddenly announces a 3-for-1 stock split. Just think, everyone who owns 100 shares will now hold 300! When the announcement gets into the newspapers (which means the news is anywhere from 24 to 48 hours late) the emotional speculator rushes in to buy even though the price of the shares has already jumped five points. The story is in the newspaper, and is true—BUT as a stock market factor it is "old stuff." The stock, reacting to gossip in the Street, may have moved up in price even before the split was formally announced. Or it jumped in price when the announcement came over one of the news tickers (still hours before you were able to get the information). If you rush to buy when you read the printed announcement in the financial pages you are, in effect, running down the pier to catch a steamer which sailed two days ago. You're likely to "take a bath."

The financial pages and the stock tables carry information essential to every investor. By all means become acquainted with them. But remember—there are a lot of people out there reading the same data. And a lot of people who knew it first. The clues are many and can be solid. But be sure you become expert in reading and analyzing them.

27

Financing
Your Retirement

The three goals most often advanced for building capital are:

1. purchase of a home;
2. college educations for children; and
3. retirement income to supplement Social Security and/or private pension income.

All three carry weight in most prudent planning even though all three are not necessarily applicable.

But *everyone* does hope to become old enough to retire if he or she pleases and *everyone* hopes for all the retirement income possible.

How to accumulate this money—for whatever purpose—is really what most of this book is all about. Making money, and making your money make more money, is the name of the game regardless of the ultimate use of the funds accumulated. You do it—if you have read so far—by buying stocks which go up in price; real estate which goes up in price; diamonds, rare violins, Picassos, Louis XIV side chairs, Tiffany lamps which go up in price or—

by marrying the boss' daughter; or

by merely piling one $5 or $10 bill weekly atop another

in your savings account . . . which is doing it the "hard way." Do it anyway you can, legally, but do it.

This chapter aims to put your hard-earned funds to work for you for your retirement, for the day you turn to this money and, in effect, say: "O.K., I've slaved for you all my working life. What can you do for me now when I need income?"

There was a time when prudent people planning for their old age based their hopes on children—sons and daughters who would continue to operate the family farm or business; or children who could provide living space in their homes as well as some financial support if need be. This is no longer true. Family farms are fast disappearing. Ditto, the small family-owned-and-operated business. And the house with the "mother-in-law" apartment, once so prominently merchandised by real-estate developers, is rarely seen in today's realty promotions. It is futile to debate filial responsibility here. Legally, children are no longer responsible for their parents' care. But anyhow, it's a fair assumption that the senior generation has come to realize that independence— at all ages—is a highly desirable state. There used to be an old saying, "When a father helps his son, both smile; when a son has to help his father, they both frown." Today, fewer and fewer of the elderly have to turn to their children for support, thanks to Social Security, pensions from previous employers and to income from funds put by during their working years.

Our senior generation has discovered that accumulated money can work . . . that if you can't earn a living by swinging a scythe, you can live from your money which was put into farm machinery and farm machinery manufacturers.

What can investments made over the years do for you in retirement? And how much can they provide? And from what sources?

At a time when money earns the highest rental (interest) in our history a retired investor primarily concerned with current income can count on getting as high as 10% a year, approximately, on his invested funds.

He can get close to that figure from Treasury bonds and Government-endorsed issues, from good-to-high quality coporate bonds, from special six-months savings accounts based on Treasury bill rates, from utility preferred and common stock issues, from some mutual funds which specialize in high-yield bond and money market investments.

The one important drawback in any such high-yielding investments is the fact that they are all expressed in terms of dollars. Therefore, bonds of all types, bank deposits of all kinds, offer no help against the rampant inflation which in fact has been one of the principal factors boosting interest rates to these historic high levels and keeping them there. Nor is it realistic to expect that any bond or other investment expressed in terms of dollars will ever prove big market gainers.

So while the high interest rate figure is both attractive and rewarding, the fine print (inflation) takes it away from you, steadily eroding the purchasing power of both those 10% annual returns and of the principal you put to work in these types of investment.

It would help, at the outset, to make clear that there are few, if any, investments providing generous retirement income which can also fight inflation to a standstill. If you want a big 10% return from your investment you can't reasonably hope that it will also rise in market price sufficiently to offset the shrinkage in the dollar. In fact, sustained high interest rates can only serve as a ceiling on the market price of dollar type investments (bonds, savings accounts, etc.). You can't have both high income and inflation protection unless—one possibility—you are skillful enough as a real estate operator to get both high current income and appreciation from property. It has been done by experienced operators. I doubt, however, that they acquired their ability from books.

Much has been made of the fact that gold and silver and

large diamonds and violin bows and Picassos have soared in value—far beyond the reaches of the Dow Jones Industrial Averages. And if you pick your spots you can make a good case for the argument—when these media are employed by people who know what they are doing in these sophisticated and highly specialized markets. But if you are depending upon the income from, say, $100,000 in resources to flesh out your Social Security check, you most likely need that $9,000–$10,000 interest or dividends coming in as frequently as you can get it . . . monthly, quarterly, semi-annually. Even if you knew enough about either field to buy a Picasso or an Amati for $100,000, what would you do for supermarket money while your rare work of art is appreciating in price? Or what if you buy gold coins or diamonds? You would, again, be passing up any current income; moreover, you would be saddled with insurance and other safekeeping expenses which would be money going out, not coming in. Not to overlook the market risks, which, from time to time, result in price drops in even so precious a commodity as gold or silver or even real estate. If you want income *now* you want securities which yield generous income now.

And if you point out that a simple 10% annual return without price appreciation is often wiped out by inflation, you are correct. That's the way the cookie crumbles.

There is *no* investment which can guarantee a perfect month-by-month, year-by-year hedge against inflation. If you are retired and dependent upon income from your investments you have a choice. Either go for the highest current return you can get at the level of risk you feel you can assume and hope for the best, or place high income in a secondary position and assume the risk which goes with playing for capital gains . . . gains you hope will be sufficient to more than offset the dwindling purchasing power of the dollar. But better be prepared for losses.

Every retiree has the right to make this choice. If there is no chance of recouping market losses the course to pursue should be obvious: high income from high-safety securities. There may be times when 50 to 75% of that annual income is eaten away by inflation; there may be times when even the entire yield is wiped out by inflation which could mean, in effect, that you are living off capital.

As negative or distasteful as it may seem, a retiree will probably be more successful in trimming his current budget to meet higher living costs than he would be in attempting to increase capital or income.

By definition, equity (ownership) investments are the only ones which can offer even a hope of offsetting inflation. If you buy common stock, or an apartment house, or a rare painting which rises 10%–20% in value during a twelve-month period when inflation is taking 10% out of the dollar, you are successfully combatting inflation. If you cash in at the end of the year you will have enough additional dollars (after paying taxes on your profit) to buy more food at the super-market, even at the 10% higher prices. Now all you have to do is to repeat the process every year.

Common shares—which represent an ownership invest-ment—have not, on average, successfully stood off inflation during the last decade (ending with 1979) when the cost of living more than doubled. As a matter of fact, the Dow Jones industrial stock average was lower at the end of the decade than it was at the beginning.

While common shares have generally been of no help, dividends paid by particular common shares were far more successful in the race with inflation. Many utility companies have established enviable records of raising dividend payout over the years. A.T.&T.'s annual $5 dividend, for example, represents several advances over the last decade which roughly paralleled the steady rise in the Bureau of Labor Statistics' "cost of living" index—the leading measure of inflation.

But this is not to say that many of these same common stock issues which increased dividends over the years have been immune to market price losses. Increased dividends are not always accompanied by higher stock prices, especially in times of high interest rates when income from bonds overshadows the return available from most commons. But if 100 shares of A.T.&T., for example, have been part of your retirement portfolio for years you will find that current dividend income from that stock (and from many others) will now give you almost as much purchasing power at the supermarket as earlier dividends did when skimmed milk and cottage cheese were selling at much lower prices.

And what you are looking for in retirement is, primarily, purchasing power—even more than a higher bottom line . . . a total market value figure for your securities portfolio. Admittedly, given your druthers, a $150,000 total market evaluation today (versus $100,000 six years ago) would be pleasant for both yourselves and your heirs. But far more important is a current income of $10,000 (or more) versus $7,500 a half-dozen years ago. As in every form of investment, successful retirement financing requires that you keep your eye on the ball to provide generous and, if possible, rising income.

Generous income today is provided mainly by debt-type securities: Treasury bonds and notes and bills; Government-endorsed bonds such as "Ginnie Maes" and other agency types; high-grade corporate bonds; preferred stocks and FDIC and FSLIC-insured savings accounts and savings certificates. These offer fixed yields: if you buy a 9¾% XYZ Corp. bond today for $1,000 you can count on getting $97.50 a year interest for as long as you hold the bond. There is *no* chance you will get more, no matter what happens to the cost of living index. That $97.50 is generous by all historic standards. And it's "safe." But that's it. If you now spend $50 a pair for shoes that annual interest income will cover the cost, approximately, of two pairs of shoes. If the shoes go up to $100 a pair, you'll have to make do with only one new pair a year (assuming the bond interest represents your shoe budget). But there's no chance you will have to go barefoot. For any portfolio "leavening" by which you hope to increase current income from that $1,000 investment, you will have to turn to equities . . . common shares. And that spells risk.

Many high-quality common stocks have doubled dividends in the last decade. Many have been forced to reduce or even eliminate their dividend. On average, stock market prices have "gone nowhere." So there can be no guaranties either as to dividend output or market price. But common shares do offer a hope of offsetting inflation. It is not at all improbable that 100 shares of a $20 utility stock which a decade ago yielded $100 in annual dividends today is yielding close to $200 even though the market price of the stock has not risen appreciably, if at all. If you were counting on that 100-share dividend to cover your shoe budget, the investment today would continue to provide the same number of pairs of shoes, even at the much higher current shoe prices.

The decision of whether your investment should be in fixed-income bonds or in the riskier equities market depends upon your age, your responsibilities, your total resources, your budget needs and, by no means last, your temperament.

The question of age can be worded another way: "How many years of inflation must you figure on?" A retiree at age 85 obviously need not concern himself with inflation as much as a person retiring at age 65. The 85-year old may reasonably feel that for the balance of his life he might be able to get by on fixed income even if it should mean trimming his budget, or, more likely, invading capital. In fact, at that age, a life annuity would not only give him a current income well in excess of bond or bank interest, but assure him of that income for as long as he lives. He will never run out of money.

The 65-year old retiree must protect himself differently. An annuity can't do the trick for him because such a contract bought at age 65 will generally not yield him as much as high-grade bonds which, in addition, would keep his capital intact. So he must shift for himself, and since inflation will most likely be a factor in his budget for many years to come, he can't afford to lock up his income now at a fixed level for the balance of his lifetime.

Risk or no, he will have to apportion some of his investable money to common shares or other equity (real estate ownership) investments. He will have to assume the risks of a fluctuating market as well as changing dividend payouts in the hope that both market price and dividends will rise in his favor.

How do you decide how much in bonds and how much in equities? Consult your conscience and your temperament. If you are the type to chew your fingernails up to the elbow over each ⅜-point movement in stock market price, keep your equity commitment to a minimum. If you can take such changes with equanimity, you can take a larger position in common shares.

Retirement years may be the "golden years" as so many preach, or they may not be. But certainly they should not be years of worry ... any worry which can be avoided. Remember the old maxims: "Better a sure dime than an uncertain dollar," and "Do you want to eat well, or sleep well?" It would seem retirement can be far more pleasant, even if you have to raise your own vegetables, if you reduce your spending for food rather than endure the sleepless nights which often accompany any attempt to wrest more income from a contrary stock market.

The size of your fortune is also a factor, and so are your pension sources. Retirees with incomes from pensions of, say, $2,000 a month are certainly better equipped to put half their investment funds, or more, into common shares than are those who have only Social Security as a basic source of income—and who must make sure of every additional dollar of revenue. With a $2,000 monthly income foundation, one can more comfortably ride out stock market fluctuations than can someone to whom every dollar of income or capital is crucial to the budget. Again, if a retiree has $200,000 or $300,000 in resources to fall back on he is far less vulnerable to the market than if his total back-up fund is only $30,000.

There are no hard and fast formulae. A 40% bond–60% equity portfolio could be "just right" for one retired couple with a comfortable pension and Social Security base, but could be far too risky for an 80-year old couple who have only a minimal pension income and need every dollar of "guaranteed" income it can get from Treasury and high-grade corporate bonds.

A word about mutual funds in retirement:

Over the working years you may have paid regularly, or even intermittently, into one or more mutual funds as a medium for building assets. The results may have been excellent, so-so, or poor. (After all, most mutual funds invested in common shares—or, at least, did in the past before generous income became available from bonds and other money market instruments. So a mutual fund record consistent with the general stock market chart could be considered a "good" record . . . and that isn't saying much.)

But regardless of what your funds did in the past, Retirement Day becomes a day of decision about them and, in fact, about all your resources which should now be directed toward supporting you in "grand style," or at least as "grand" as you can manage.

If you hold growth-type mutuals which have had satisfactory records over the years you might continue to hold them, reinvesting capital gains and/or dividends *only* if you do not need every dollar of income you can lay your hands on. If you do need additional current income, tell the fund to send you capital gains and dividends by check. If the fund has not demonstrated any ability long-term to rack up capital gains with any consistency, you should either redeem the shares for their cash asset value and reinvest elsewhere (in bonds, common shares, whichever provide the most comfort), or ask the fund management if it has an income-oriented fund in its stable to which you can transfer your investment for a nominal fee of $5 total. If there is no such fund, *or* if management insists on your paying another full buying commission of about 9% to make the transfer you should show your displeasure by taking your money out and reinvesting elsewhere.

At retirement, your attitude toward any mutual fund investment you may have built over the years should be identical with your attitude toward all other assets at your command: "it's time for you to go to work providing me with income, inflation protection, or both."

Either the fund must display a consistent record of 10 to 15% a year appreciation in gains plus dividends, or your money should go to work elsewhere. Don't permit inertia to keep you in any investment in retirement which doesn't do the retirement job you need. You are no longer interested in building a fortune for the future. Your future is now. What you want is to now enjoy the results of years of self-denial (which is what savings represent). What you want is, within reason and within the bounds of your fortune, to be able to order the restaurant meal you want, rather than the one which is "priced reasonably."

It's now time to look out for No. 1 . . . which leads directly to the one factor in retirement investing which, I have found over the years, must be stressed time and again: selfishness, and the common fear of it.

You have spent decades rearing and educating children, perhaps also taking care of elderly parents, contributing to various other worthy causes. Now, in your retirement, and increasingly as the years pass, you become unduly concerned with the size of the estate you are going to leave to your children and grandchildren. From the Olympian peak of age 76 you look down upon the efforts of your 39-year old son-in-law and decide that he and your daughter, combined, haven't enough financial savvy to be trusted alone in the supermarket, much less to finance the education of your 7- to 10-year old grandchildren. It's urgent, you decide, that you accumulate a fund to pay their college bills and set them up in business or their professions thereafter, even if it means that you now pass up a new car, a cruise, or a new hi-fi set.

Utter nonsense! The belief that by denying yourselves a few thousand dollars now you can materially alter the life-style of your grandchildren five, ten or fifteen years hence is nothing more than a grand illusion. The dollars you save now by doing without some well-deserved pleasure will most likely lose 25 to 50% of their purchasing power by the time the kids get around to using them. If they're going to make it in life, they're going to have to do it without your few thousand dollars. Your first duty is to yourselves. Your future is *now*. Display an "I'm for No. 1" bumper sticker and live up to it.

And if your means are so limited that indulging your-selves may require invading your capital . . . even exhausting it during your lifetime (via a lifetime annuity, for example) so what? That's O.K., too.

Financials, Taxes,
and Terms

A Special Appendix by the NYIF Editorial Staff

A

How to Read a Company's "Financial Reports"

WHAT IS A BALANCE SHEET?

Periodically, a corporation needs to demonstrate to its shareholders what the company is worth. The company simply lists everything it owns (assets) and everything it owes (liabilities). *Assets* are items of value—things that a company *owns* or has *owed to it;* assets are a corporation's possessions, or its pluses! *Liabilities* are the company's obligations—its debts, what the company *owes!* The difference between assets and liabilities represent the company's net worth or the stockholders' net ownership, called *stockholders' equity.* This tabulation of assets, liabilities, and net worth is known as a *balance sheet.* Traditionally, the balance sheet is arranged as follows:

$$\text{ASSETS} = \text{LIABILITIES} + \text{STOCKHOLDERS' EQUITY}$$

Both sides "balance," of course, because a corporation's stockholders have a stake in their corporation equal to the amount by which the corporation's assets exceed its liabilities. Expressed another way, what a company owns (assets) minus what it owes (liabilities) is equal to its net worth. The net worth (stockholders' equity) represents the value of the shareholders' investment in the corporation: it is the amount of money invested in the business by stockholders, plus the profits that have *not* been paid out as dividends. The basic balance sheet equation is:

Total assets = Total liabilities + Stockholders' equity

Since a firm's financial state is continually changing, the balance sheet must be dated. The balance sheet's date shows on what day the tabulations were made. The assets, liabilities, and stockholders' equity are listed at their values *at the close of business* on the date shown at the top of the statement. A *simplified* balance sheet appears in Figure 1.

The value of the items owned—of the assets—can be figured many different ways. In actuality, the amount of money received from buyers, should all the assets be sold (liquidated), may differ dramatically from the values shown on the balance sheet. The shareholders' (stockholders') equity therefore represents the amount of money that *would* go to the preferred and common stockholders if all the company's assets were sold at the values at which they are carried on the balance sheet and if all liabilities were paid off as well. Thus, in another form, the balance sheet equation is:

Shareholders' equity = Total assets − Total liabilities

FIGURE 1

BALANCE SHEET
ROXBURY MANUFACTURING COMPANY
December 31, 1978

Assets

Cash	$ 75,000	
Marketable securities	150,000	
Accounts receivable	375,000	
Inventory	400,000	
Total current assets		$1,000,000
Property, plant, and equipment		$ 605,000
Prepayments		20,000
Intangibles		10,000
Total assets		$1,635,000

=

Liabilities

Accounts payable	$200,00u	
Accrued expenses	150,000	
Accrued taxes	50,000	
Total current liabilities		$400,000
Bonds—8%, due 1995		500,000
Total liabilities		$900,000

+

Stockholders' Equity

Preferred stock—6% ($100 par)	$ 75,000	
Common stock ($10 par)	300,000	
Capital surplus	100,000	
Retained earnings	260,000	
Total stockholders' equity		$ 735,000
Total liabilities and stockholders' equity		$1,635,000

HOW IS A BALANCE SHEET PUT TOGETHER?

Let us "build" a sample balance sheet for a typical manufacturing corporation, a block at a time, explaining each item separately.

ASSETS

A corporation's assets are traditionally listed, by type, in the following order:

> Current assets
>
> Fixed assets
>
> Sundry assets
>
> Intangibles

Current Assets

These are items that a company owns or has owed to it and that, in the normal course of business, will be converted into cash within a year or less. This category includes:

Cash. In addition to bank deposits, these are the bills and coins in the corporate "till." Such deposits are usually of the demand type, such as *checking* account balances.

Marketable Securities. Cash that the company does not need immediately is put to work by investing it, usually in short-term instruments such as Treasury bills. The value of such investments is shown on the balance sheet at the *lower* of their cost or their market value; in the vast majority of cases the market value of the securities is higher than their cost, so cost usually appears on the balance sheet. An indication elsewhere, possibly in a footnote, cites the current market value of the securities.

Accounts Receivable. Most manufacturing companies

sell to wholesalers or distributors. Goods are usually shipped with payment expected within 15 to 90 days. The total amount of billings outstanding represents the amount of money due the company for goods already shipped. Since the *entire* amount of the billings will probably not be collected for various reasons (for example, bankruptcy of the buyer), an estimate of bad debts is made. This *allowance for bad debt* is deducted from the total accounts receivable, and the leftover figure is shown on the balance sheet. This net figure represents an estimate of the amount that will be collected eventually.

Inventory. This category includes raw materials, work in progress, and finished goods. Like marketable securities, inventories are carried on the balance sheet at the lower of cost or market value. Except in very unusual situations, the market value of the inventory is expected to be higher than its cost: a manufacturing corporation makes its profit selling its finished goods for more than it costs to produce them. Cost accounting for inventory is based on two popular methods: FIFO (first-in/first-out) and LIFO (last-in/first-out). The method that a company chooses can have a dramatic effect on its earnings and on the value of the inventory remaining after a sale.

During inflationary periods, the FIFO method yields higher profits (and higher taxes!) than LIFO. FIFO also results in higher inventory evaluation. During *deflationary* periods, the results are just the opposite. Here is a visual aid in remembering the effects of LIFO over FIFO during inflationary periods.

LIFO = Lower gross profits
      Lower taxes
      Lower inventory valuation

Total Current Assets. The sum of these four types of

current assets is the corporation's *total current assets.* Now more detail can be added to the current asset portion of the sample balance sheet in Figure 1. Compare the section below with the first section in that figure.

Current Assets:	
Cash	$ 75,000
Marketable securities at cost	
(Market Value – $156,000)	150,000
Accounts receivable	
($390,000 less $15,000 allowance	
for bad debt)	375,000
Inventory (first-in/first-out)	400,000
Total current assets	$1,000,000

Current assets are in constant motion! When a company sells its products, an appropriate amount is deducted from inventory and goes into accounts receivable. When buyers pay their bills, accounts receivable become cash and the cash may then be used to pay debts. Or, a company may add to inventory and thus repeat the cycle.

Also, when an item is sold for more than its inventoried value, the difference (that is, the *gross profit*) automatically increases the total current assets by the amount of the profit. (We shall demonstrate how this profit is reflected on the *other* side of the balance sheet later.) Since both sides must balance, this profit is reflected by a corresponding increase in shareholders' equity. The company has made a profit, and the shareholders are therefore better off!

Quick Assets. The total current assets that may be *quickly* converted into cash, should the company deem it necessary, are called *quick assets.* The only item under current assets that is *not* considered very liquid is inventory. Therefore, to figure *quick assets,* merely subtract inventory from total current assets.

Example:

Cash	$ 75,000
Marketable securities	150,000
Accounts receivable	375,000
Inventory	400,000
Total current assets	$1,000,000

Subtracting inventory ($400,000) from the total ($1,000,000), we arrive at a figure of $600,000 for quick assets. Of course, the same amount may be derived by adding together cash, marketable securities, and accounts receivable—if these figures are all you have to work with. The formulas are as follows:

$$Quick\ assets = Total\ current\ assets - Inventory$$

$$Quick\ assets = \$1,000,000 - \$400,000$$
$$= \$600,000$$

or

$$Quick\ assets = Cash + Marketable\ securities + Accounts\ receivable$$

$$Quick\ assets = \$75,000 + \$150,000 + \$375,000$$
$$= \$600,000$$

Current Liabilities

Now shift to the *other* side of the balance sheet to look at the debts of the corporation that are scheduled for payment within one year. This quick comparison determines in a shorthand way, as accountants do, whether enough money is available to stay in business: since current assets, at least in theory, represent the source from which current liabilities are paid, we want to know how the debts compare with the assets.

Current liabilities might include: *accounts payable,* the amount the company owes to its business creditors; *accrued expenses,* amounts owed to its salespeople in salaries and wages, interest on debt, and all other unpaid items; *accrued taxes,* Federal, state, and local taxes owed, Social Security (FICA) deductions, and local government levies withheld from employees; *notes payable,* monies owed to banks, to other lenders, or on outstanding bonds that are due to be paid within the year. The current liabilities section of the balance sheet of our typical manufacturing corporation reads:

Accounts payable	$200,000
Accrued expenses	150,000
Accrued taxes	+ 50,000
Total current liabilities	$400,000

Relating Current Assets to Current Liabilities

Working Capital. The relationship between current assets and current liabilities is quite important. After all, it is certainly necessary for a corporation to be able to keep current on its obligations. At a minimum, there should be an excess of current assets over current liabilities. This excess, called *working capital,* represents the amount of money that would be left from the current assets if all current liabilities were paid off. This important figure is derived by subtracting current liabilities from current assets, thus:

$$\text{Working capital} = \text{Current assets} - \text{Current liabilities}$$

A company's ability to meet its obligations is measured, at least in part, by the amount of its working capital. Working capital is also known as *net working capital* or *net current assets.*

Example:

Assets		Liabilities	
Cash	$ 75,000	Accounts payable	$200,000
Marketable securities	150,000	Accrued expenses	$150,000
Accounts receivable	375,000	Accrued taxes	50,000
Inventory	+400,000		+
Total current assets	$1,000,000	Total current liabilities	$400,000

For our typical corporation:

$$\text{Working capital} = \text{Current assets} - \text{Current liabilities}$$
$$= \$1,000,000 - \$400,000$$
$$= \$600,000$$

Current Ratio. Working with a *dollar* figure for working capital is rather difficult, especially when comparing one company with another. Dollars alone do not tell the whole story. A company may have only a modest amount of current liabilities, requiring a relatively small amount of working capital. Or its current liabilities may be very large, requiring many more dollars of working capital for safety's sake. Of primary importance, therefore, is the *proportion* by which current assets exceed current liabilities. This ratio, called the *current ratio,* is arrived at by dividing current assets by current liabilities. Thus:

$$\text{Current ratio} = \frac{\text{Current assets}}{\text{Current liabilities}}$$

Using the figures from the previous section on working capital:

$$\text{Current ratio} = \frac{\$1,000,000}{\$\ 400,000} = 2.5$$

The current ratio, 2.5, means that our typical corporation can cover its current liabilities two and a half times over. In other words, for every dollar of current liabilities, it has 2½ dollars of current assets.

This current ratio is expressed in a variety of ways:

2.5 or 2½ or 2.5 × or 2½ times or

2.5 to 1 or 2½ to 1 or 2½/1

A "good" current ratio, for the typical manufacturing company, is 2 to 1 or higher. For a company with easily collectable receivables, like a public utility, a current ratio as low as 1 to 1 may be acceptable.

Quick Asset Ratio. An even more stringent test of a company's ability to meet its current obligations is the *quick asset ratio,* also called the *liquidity ratio* or *acid test ratio.* This ratio indicates the relationship between *quick assets* and current liabilities:

$$\text{Quick asset ratio} = \frac{\text{Quick assets}}{\text{Current liabilities}}$$

Example:

Using the ongoing figures for our corporation:

Quick assets = Total current assets − Inventory

Quick assets = $1,000,000 − $400,000
  = $600,000

$$\text{Quick asset ratio} = \frac{\text{Quick assets}}{\text{Total current liabilities}}$$

$$\text{Quick asset ratio} = \frac{\$600,000}{\$400,000} = 1.5$$

The quick asset ratio of 1.5 indicates that our corporation had one-and-one-half times the total of its short-term liabilities in quick assets alone. A "safe" quick asset ratio for the average manufacturing concern is 1 to 1. In other words, the corporation should have enough *quick* assets to pay off all the current liabilities.

Fixed Assets

Now that we have addressed both current assets and current liabilities, let us turn our attention to the remainder of the left-hand (asset) side of the balance sheet.

The items of value used in current operations that can be expected to generate revenue are referred to as *fixed assets.* Included in this category are such items as improved land, buildings, furniture and fixtures, machinery, tools, and transportation equipment—sometimes referred to collectively as *property, plant, and equipment.* These assets are normally not considered as items to be sold but rather as "tools of the trade" with which the manufactured product is produced, displayed, and transported. Most fixed assets are listed on the balance sheet at *cost minus accumulated depreciation.* For our typical manufacturing corporation, the fixed assets are $605,000, as shown on the balance sheet under property, plant, and equipment. (See Figure 1.)

Depreciation. As fixed assets grow older, they decrease in value due to ordinary wear and tear, action of the elements, or obsolescence. Since our balance sheet attempts to list everything owned by the corporation at current value, the value at which fixed assets are shown declines as the assets get older. When a fixed asset is acquired by the corporation, it is *not* charged as a business expense in the year it is purchased. Since a fixed asset is expected to last quite a few years, the company charges it as an expense, *a little bit at a time,* spread over the years it is supposed to be usable to the company. By way of analogy, assume you as an individual (were it legal!) could *spread out* a deductible personal expense of $5,000, for a car. Instead of taking the full $5,000 deduction in the year in which you incurred the actual expense, you might instead deduct $1,000 a year for five consecutive years, thus *spreading out* the expense. Spreading out the expense *is* quite legal for the corporation! The amount by which the fixed assets are lowered each year is the portion of the cost of fixed assets charged as an expense for a given year; that portion is called *annual depreciation* and is listed as such.

Three Methods for Determining Amount of Depreciation. Fixed assets may be depreciated by three principal methods:

1. straight-line,
2. sum-of-years' digits, and
3. double declining balance.

When a fixed asset is purchased, the company determines how long the asset is expected to be used (*useful life*). It also determines the value that it expects to receive when the asset is scrapped (*salvage value*). The cost of the asset is considered to be the initial price *minus* the salvage value, because the salvage value will be received some time after the item is purchased. In most cases, this net cost figure is the amount depreciated over the item's useful life, not the full price paid. The simple equation is:

$$\text{Net cost} = \text{Actual cost} - \text{Salvage value}$$

Comparing the Three Methods for Determining Depreciation. The effect of each method for calculating annual depreciation is different. With the straight-line method, you even out profits over several years, and you list a high remaining value for the asset in the later years. With the sum-of-years' digits method and the double declining balance method, you take a large writeoff in early years, thus lowering your early profits as well as your early taxes. With both of these methods, you consequently list a lower remaining value in the later years. Since the double declining balance method accelerates depreciation the most of all three, it is used when your chief concern is to lower taxes in the early years of an asset's useful life.

It is permissible to use one method of depreciation for reporting to stockholders and another for purposes of filing a tax return. Very often a company reports to its stockholders on a straight-line basis and files its tax return on double declining balance, since it produces a higher expense and, therefore, a lower tax.

Sundry Assets

This is a *miscellaneous* category, generally including unimproved land, prepaid expenses, deferred charges, and other items that are usually considered investments for the future. *Prepaid expenses* include payments for materials or services in *advance* of their receipt or use, such as early rent payments and insurance premiums. *Deferred charges* are used to "charge off" major expenses, such as those incurred in the introduction of a new product or the formation of a new subsidiary company.

Example:

A company spends $1,000,000 to purchase a ten-year lease in a given year. It includes $900,000 in the sundry assets section so that the *total assets* section shows a decline of only $100,000 that year; that is, the company considers $900,000 of the total amount spent as an asset in terms of having a lease. The balance sheet shows cash minus $1,000,000 and sundry assets plus $900,000. The company then reduces the $900,000 in each subsequent year for the next nine years so that it spreads out the $1,000,000 cost for the lease over a ten-year period.

Intangible Assets

Included in this category are items of value that have no physical existence, such as patents, franchises, and goodwill. Such items are very difficult to quantify. Traditionally, intangibles are the last item shown on the asset side of the balance sheet.

LIABILITIES

Liabilities

Let us now turn our attention again to the *right* (debit) side of the balance sheet. Here are listed the corporation's debts and, further down, the stockholders' equity.

Current Liabilities. The first category, *current liabilities,* includes all obligations that fall due within the year.

Fixed Liabilities. The fixed liabilities appear below current liabilities on the balance sheet. The major item, ordinarily, is the corporation's funded debt, usually outstanding bonds maturing five years or more in the future. This category may also include long-term promissory notes, bank loans, and other obligations.

Bonds are carried on the balance sheet at their par value. Keep in mind that the actual market prices of the company's own bonds *could* be either at a premium (above par) or at a discount (below par). The coupon rate and maturity date are usually indicated for each bond outstanding. The liabilities section of the balance sheet of our typical manufacturing corporation looks like this:

Liabilities

Accounts payable	$200,000
Accrued expenses	150,000
Accrued taxes	+ 50,000
Total current liabilities	$400,000
Convertible debentures	+ 500,000
8% interest, due 1995	
Total liabilities	$900,000

SHAREHOLDERS' EQUITY

Stockholders' (Shareholders') Equity

As we know, the difference between the corporation's total assets and total liabilities is referred to as *stockholders' equity* or net worth. The final section of the balance sheet therefore represents the stockholders' equity, which is the stake that the stockholders, both common and preferred, have in their corporation. This section itemizes the amount of equity or *ownership* of the *true owners* of the corporation, the shareholders. It might be thought of as the money the corporation "owes" the owners. The items in this category are:

1. preferred stock,
2. common stock,
3. paid-in capital (capital surplus), and
4. retained earnings (earned surplus).

Preferred Stock. Preferred stock, like common stock, is an equity security. Holders of such stock are considered to be owners of the corporation in contrast to bondholders who are considered creditors. Fittingly, preferred stock, which is ordinarily senior to common stock with respect to dividends and liquidation rights, is listed first. Such stock is "carried" *not* at its market value, but at its total par value, which in most instances is approximately equal to the amount the company received when the stock was first sold to the public. This listed figure usually approximates the amount that the preferred stockholders are entitled to receive if the company is dissolved. Most balance sheets detail information about any preferred stock listed, such as par value, convertibility (if any), dividend rate, and the number of shares authorized, issued, or outstanding.

Example:

Preferred stock	$75,000
6% Cumulative—$100 par	
Authorized, issued, and outstanding	
750 shares	

All 750 authorized shares of preferred stock are issued and outstanding.

750 Shares × $100 Par = $75,000 Book value
(Total par value)

Each share of $100 par preferred stock is entitled to a dividend at 6 percent of the par value each year. In other words, 6 percent of $100 equals a $6-per-share annual dividend. The balance sheet indicates that such dividends are cumulative. In the event that any preferred dividends are "skipped," the company may not pay dividends on the common stock until all back dividends on the preferred stock (arrearages) have been paid.

Common Stock. The balance sheet shows the number of shares of common stock outstanding and their par value. Historically, par value represented the price at which the shares were first sold by the corporation. After the initial offering, par value has very little real significance. For our purposes, let's consider the amount shown on the balance sheet as "common stock" to represent the company's "seed money" —the amount of money, *at par value,* that the company first received from the sale of stock. In recent years, because stock transfer taxes are based on par values, corporations have been assigning par value well below the price at which the shares are sold. Today, par value has little or no meaning in terms of the value of the shares.

Example:

Common stock	$300,000
$10 par Authorized, issued, and outstanding 30,000 shares	

Paid-In Capital. This item, also called *capital surplus,* shows the amount of money the company received from the sale of shares of common stock to the public *in addition to* the par value.

Example:

Our corporation, Roxbury Manufacturing, starts in business by selling 20,000 shares of stock at their original par value of $10 each. After this initial offering, the common stock section of the balance sheet shows $200,000. At least at this point in time, there is *no* paid-in capital. If, at a later date, the company issues another 10,000 shares at $20 each, the "extra" monies received—the amount *over* par value—are indicated in the paid-in capital section of the balance sheet. The *basic* amount received ($10 par value) is added to the common stock account. The overage (the $10 which exceeded par value) goes into the paid-in capital account.

Common stock	$300,000
$10 par Authorized, issued, and outstanding 30,000 shares	
Paid-in capital (capital surplus)	$100,000

This entry indicates that the founders of the business invested a total of $400,000 in common stock, of which $100,000 exceeded the total par value of $300,000. Generally, therefore, the *total* of these two accounts (common stock and paid-in capital) indicates the amount of money the company has received through the sale of its common stock to investors.

Retained Earnings. Also known as *earned surplus,* this section shows the amount of profit that the company retains in the business *after* paying any dividends on the common stock. In a sense, retained earnings represent profits that have not yet been paid out to the common stockholders in the form of dividends.

Example:

A company is formed by selling a share of common stock at $100 per share to 10 different people. The total amount collected is used to purchase goods at wholesale—for subsequent resale. An early balance sheet is as follows:

Assets		*Liabilities*	
Inventory	$1,000		-0-
		Stockholders' Equity	
		Common stock $100 par	$1,000

At this point, total assets ($1,000 in inventory) equal total liabilities (zero) and stockholders' equity ($1,000). The company then sells the inventory for a total of $2,000 and uses all the cash to purchase still more inventory. Situation is now:

Assets		*Liabilities*	
Inventory	$2,000		-0-
		Stockholders' Equity	
		Common stock $100 par	$1,000
		Retained earnings	$1,000

The $1,000 earned profit, over and above its initial invest-
ment, appears in the retained earnings account.

The total of $2,000 under stockholders' equity, how-
ever, does not mean that the shareholders will receive $20
back for their $10 investments. These retained earnings are
not cash: the profit has already been reinvested in additional
inventory. Since the average balance sheet lists many items
at *other than* their liquidation values, the chances of the
shareholders' receiving cash equal to the net worth (shareholders' equity) portion of the balance sheet are small. Remember that shareholders' equity represents the amount
that the stockholders *would* receive, *if* all assets were sold at
the values at which they are carried on the balance sheet
(book value) and *if* all liabilities were paid off at their balance
sheet figures.

Example:

A company is formed through the sale of 1,000 shares of preferred stock at $100 per share and 500,000 shares of com-
mon stock at $1 per share. It uses some of the cash received
to purchase machinery and raw materials, but it does not pay
for all the items in full. Our balance sheet looks like this:

Assets		Liabilities	
Cash	$160,000	Accounts payable	$ 50,000
Inventory	+ 85,000		
Total current assets	$245,000	*Stockholders' Equity*	
Property, plant, and		Preferred stock	
equipment	+405,000	$100 par	100,000
Total assets	$650,000	Common stock	
		$1 par	+500,000
		Total liabilities and stockholders' equity	$650,000

At this early period of the company's development, it
has no profits and therefore no retained earnings. But it oper-

ates successfully over time and increases its assets by $200,000 through sales and its liabilities by only $50,000. The difference between the value of the newly acquired items and the additional debt—$150,000—represents a "gain" for the company's owners. At least in theory, the stockholders are "worth" $150,000 more, a profit shown as retained earnings. Keep in mind that the $150,000 thus "earned" is spread out among various assets. To realize this sum in cash, the company would have to liquidate some assets. The balance sheet now looks like this:

Assets		Liabilities	
Cash	$ 80,000	Accounts payable	$ 60,000
Accounts receivable	135,000	Accrued expenses	+ 40,000
Inventory	+140,000	Total liabilities	$100,000
Total current assets	$355,000		
Property, plant, and		*Stockholders' Equity*	
equipment	470,000	Preferred stock	
Prepaid expenses	+ 25,000	$100 par	100,000
		Common stock	
		$1 par	500,000
		Retained earnings	+150,000
		Total liabilities	
		and stockholders'	
Total assets	$850,000	equity	$850,000

The balance sheet balances! If the company decides to liquidate, it realizes $850,000 in cash from the sale of the assets, at least in theory. If it next pays off all obligations ($100,000 for all liabilities), it would have a total of $750,000 to be distributed to the owners of the company, its shareholders. The preferred stockholders are entitled to receive par for their stock ($100,000), leaving $650,000 for the common stockholders. The common stockholders' stake in the company can be found by adding together the common stock listing ($500,000), paid-in capital ($0), and retained earnings ($150,000). The sum of these three figures shows the *common* stockholders' equity.

On the other hand, let us assume the company decides to continue operations for future profits. To reward the stockholders, it decides to distribute a dividend. Since the term "retained earnings" means earnings retained in the business, any distributed earnings in the form of dividends *decreases* retained earnings.

BALANCE SHEET ANALYSIS

In this section we shall analyze our balance sheet by looking at capitalization and book value. We have already compared current assets with current liabilities on pages 210–212. We suggest that you review that section now, and consider it as part of our balance sheet analysis.

Capitalization (Capital Structure-Invested Capital)

A company's *capitalization* is simply the sum of the balance sheet values for the corporation's bonds, preferred stock, and common stock. All *three* elements of the common stock are added: common stock, paid-in-capital, and retained earnings. Thus, capitalization represents the monies invested in the company by the *original* purchasers of the bonds, preferred stock, and common stock. It also reflects retained earnings, which is the capital that has *not* been paid out as dividends but that rather has been reinvested in the company. Capitalization thus tells us how a company got its funds and, secondarily, how it is handling them.

Capitalization is expressed in terms of three ratios, one each for bonds, common, and preferred stock. Each of these *capitalization ratios* represents the proportion of money collected through each vehicle to the *total* capitalization amount, assuming the total amount is equal to 100 percent.

Example:

FIGURE 2

BALANCE SHEET
ROXBURY MANUFACTURING COMPANY
December 31, 1978

Assets

Cash	$ 75,000
Marketable securities	150,000
Accounts receivable	375,000
Inventories	+400,000
Total current assets	$1,000,000
Property, plant, and equipment	605,000
Prepayments	20,000
Intangibles	+ 10,000
Total assets	$1,635.000

Liabilities

Accounts payable	$200,000
Accrued expenses	150,000
Accrued taxes	50,000
Total current liabilities	$400,000
Bonds 8%—Due 1995	500,000
Total liabilities	$900,000

Stockholders' Equity

Preferred stock—6% ($100 par)	$ 75,000
Common stock ($10 par)	300,000
Capital surplus	100,000
Retained earnings	260,000
Total stockholders' equity	$ 735,000
Total liabilities and stockholders' equity	$1,635,000

In Figure 2, Roxbury's capitalization is shown to be $1,235,000, calculated as follows:

	Preferred		Common		Capital		Retained		Capitali-
Bonds +	stock	+	stock	+	surplus	+	earnings	=	zation
$500,000 +	$75,000	+	$300,000	+	$100,000	+	$260,000	=	$1,235,000

The *bond ratio* is derived by dividing total capitalization into the bonded debt, usually outstanding bonds maturing five years or more in the future.

$$\text{Bond ratio} = \frac{\text{Bonds}}{\text{Total capitalization}}$$

$$\text{Bond ratio} = \frac{\$\ 500,000}{\$1,235,000} = 0.405 \text{ or } 40.5\%$$

The *preferred stock* ratio is found by dividing total capitalization into the par value of the preferred stock.

$$\text{Preferred stock ratio} = \frac{\text{Preferred stock}}{\text{Total capitalization}}$$

$$\text{Preferred stock ratio} = \frac{\$\ 75,000}{\$1,235,000} = 0.061 \text{ or } 6.1\%$$

The *common stock ratio* is found by dividing total capitalization into *all three parts* of the common stock account.

$$\text{Common stock ratio} = \frac{\text{Common stock} + \text{Capital surplus} + \text{Retained earnings}}{\text{Total recapitalization}}$$

$$\text{Common stock ratio} = \frac{\$300,000 + \$100,000 + \$260,000}{\$1,235,000} = 0.534 \text{ or } 53.4\%$$

All three capitalization ratios add up to 100 percent.

FIGURE 3
Breakdown of Roxbury's Capitalization Ratios

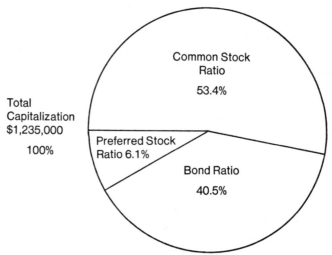

There are certain capitalization ratio "yardsticks." For example, if the bond and preferred stock ratios combined exceed 50 percent of the total capitalization, an industrial company is generally considered by industry standards to have a leveraged capital structure. This condition may be considered speculative.

Book Value

The net tangible assets backing each share of common stock is known as *book value*. Calculating book value is easy: since the balance sheet always shows the theoretical value of the common stockholders' equity (common stock + paid-in capital + retained earnings), just subtract the *intangible* assets (if any) and divide by the number of outstanding common shares. The formula, applied to the sample balance sheet from the previous section on capitalization, is as follows:

$$\begin{array}{ll} \text{Book} \\ \text{value} \end{array} = \left[\begin{array}{l} \text{Common} \quad \text{Capital} \quad \text{Retained} \\ \quad \text{stock} \; + \text{surplus} + \text{earnings} - \text{Intangibles} \end{array} \right] \begin{array}{l} \text{Number of shares} \\ \div \text{of common stock} \\ \quad \text{outstanding} \end{array}$$

$$\begin{array}{l} \text{Book} \\ \text{value} \end{array} = (\$300,000 + \$100,000 + \$260,000 - \$10,000) \div \$30,000 = \begin{array}{l} \$21.67 \\ \text{per share} \end{array}$$

The book value per common share represents the amount of cash that would be available for each share of common stock if all the assets (excepting intangibles) were sold *at the values at which they are carried on the balance sheet* and if all liabilities, bondholders, and preferred stockholders are "paid off." For our purposes, assume that the company must pay the bondholders and preferred stockholders the total par value of their securities as shown on the balance sheet. (However, accountants would most probably use the higher value between the total par value as shown on the balance sheet and the total market value based on the call price of their securities.)

A company's book value can be of great significance, despite the fact that, in the real world, liquidating the company at balance sheet values is virtually impossible. An increasing book value is generally considered to be a healthy sign for a company; a decreasing book value may indicate a weakening financial situation. To the securities analyst, whether a company's book value is *increasing* or *decreasing* is especially significant; while normally a company's *book value* and its *market value* bear no correlation (with some exceptions mostly for financial service companies, such as insurance firms), these values do usually move in concert. For example, the "bid" shown in the newspaper for mutual funds is actually the book value of a share of the fund!

Summary Comment

As we have seen, the balance sheet reflects the company's financial position at a particular point in time—what it owns, what it owes, and what the shareholders are worth. It is like a snapshot of a subject "on the run"—the action is frozen, and the values are reflected as of the close of business on the balance sheet date.

While one balance sheet can be very revealing, a *series* of balance sheets, possibly covering the previous five or six years of operations, can be of even greater significance. The *trends* are extremely important. Is this year's current ratio better or worse than it has been over the last several years? Is the book value per common share going higher or lower? A study of the ratios *over a period of a few years* can reveal much about the company's future prospects.

INCOME STATEMENT CONSTRUCTION

Corporate annual reports traditionally show a balance sheet representing the corporation's financial picture on a particular day, usually the final day of the company's fiscal year. Most annual reports contain another financial statement in addition to the balance sheet—the income statement. The *income statement* (also known as the *profit and loss statement*), a statement of income and expenses usually over the *entire* year, shows how much the company made or lost during the year. A typical, simplified, income statement appears in Figure 4. (Assume 30,000 shares of common stock outstanding.) Review that statement briefly before we examine it entry by entry.

Net Sales
The *net sales* listing shows the amount of money that the company took in as the result of its manufacturing activities. "Net" reflects the fact that returned goods and discounts have been taken into account. Were this a nonmanufacturing enterprise (such as an airline or utility), this item might be called *operating revenues*.

FIGURE 4

STATEMENT OF INCOME
ROXBURY MANUFACTURING COMPANY
January 1–December 31, 1978

Net sales	$2,000,000
Cost of goods sold	− 1,590,000
Selling, general, and administrative expenses	− 154,000
Depreciation	− 56,000
Operating income	$ 200,000
Other income	+ 7,500
Total income (EBIT)	$ 207,500
Interest on bonds	− 40,000
Taxes (50% rate)	− 83,750
Net income	$ 83,750
Preferred dividends	− 4,500
Net earnings	$ 79,250
(earnings available for common stock)	

Cost of Goods Sold

Think of this item as "factory" costs. It includes such factors as the costs of maintaining the manufacturing facilities, raw materials, and labor.

Selling, General, and Administrative Expenses

This item includes the cost of running the *sales* office of the company: office payroll, salespersons' commissions, advertising, and other such nonmanufacturing expenses.

Depreciation

The annual depreciation of the fixed assets appears in this category. You may consider this a *noncash expense* because the assets may have been paid for well in the past but are being "charged off" in small increments each year.

Operating Income

Subtracting the operating costs from net sales gives

operating income. It is "factory" profit, because we have not yet considered bond interest, taxes, or income from sources other than manufacturing.

Other Income

The income the company receives as dividends and/or interest on the marketable securities it may own appears here. This item may also include other sources of income not related directly to the firm's operations, such as the sale of real estate (above book value) or rental income on unused land held for future use.

Total Income

Also known as *earnings before interest and taxes* (EBIT), this category is fairly self-explanatory.

Interest on Bonds

Almost as self-explanatory is the amount of money that the corporation pays out each year to service its outstanding bonds.

Taxes

Federal and state income taxes, for our purposes, can be figured at roughly 50 percent. Thus, 50 percent of ($207,500 − $40,000) gives us $83,750 in taxes.

Net Income

This item is also known as *net profit*. All income and all expenses have now been weighed against each other. Only the stockholders remain to be satisfied.

Preferred Dividends

Note that the corporation deducted its bond interest payments *before* figuring its tax liability. Preferred dividend payments, however, are *not* a deductible item and do not lower taxes.

Net Earnings

Such earnings, also known as *earnings available for common stock,* may be reinvested in the company and/or paid out to the common stockholders as cash dividends. Any amount *not* paid out as dividends, at least in theory, increases the retained earnings account.

INCOME STATEMENT ANALYSIS

Just as balance sheet ratios measure a company's financial strength, so too do important income statement ratios reflect a company's state of affairs. In the following analysis, use the income statement shown in Figure 4.

Expense Ratio (Operating Ratio)

The *expense ratio,* also known as the *operating ratio,* is an excellent measure of corporate efficiency and should therefore be compared with the results of prior years. An increasing expense ratio could indicate a company's loss of control over cost.

$$\text{Expense ratio} = \frac{\text{Operating costs}}{\text{Net sales}}$$

$$\text{Expense ratio} = \frac{\text{Cost of goods sold} + \text{Selling, general, and administrative expenses} + \text{Depreciation}}{\text{Net sales}}$$

$$= \frac{\$1,590,000 + 154,000 + 56,000}{2,000,000} = 0.9 \text{ or } 90\%$$

Margin of Profit Ratio

The complement of the expense ratio, this ratio shows the percentage of the sales dollar *not* eaten up by operating costs. It is derived by dividing operating income by net sales.

$$\text{Margin of profit ratio} = \frac{\text{Operating income}}{\text{Net sales}}$$

$$= \frac{\$\ 200,000}{2,000,000} = 0.10 \text{ or } 10\%$$

Note that the margin of profit ratio plus the operating ratio equals 100%.

Cash Flow

Realizing that one of the operating expenses—depreciation—is "artificial," we might ask how much actual cash the company has available before it pays out any monies on preferred or common stock cash dividends. Depreciation is not actually "spent," at least not in the current year, and therefore cash flow is equal to the sum of net income and annual depreciation.

Cash flow = Net income + Annual depreciation
= $83,750 + 56,000 = $139,750

Interest Coverage

When examining a company we want to know how well it provides for the payment of interest coupons on its outstanding bonds. To find out, divide total income (EBIT) by the interest on the bonds:

$$\text{Interest coverage} = \frac{\text{Total income (EBIT)}}{\text{Interest on bonds}}$$

$$= \frac{\$207,500}{\$\ 40,000} = 5.2 \text{ times}$$

Interest coverage of over four times is usually considered a safe margin for the protection of a company.

Preferred Dividend Coverage
Another question is: How well are the preferred dividends covered by earnings? To find out, simply divide the net income by the preferred dividend requirements.

$$\text{Preferred dividend coverage} = \frac{\text{Net income}}{\text{Preferred dividends}}$$

$$= \frac{\$83,750}{\$\ 4,500} = 18.6 \text{ times}$$

The calculation shows that the earnings cover the preferred dividends 18.6 times over.

Primary Earnings Per Share
The earnings per share ratio is probably the most widely used measure of how well a company's fortunes are faring. As a result, it is almost the most widely advertised measure—the "bottom line." This most important measurement is determined by dividing the net earnings (which is equal to net income minus preferred dividends) by the number of common shares outstanding.

$$\text{Primary earnings per share} = \frac{\text{Net earnings}}{\substack{\text{Number of shares} \\ \text{of common stock outstanding}}}$$

$$= \frac{\$79,250}{30,000} = \$2.64$$

The expression "earnings per share" has practically been replaced by the more modern expression *primary earnings per share*. The newer term reflects earnings as they would be if all "common stock equivalents" were issued and outstanding as common stock, thus diluting "ordinary" earnings per share by 3 percent or more. Common stock equivalents include warrants, stock options, and *certain* convertible bonds and convertible preferred shares. Common stock equivalents, if they exist, are clearly labeled. Corporations now report primary earnings per share so that the investing public does *not* have to refigure the "ordinary" earnings per share. Nor does the public have to determine which convertible items are considered common stock equivalents. When earnings are figured to include *all* possible additional shares of common stock, whether common stock equivalents or not, then such earnings are reported as "fully diluted."

Fully Diluted Earnings Per Share

A corporation may have convertible bonds and/or convertible preferred stock outstanding. Investors realize that earnings per common share would be affected if such securities were to be converted. Fully diluted earnings reflect the per-share results as they *would* be if all *potential* common shares were added to the outstanding common stock. Under this method all warrants, stock options (options issued *privately* by the corporation), and convertible issues are considered as exchanged for additional common stock.

Figure 5 contains the same basic figures as Figure 4, but they have been recalculated on the assumption that the outstanding bonds are convertible and that they *have been* converted. The bonds are convertible into 20,000 additional shares of stock, and, again, the corporate tax rate is 50 percent. Assuming that the convertible bonds are exchanged for common stock, the interest on bond entry disappears. With that deduction of $40,000 gone, the income *before* tax rises from $167,500 to $207,500. At a tax rate of 50 percent, the tax burden under fully diluted conditions is $103,750 instead of $83,750, thus *raising* net earnings from $79,250 to $99,250. Again assuming that the bonds are converted, we must take into account the additional shares thus created. If 30,000 shares were outstanding before the conversion, then the fully diluted earnings figure is calculated by dividing the "new" net earnings by 50,000 shares of common stock (30,000 outstanding + 20,000 after conversion). Of course, all these changes affect the "ordinary" earnings per share of the corporation:

$$\text{Fully diluted earnings per share} = \frac{\text{Net earnings}}{\text{Number of shares of common stock outstanding after conversion}}$$

$$= \frac{\$99,250}{50,000} = \$1.99$$

FIGURE 5

INCOME STATEMENT
(Fully Diluted)
ROXBURY MANUFACTURING COMPANY
January 1–December 31, 1978

Net sales	$2,000,000
Cost of goods sold	− 1,590,000
Selling, general, and administrative expenses	− 154,000
Depreciation	− 56,000
Operating income	$ 200,000
Other income	+ 7,500
Total income (EBIT)	$ 207,500
Taxes (50% rate)	− 103,750
Net income	$ 103,750
Preferred dividends	− 4,500
Net earnings	$ 99,250
(earnings available for common stock)	

OTHER ANALYSES

Most corporations pay out at least a part of their net earnings to common shareholders through cash dividends. The percentage of earnings so distributed is known as the *payout ratio.* As a rough guideline, growth companies may be expected to have low payout ratios (10 percent), compared with a typical manufacturing company payout of approximately 50 percent. This ratio is derived by dividing the total common dividends paid by the total net earnings, which is net income minus preferred dividends.

Example:

$$\text{Payout ratio} = \frac{\text{Common stock dividends}}{\text{Net income} - \text{Preferred dividends}}$$

A corporation with $1,000,000 in net income pays $50,000 in preferred dividends and $375,000 in common stock dividends. Its payout ratio is:

$$\text{Payout ratio} = \frac{\$375,000}{1,000,000 - 50,000} = 0.394 \text{ or } 39.4\%$$

Yield on Common Stock

To determine *current yield*, divide a security's annual dividends (or coupons) by its current market price.

$$\text{Current yield} = \frac{\text{Annual dividend rate}}{\text{Market price}}$$

Generally speaking, companies with greater prospects for growth have lower yields, because growth companies usually reinvest most of their earnings in their own businesses.

Example:

A common stock has a current market price of 42 and pays annual dividends of $1.80. Its current yield is 4.3%, calculated thus:

$$\text{Current yield} = \frac{\$1.80}{42} = 0.043 \text{ or } 4.3\%$$

Inventory Turnover Ratio

We can measure how effectively the company is selling its products by determining how often its supply of inventory is manufactured and sold. Of the several methods for calculating this ratio, the simplest (and probably least professional) is as follows:

$$\text{Inventory turnover ratio} = \frac{\text{Net sales}}{\text{Year-end inventory}}$$

This method is presented because it is simple and workable. Other methods use the cost of goods sold, rather than net sales, as the numerator and the *average* inventory, rather than year-end inventory, as the denominator. As a general guide, a "good" inventory turnover ratio for an average manufacturing company is 6 times per year.

Example:

A corporation's annual report shows net sales of $14,000,000 (on the income statement) and an inventory of $2,682,000 (on the balance sheet). The inventory turnover is 5.2 times, determined as follows:

$$\text{Inventory turnover ratio} = \frac{\$14,000,000}{2,682,000} = 5.2 \text{ times}$$

Price Earnings Ratio

The *price earnings,* or *P/E,* ratio is one of the most significant measurements. It relates a corporation's profitability to the market price of its common shares, thus affording a measure of the *relative* "expensiveness" of the common stock. Typically, growth stocks have high P/E ratios; companies with poorer prospects sell at lower earnings multiples. To obtain this ratio, divide the market price of the company's common stock by the earnings per share.

$$\text{Price earnings ratio} = \frac{\text{Current market price of the common stock}}{\text{Common stock earnings per share}}$$

Example:

Company A earned $1.04 per share. Its common stock is selling in the open market at 23¼.

$$\text{Price earnings (P/E) ratio} = \frac{\$23.25}{\$\ 1.04} = 22.4$$

Each share of common stock is selling for about 22 times the amount of earnings generated by each share.

Return on Equity

An informative measure of management's efficiency is the *return on equity*, derived by dividing net income by shareholders' equity. (Shareholders' equity is the sum of preferred stock, common stock, paid-in capital, and retained earnings.)

$$\text{Return on equity} = \frac{\text{Net income}}{\text{Shareholders' equity}}$$

Example:

Turn back to the balance sheet in Figure 1 and to the income statement in Figure 8. Using information from those state-ments, the return is figured as follows:

$$\text{Return on equity} = \frac{\$\ 83{,}750}{\$735{,}000} = 0.114 \text{ or } 11.4\%$$

Return on Invested Capital

A measure of how well the company is utilizing its entire capitalization is the *return on invested capital*. (For a review on how the total capitalization figure is derived, see Section C1.) The formula is:

$$\frac{\text{Return on}}{\text{invested capital}} = \frac{\text{Net income} + \text{Interest on debt}}{\text{Total capitalization (invested capital)}}$$

Example:

Again using the balance sheet and the income statements in Figures 1 and 4, you can calculate the interest on bonds ($40,000) by multiplying the coupon rate, 8 percent, by the total par value, $500,000. After that, simply fill in the formula:

$$\frac{\text{Return on}}{\text{invested capital}} = \frac{\$83{,}750 + \$40{,}000}{\$1{,}235{,}000}$$

$$= 10.0\%$$

"FINANCIAL REASONING" PROBLEMS

Let us apply our knowledge of accounting by following the effects of a managerial decision on the corporation's fi-nancial statements! In each instance, we shall trace the course of events, noting the impact on the company's assets, liabilities, shareholders' equity, and several of the more common ratios.

Stock Splits

When a common stock is split, the *number of shares* of common stock *increases* and the *par value* of the common stock *decreases* in the same proportion.

A "beginning" common stockholders' equity before a split consists of:

Common stock: at $.40 par value, 600,000 shares authorized, 300,000 shares issued and outstanding	$120,000
Paid-in capital	40,000
Retained earnings	+ 135,000
Total common stockholders' equity	$295,000

In a 2-for-1 split, the number of issued and outstanding shares doubles (from 300,000 to 600,000) and the par value is halved (from $.40 to $.20). The *new* common stockholders' equity looks like this after the split:

Common stock: at $.20 par value, 600,000 shares authorized, 600,000 shares issued and outstanding	$120,000
Paid-in capital	40,000
Retained earnings	+ 135,000
Total common stockholders' equity	$295,000

Because of the 2-for-1 split, the par value changes from $.40 to $.20 but the number of outstanding shares doubles! No *real* change occurs in the balance sheet! The common stock account *still* comes out to $120,000:

300,000 shares @ $.40 par = $120,000 *and*
600,000 shares @ $.20 par = $120,000

Certainly a greater number of shares are outstanding;

but, at least in theory, the shareholders are no better off (and no *worse* off!) than they were before the split. Traditionally, a flurry of buying follows a stock split. The market theory is that the stock will sell better at a lower price after the split be-cause it is more "marketable." People tend to favor lower-priced issues even though a lower-priced security bears no more intrinsic value than a higher-priced security. The actual net effect of the split is nil, because the book values on the balance sheet do not change.

Stock Dividends

Classically, stock dividends require the issuance of addi-tional shares, but the par value of the common stock does *not* change.

Example:

Using the same stockholders' equity statement from the pre-vious section, let us restate the figures as they appear after the payment of a 30 percent stock dividend, that is, 90,000 shares (30% of 300,000):

Common stock: at $.40 par value, 600,000 shares authorized, 390,000 shares issued and outstanding	$156,000
Paid-in capital	40,000
Retained earnings	+ 99,000
Total common stockholders' equity	$295,000

Compare the previous figures with these. The *total* equity does not change. Nevertheless, the common stock account increases by $36,000 (from $120,000 to $156,000), and the retained earnings account decreases by $36,000 (from $135,000 to $99,000). Our common stockholders are no richer or poorer, but the balance sheet changes in that the common stock account increases at the expense of the retained earnings account.

Smaller stock dividends (generally less than 25 percent)

are treated differently. Paid-in capital may also be increased, and the market value of the common stock may be taken into account.

FIGURE 6

DOKTABESSIE CORPORATION
BALANCE SHEET
June 30, 1979

Assets		*Liabilities*	
Cash	$165,000	Accounts payable	$166,000
Marketable securities	18,000	Accrued taxes	70,000
Accounts receivable	260,000	Notes payable	84,000
Inventory	455,000	Accrued expenses	151,000
Total current assets	$898,000	Total current liabilities	471,000
		First mortgage bonds: 7½% due 1/1/94	500,000
Property, plant, and equipment:		Total liabilities	$971,000
Land	$ 75,000		
Buildings	506,000	*Stockholders' Equity*	
Equipment	89,000	Preferred stock ($100 par,	
Machinery	164,000	1,000 shares authorized,	
	834,000	issued, and	
Less: Accumulated depreciation	−217,000	outstanding)	100,000
		Common stock ($25 par,	
Net property, plant, and equipment	$617,000	12,000 shares authorized, issued, and	
		outstanding)	300,000
		Paid-in capital	58,000
		Accumulated retained earnings	290,000
		Total stockholders' equity	$748,000
Intangibles	204,000	Total liabilities and stockholders' equity	$1,719,000
Total assets	$1,719,000		

Declaration of Cash Dividends

For the remainder of this section use the balance sheet in Figure 6.

A board of directors announces a cash dividend payment of $0.50 per common share approximately two months before the dividends are actually paid out to the stockholders. As a result, the Doktabessie Corporation balance sheet undergoes changes between the time the corporation declares a cash dividend and the time it actually pays it.

The declaration of a cash dividend creates a current liability of $6,000 ($0.50 × 12,000 common shares). Current liabilities must be adjusted to include this *new* obligation, which must be paid out within the next year. An item (probably labeled "dividends payable") is added to current liabilities, raising the total by $6,000 to $477,000. Where does this $6,000 come from? From the accumulated retained earnings! As you will recall, retained earnings may be thought of as unpaid dividends. Management has now decided to pay some of this accumulated value to the common stockholders. So we now *reduce* retained earnings by $6,000 (from $290,000 to $284,000). The overall "change" on the balance sheet is an increase in current liabilities and a decrease in retained earnings.

Since current assets remain the same while current liabilities have increased, several ratios are adversely affected. The dividend reduces:

- the working capital (net current assets),
- the quick asset ratio (acid test ratio),
- the current ratio, and
- the book value.

Logically, the dividend also reduces the common stockholders' stake in the company, because part of their accumulated profits is paid out to them! Understandably, the value remaining after they receive their dividends is reduced by the amount of such dividends.

Payment of Cash Dividends

When the Doktabessie Corporation actually pays out the cash dividends, the company is actually dispersing cash in the amount of the current liability established for such payment. The following changes occur:

- *cash* decreases and
- *dividends payable* disappears.

Cash is now $159,000 ($165,000 − $6,000), and total current assets decreases to $892,000. The total current liabilities entry goes back to $471,000. Note where the *ultimate* change occurs: cash is reduced, and the payment comes from retained earnings! The shift was done in two stages:

1. When the dividend is *declared,* retained earnings decrease and current liabilities increase.
2. When the dividend is *paid,* cash decreases and that particular current liability disappears.

Retiring Debt at a Discount

If the corporation's bonds are trading in the open market at a discount, the management may possibly elect to buy them back. Thus they can retire the obligation at a bargain rate rather than pay the holders full par value at maturity.

The Doktabessie Corporation buys $50,000 of its own bonds in the open market for a total of $40,000. The balance sheet changes as follows:

- Cash decreases by *$40,000.*

- Total current assets and *total* assets also decrease by the same amount.
- Working capital, quick assets, current ratio, and acid-test (quick asset) ratio all decline because current assets are reduced while current liabilities remain unchanged.
- Bonds are reduced by *$50,000*.
- Stockholders' equity *increases* by $10,000 because we have reduced assets (cash) by *$40,000* and liabilities by *$50,000*. Thus we gain $10,000, which is reflected in increased net worth. Since the company has "paid off" a $50,000 debt at a cost of only $40,000, the stockholders have gained!

While the *cash* picture is not as good as it was and although some ratios have declined, the overall effect is "good" in that the stockholders' equity increases.

Retiring Debt at a Premium

The Doktabessie Corporation elects to retire some of its bonds through the exercise of a "call" provision. The call price is usually above par, so our corporation is paying a premium price for the early retirement of part of its debt. Calling $100,000 par value of bonds at a price of 102 ($1,020 per bond) costs the corporation $102,000. The management is eliminating a $100,000 debt (liabilities), but the cost is $102,000 in cash (assets)! It pays the "extra" $2,000 from retained earnings.

Note the effects on the corporation's balance sheet. Cash decreases from $165,000 to $63,000. Current assets, of course, now total only $796,000 and total assets, $1,617,000. On the liabilities side of the balance sheet, the bonds go down from $500,000 to $400,000 and total liabilities from $971,000 to $871,000. Retained earnings reflect the $2,000 "loss" the company suffered and decreases from $290,000 to $288,000. The "new" balance sheet shows:

Total assets = Total liabilities + Net Worth
$$\text{(stockholders' equity)}$$
$1,617,000 = 871,000 \qquad + 746,000$

The cash spent also adversely affects working capital, current ratio, quick assets, and the liquidity (quick asset) ratio.

Sale and Lease-Back of Fixed Assets

The Doktabessie Corporation decides to raise cash by selling and leasing back some of its expensive machinery. The corporation sells machinery carried on its balance sheet at $30,000. This sale reduces the property, plant, and equipment from $617,000 to $587,000. At the same time it increases current assets from $898,000 to $928,000 because cash goes up to $195,000.

The effects on the balance sheet depend on whether the sale is made at a price greater or lower than the value at which the assets are carried on the balance sheet. Essentially, if the sale is made for more than the book value of the asset, the corporation makes a "profit." For sales of assets at prices below their book value, the corporation sustains a "loss." In essence, the company is exchanging a *fixed* asset (machinery) for a *current* asset (cash). This shift increases current assets at the expense of fixed assets and thus improves working capital and the current ratio. Since current assets increase while the current liabilities remain the same, the corporation's working capital increases (current assets — current liabilities). Also, the current ratio (current assets ÷ current liabilities) also improves. In short:

- *If the asset is sold at a profit, total* assets increase, and the increase is also reflected in the retained earnings account.
- *If the asset is sold at a loss, total* assets decrease (by

the difference between the book value and the sale price of the asset sold). The decrease also lowers the retained earnings account by the same amount.

CONCLUDING COMMENTS

We have explained, in simple fashion, the construction of the two most basic financial statements, the balance sheet and the income statement. We trust that you now understand the basic purpose of each document and can examine such statements with an eye toward evaluating a company's future prospects.

These documents detail a corporation's financial position and its earnings. They show the end result of the management's efforts to run a profitable business. Knowing how to interpret this information is absolutely essential to a professional analysis of the company—the key ingredient to enable you to decide whether to buy or sell the company's securities.

B

Considering Taxes

Many investment decisions are based, quite understandably, on the tax implications involved. This chapter will attempt to give you a *basic* understanding of Federal taxation as it applies to securities transactions. The reader is cautioned that this chapter will in no way attempt to treat this subject in its entirety. Investors are urged, even *cautioned,* to seek competent tax advice from a professional in this complicated area. Please do not use the information in this chapter as a taxation "cookbook." The information is accurate enough to serve as a general guideline—please don't attempt to prepare a full meal from the "recipes" given.

Let us further warn you that we will not be delving into the ramifications of gifts and estates. The tax laws in these areas have changed in recent years and will continue to change for at least several years after the initial publication of this book. Before making a significant investment decision, please—please—please consult with your attorney/accountant/tax counselor.

When you purchase a security, and subsequently sell it, you may wind up with either a capital gain or a capital loss. Let's not concern ourselves with those rare trades where you wind up exactly even.

By "security" we mean, generally, stocks and bonds. Also excluded from these comments are Treasury bills. Treasury bills are *not* considered capital assets. When you purchase a T bill and subsequently sell it (or have it mature) such "gain" is considered interest income and not capital gain. The same tax reasoning applies to accrued interest on E or EE Savings Bonds. If you bought a $50 face-value E bond for $37.50 and cashed it in before maturity for, say, $42.50, the $5 gain is considered as current income for income tax purposes. If you hold the bond until maturity, the entire $12.50 rise in value is taxed as current income.

A gain can be either short-term or long-term. Short-term gains are those which arise from the sale of a security which has been held for one year or less. When you sell, at a profit, a security which you have held for more than one year, such gain is long-term. With a few rare exceptions—much beyond the scope of this work—all profits and losses resulting from short sales are considered to be short-term. (This is probably a good reason for most people *not* to engage in short selling— in the vast majority of instances, even when you are right, your gain is fully taxable at short-term rates.)

Short-term gains are taxed at ordinary income rates. Such rates run from 14% to 70%. In effect, short-term gains are taxed in the same manner as dividend or interest income. No "special" tax treatment applies here; short-term gains are fully taxable.

Short-term losses may be deducted from your otherwise taxable income—up to a maximum of $3,000 in any one year. If you suffer more than $3,000 of short-term loss in a single year, the excess over $3,000 is "carried forward" to the following year (or years).

Long-term capital gains enjoy a tax advantage. Only 40% of your long-term gains are taxed. Obviously a long-term gain is much more desirable than a short-term gain. Only 40% of the former is taxable—100% of the latter is taxable! So let those profits run!

Obviously, since long-term gains are much more desirable, please check carefully the original purchase date when you anticipate selling a security. If it has been less than one year since you bought the security, you might very well want to consider waiting until you have held it more than one year in order to receive better tax treatment on the gain. Don't cut off your nose to spite your face! However, if you feel that the security should be sold *now* for good and sufficient reasons, don't delay in order to lower your ultimate tax bill. Your profit could very well dissipate by the time the required holding period of one year has elapsed.

Long-term losses may be deducted from your ordinary income, but only in an amount equal to 50% of such loss. In other words, for every $2.00 of long-term loss you may only deduct $1.00 from your taxable income. It should be obvious that long-term losses are not nearly as desirable as short-term losses since you can deduct the entire amount of any short-term loss, but only 50% of the amount of any long-term loss. Remember that $3,000 tax loss maximum? It applies here too. An investor can only deduct a *maximum* of $3,000 of tax losses in any one year—whether such losses are short-term or long-term—or some of each.

Thus far we have addressed the Federal tax consequences of a single transaction. When you sell a security (or cover a short) you will have either a gain or loss, short-term or long-term. We have addressed how you should treat, taxwise, each of these situations. Keep track of your gains and losses on a continuing basis! Your personal records should show the gain or loss on each of your transactions during the year—and you should show a continuing *net total* record of both your short-term and your long-term gains or losses. Keep everything in these two piles. Short-term profits and losses can be "laid off," one against the other. It is only necessary for you to keep the net total. You do not have to keep a separate list of short-term gains and short-term losses, just one net total. The same thing applies to your long-term gains and losses—keep a net total of your long-term gains and losses.

Let's complicate the picture a little bit to make it more realistic. Let's suppose that you were involved in several trades during the taxable year and have some short-term situations *and* some long-term situations. Your position would reflect one of the following:

A. Short-term gains and long-term gains
B. Short-term gains—long-term losses
C. Short-term losses and long-term losses
D. Short-term losses—long-term gains

Now what? In situation (A), simply add the short-term gains to your ordinary income and add 40% of your long-term gain to ordinary income. For situation (B), net them out! Yes, that's right, add both the short-term gains and the long-term losses together to arrive at a net figure which will either be a short-term gain or a long-term loss. If you arrive at a net short-term gain, merely add this to your ordinary income. If you net out to a long-term loss, subtract 50% of this loss from your ordinary income, up to a maximum of $3,000. Situation (C): deduct the amount of any short-term losses from your ordinary income, up to a maximum of $3,000. Then, if you have not "used up" your $3,000 annual deduction, deduct 50% of your long-term losses. Use your short-term losses first! You must carry forward any unused short-term losses to the next tax year. Please be aware that any such short-term tax loss carried forward retains its short-term character. Any unused long-term losses are carried forward as well. In situation (D), net out both figures as you did for (B). If you net out to a short-term loss, subtract any such loss from your ordinary income. If you net out to a long-term gain, declare 40% of such gain.

Short-term losses are better than long-term losses; long-term gains are better than short-term gains. The lesson here is quite obvious. Whenever possible, cut your losses short and let your profits run! Remember that short-term losses can afford you a dollar–for–dollar deduction. Only 40% of your long-term gains are taxable.

Now that we know, basically, *what* to do with a profit and/or a loss, let's find out *when* to do it! There is an interesting fillip to the tax law which says that you can take your losses in the year in which you *sell* the stock involved. This means that you can sell securities, at a loss, during Christmas week and have such losses considered for the then-current year. *Profitable* trades, however, are considered to have been effected in the year in which the trades *settle.* This means that if you sell a security, at a profit, during Christmas week of 1980—in the regular way—your profit is considered to have been taken in the year 1981!!! This point is really only important for trades very late in the year since most trades effected during the year will *settle* that same year.

By the way, if you get "caught short" during Christmas week and wish to have a profitable transaction figure in your tax picture that same year, please so inform your stock broker. He may be able to sell your stock next-day or cash delivery, which will cause the profitable transaction to settle in the same year. This may cost you something, as such special trades are usually effected at a slightly lower price than the then-current market.

Wash sales. No, we are not talking about selling freshly-laundered clothing at a discount! A *wash sale* is involved should you sell a security at a loss and re-purchase that same security (or an equivalent one) within 30 days before or 30 days after such sale. In such a case you are not permitted to take that tax loss right away. Rather, the amount of the loss is added to the new purchase price to establish your tax cost for the reacquired security.

Sound complicated? It is!

Example

You purchased 100 shares of XYZ several years ago at a cost of $5,000. It is currently selling for $3,000 and you decide to sell it, thinking that you will take the $2,000 long-term loss in the current tax year. You sell it and then you change your mind. You decide that XYZ is going to go places at long last and you rue the day, two weeks ago, when you sold it in a fit of pique. You buy back the XYZ at a cost of $3,500—yes, it went up $500 in price since you sold it two weeks ago. You are now in a wash sale situation by virtue of the fact that you sold a security at a loss and re-purchased it less than 30 days after the sale. You cannot take the $2,000 tax loss. Rather, the $2,000 loss must be added to the new purchase cost of $3,500 so that your new tax basis for the XYZ is now $5,500. Should you ultimately sell the stock for $7,000, you would declare a gain of $1,500 (your "new" cost of $5,500 compared with your sale at $7,000). See what happened? You were not permitted to take the $2,000 loss but rather were limited to only an overall profit of $1,500. This isn't as bad as it seems. You merely were not permitted first to take a $2,000 loss ($5,000 minus $3,000) and then to take a $3,500 profit ($7,000 minus $3,500). Your Uncle Sam wants you to do it in one step only. There's a logic here. The "Revenooers" would frown upon your taking your losses late in the year, thus benefitting from their deductibility, and reacquiring such securities right away in order to sell them at a profit, with such profits (long-term) taxable only at the 40% rate.

What happens when several "lots" of stock are owned— purchased at different times and/or prices—and one of the lots is sold? Unless you indicate otherwise at the time you give the sell order to your broker, you are considered to have sold the first lot that you purchased. This is the so-called FIFO method. Suppose you buy 100 shares of ABC in 1977, another 100 in 1978 and a third lot in 1979. Should you sell 100 shares in 1981, without specifying which particular lot you are selling, you are considered to have sold the block of stock you purchased in 1977, and you must figure your gain or loss against the price you paid for those shares in that year. Should your particular tax situation dictate that it would be to your benefit to sell the 1978—or 1979—block of stock rather than the 1977 purchase, then so instruct your broker at the time you give him the sell order. He can mark the order "versus purchase 1978"—or "versus purchase 1979" as per your instructions. Such instructions must be given to the broker when the order is entered.

Stock dividends and stock splits. Normally there is no tax due upon your receiving a stock dividend or a stock split. Shares so received have a holding period of the original purchase date of the stock. Thus, if you have owned a security more than one year and then receive additional shares through a stock dividend or stock split, the sale of these additional shares will represent a long-term situation— the holding period of the shares so received dates back to the *original* purchase date for the stock.

There is one variation, however, in that a stock dividend which is *optional* IS taxable upon receipt. The mere fact that you were given the option as to whether you wished to receive the dividend in shares or in stock makes it taxable to you upon receipt. Even if you elect to receive your dividend in shares, and not in cash, you must pay tax on the shares so received.

The holding period for any shares you obtain through the exercise of rights or warrants begins at the time you exercise, not the point in time at which you bought or received the right or warrant itself.

SHORT AGAINST THE BOX

It is possible to "lock in" a profit on a security and to delay the tax consequences of such profit. A situation might occur wherein you have a handsome profit toward the end of a particular year but are reluctant to take the profit in that year because you are suffering an embarrassment of riches. So you think: "Boy, I'd love to sell that stock right now while I still have a large profit but, darn it, I wish that it were next year when paying the tax on that profit wouldn't be quite so onerous as it is this year."

Here's how you can do it. Instruct your broker to sell your position short against the box. He will execute a bonafide short sale which will result in your account being both long (your original position remains untouched) *and* short at the same time. Your account will remain in this position until you instruct your broker to "flatten" the long and the short, one against the other. You are not considered to have sold the stock, for tax purposes, until such time as the position is "flattened." The profit that you enjoyed at the time you executed the short sale cannot be taken away from you. Such profit was "locked in" at the time of the short sale. The other side of the coin is that you cannot benefit by any further rise in the price of the security that you sold short. You cannot change a short-term profit into a long-term profit using this ploy. It should only be used to *postpone* the tax consequences of a profitable transaction from one year to the next.

The self-employed person and/or the individual who works for an employer that does *not* offer a retirement plan should investigate the possibility of establishing either a Keogh or an IRA Plan in order to build for their futures. The tax advantages are rather dramatic! For those of you in a position to open either one of these plans, we strongly urge you to seek competent tax advice.

We trust that these brief explanations will guide you in your future investment decisions. We have given you, we hope, just enough information to make you at least vaguely aware of the possibilities that can exist for the average investor to improve his portfolio performance by the conscientious, and correct, utilization of acceptable taxation planning.

Readers should not jump to investment conclusions without first checking out any of their interpretations of tax ploys with an expert in the field. At the very least, ask your broker whether your independently-arrived-at judgments are valid—whether there isn't something "special" in your particular case which requires a different interpretation from the widely accepted "book" interpretation. It will never hurt to check and see whether there is some important special factor you may have overlooked.

This chapter can't make you a tax expert, but it will give you an insight into the various tax avenues open to you and therefore encourage you to seek professional advice before making any securities decision based on tax considerations. The very least you should do is to set the problem before your broker who can easily ask his firm's tax expert for money saving maneuvers. Don't act first and then learn the tax consequences later.

C

Glossary

ABC AGREEMENT: A contract by which an individual purchases a seat on the Exchange through funds advanced by a partnership (or corporation). The agreement stipulates, among other things, whether the seat will be (A) retained by the individual and another bought for the company; (B) sold and the proceeds remitted to the firm; or (C) transferred to the firm for a nominal consideration should the individual leave the firm or die.

ACCOUNTS PAYABLE: A current liability showing the amounts due others within a period of one year where such liability resulted from the purchase or manufacturing of inventory.

ACCRUED EXPENSES: A liability, current or long-term, showing the estimated amounts due others for services rendered or goods received.

ACCRUED INTEREST: (1) The amount of interest due the seller, from the buyer, upon settlement of a bond trade; (2) prorated interest due since the last interest payment date.

ACCUMULATED DEPLETION (DEPRE-CIATION): See Allowance for Depletion.

ACCUMULATION UNIT: A share of a variable annuity fund, the value of which is calculated to be the value of the entire fund divided by the number of accumulation units. The term is generally used during the accumulation phase of the annuity. See Annuity Unit.

ACID TEST RATIO: The value of cash, cash equivalents and accounts receivable divided by current liabilities. See Liquidity Ratio.

ACTIVE BONDS (THE "FREE" CROWD): A category of debt securities that the NYSE Floor Department expects to trade frequently and that are consequently handled "freely" in the trading ring in much the same manner as stocks.

ACTIVE BOX: A physical location where securities are held awaiting instruction.

ADJUSTED DEBIT BALANCE: The net money borrowed by a brokerage customer in a margin account as a result of both settled and unsettled transactions.

ADJUSTMENT BONDS: See Income (Adjustment) Bonds.

ADMINISTRATOR: A court-appointed person or institution charged with the maintenance and distribution of the assets and liabilities of a deceased.

ADR: See American Depository Receipt (ADR).

ADVERTISING PRACTICES: In accordance with Section 1 of the NASD Rules of Fair Practice, any communication designed for public consumption—including sales literature, market letters, and recruiting materials—must not contain false or misleading statements of any material facts. All such communications must be considered in terms of their reasonableness and accuracy. Each item must be initialed or signed by a registered principal of the firm that is advertising, and filed for three years; further, it must be filed with the NASD Executive Office in Washington, D.C., for review within five days after its initial usage, unless it is a tombstone ad or is approved by a registered stock exchange or other regulatory body whose standards are similar to the NASD's.

AFTERMARKET: A market for a security either over-the-counter or on an exchange after an initial public offering has been made. *See* Free-Riding; Hot Issue; Stabilization; Withholding.

AGENCY TRANSACTION: *See* As Agent.

Agreement Among Underwriters: An agreement among members of an underwriting syndicate specifying the syndicate manager, his duties, and his privileges, among other things. *See* Underwriting Agreement; Underwriter's Retention.

All-Or-None Offering: A "best-efforts" offering of newly issued securities in which the corporation instructs the investment banker to cancel the entire offering (sold and unsold) if all of it cannot be distributed.

All-Or-None (AON) Order: An order to buy or sell more than one round lot of stock at one time and at a designated price or better. It must not be executed until both of these conditions can be satisfied simultaneously.

ALLOWANCE FOR DEPLETION (Also called "Accumulated Depletion"):   The portion of the cost of acquiring and putting into production a natural asset (i.e., oil wells, gold mines) which has been written off against income (expensed). A balance sheet account showing the amount of the cost of a natural wasting asset which has been charged against income. For example:

Gold Mine, at cost	$100,000
Less: Allowance for Depletion	25,000
Net Book Value	$ 75,000

ALLOWANCE FOR DEPRECIATION (Also called "Accumulated Depreciation"): That portion of the cost of acquiring and putting into production buildings and equipment which has been written off against income (expensed). A balance sheet account showing the amount of an asset's cost which has been charged against income since its acquisition. For example:

Machinery at cost	$10,000
Less: Allowance for Depreciation	3,000
Net Book Value	$ 7,000

ALTERNATIVE (EITHER/OR) ORDER: An order to do either of two alternatives such as either buy at a limit or buy stop for the same security. Execution of one part of the order automatically cancels the other.

AMERICAN DEPOSITORY RECEIPT (ADR):   A receipt showing evidence that shares of a foreign corporation are held on deposit or are under the control of a U.S. banking institution; it is used to facilitate transactions and expedite transfer of beneficial ownership for a foreign security in the United States.

AMERICAN STOCK EXCHANGE CLEARING CORPORATION: A wholly owned subsidiary of the American Stock Exchange charged with the responsibility of assisting member firms settle trades. The Corporation has contracted with the Securities Industry Automation Corporation to perform all its duties except the rules-making function.

AMERICAN STOCK EXCHANGE MARKET VALUE INDEX: A market index for all common stocks listed on the ASE, prepared daily and grouped by geographic locale and industrial category.

AMERICAN STOCK EXCHANGE PRICE CHANGE INDEX: An "unweighted" market index for all common stocks listed on the ASE, prepared hourly.

AMEX: An Acronym for *American Stock Exchange, Inc.*

AMEX RULE 411: The American Stock Exchange's version of the "know your customer" rule of the NYSE. See *Rule 405*.

AMFOD: An acronym for *Association of Member Firm Option Departments.*

AMORTIZATION: A generic term including depreciation, depletion and write-offs of intangibles, prepaid expenses, and deferred charges.

"AND INTEREST": A bond transaction in which the buyer pays the seller a contract price plus interest accrued since the corporation's last interest payment.

ANNUAL DEPRECIATION: That portion of the cost of fixed assets charged as an expense for a given year.

ANNUAL REPORT: A formal statement issued yearly by a corporation to its shareowners. It shows assets, liabilities, equity, revenues, expenses, and so forth. It is a reflection of the corporation's condition at the close of the business year, and the results of operations for that year.

ANNUITY: A contract between an insurance company and an individual whereby the insurance company agrees to make period payment to the individuals.

ANNUITY UNIT: A term used to describe Accumulation Units of a variable annuity once distribution has begun.

ANNUNCIATOR BOARD: A paging system on the New York Stock Exchange by which telephone clerks summon brokers, using numbers with colored markers attached.

AON ORDER: See All-Or-None (AON) Order.

ARBITRAGE: The simultaneous purchase and sale of the same or equal securities in such a way as to take advantage of price differences prevailing in separate markets. See Bona Fide Arbitrage; Risk Arbitrage.

AS AGENT: The role of a broker/dealer firm when it acts as an intermediary, or broker, between its customer and another customer or a market-maker or contra-broker. For this service the firm receives a stated commission or fee. See As Principal.

AS PRINCIPAL: The role of a broker/dealer firm when it buys and sells for its own account. In a typical transaction, it buys from a market-maker or contra-broker and sells to a customer at a fair and reasonable markup; if it buys from a customer and sells to the market-maker at a higher price, it is called a markdown.

ASSETS: Everything of value that a company owns or has due: cash, buildings and machinery—fixed assets; and patents and good will—intangible assets. See Equity; Liabilities.

ASSOCIATE SPECIALISTS: Assistants to regular specialists who do not solicit orders or stabilize markets as principals. They may act as agents, but only in the presence and under the supervision of a regular or relief specialist.

AT-THE-CLOSE ORDER: An order to be executed, at the market, at the close or as near to the close as practicable of trading for the day.

AT-THE-MARKET: (1) A price representing what a buyer would pay and what a seller would take in an arm's-length transaction assuming normal competitive forces; (2) An order to buy or sell immediately at the currently available price.

AT-THE-OPENING (OPENING ONLY) ORDER: An order to buy or sell at a limit price on the initial transaction of the day for a given security; if unsuccessful, it is automatically cancelled.

AUCTION MARKETPLACE: A term used to describe an organized exchange where transactions are held in the open and any exchange member present may join in.

AUTHORIZED STOCK: The maximum number of shares permitted by the state secretary to be issued by a corporation.

AUTOMATIC RE-INVESTMENT OF DISTRIBUTIONS: A feature of voluntary and contractual accumulation mutual fund plans by which shareholders can re-invest dividends and/or capital gains by acquiring new shares.

AUTOMATIC WITHDRAWAL: A privilege of participants in a voluntary accumulation or completed contractual mutual fund plan by which the custodial bank disburses to the planholder a specified sum of money each month or quarter. If mutual fund distributions are insufficient to meet this demand for money, an appropriate number of shares will be redeemed.

AVERAGE: A stock market indicator based on the sum of market values for a selected sample of stocks, divided either by the number of issues or by a divisor that allows for stock splits or other changes in capitalization. The most widely used average is issued by Dow-Jones.

AVERAGE DOWN: The practice of purchasing additional shares of the same issue as its market price declines so that the investor's cost per share for his entire holding will also decline.

AVERAGE UP: The practice of purchasing additional shares of the same issue as its market price rises so that the investor's cost per share for his entire holding will also rise.

B: A symbol on the ticker tape that means a quote report rather than a trade report.

BABY BOND: A bond with a face value of less than $1,000, usually in $100 denominations.

BACK OFFICE: An industry expression used to describe non-sales departments of a brokerage concern. Its particular reference is usually to a firm's P&S and Cashiering Departments.

BACKING AWAY: The practice of an OTC market-maker who refuses to honor his quoted bid-and-asked prices for at least 100 shares, or 10 bonds, as the case may be. This action is outlawed under the NASD Rules of Fair Practice.

BALANCE ORDERS: The pairing off of each issue traded in the course of a day by the same member to arrive at a net balance of securities to receive or deliver.

BALANCE SHEET: A condensed statement showing the nature and amount of a company's assets, liabilities, and capital on a given date. It shows in dollar amounts what the company owns, what it owes, and the ownership interest (shareholders' equity).

BALANCE SHEET EQUATION: Total assets equal the total of liabilities and shareholders' equity.

BALANCE COMPANIES (FUNDS): Investment companies that strive to minimize market risks while at the same time earning reasonable current income with varying percentages of bonds, and preferred and common stocks.

BALLOON EFFECT: A term used to describe a serial bond issue having lower principal repayments in the earlier years of its life and higher principal repayments due in the later years.

BANK FLOAT: The financial advantage for banks realized from the normal delay in transferring funds between banks in processing transactions.

BANKERS' ACCEPTANCES: Bills of exchange guaranteed (accepted) by a bank or trust company for payment within one to six months, to provide manufacturers and exporters with capital to operate between the time of manufacturing (or exporting) and payment by purchasers. Bids and offers in the secondary marketplace are at prices discounted from the face value.

BANKS FOR COOPERATIVES (CO-OP): An agency under the supervision of the Farm Credit Administration that makes and services loans for farmers' cooperative financing. The agency is capitalized by the issuance of bonds whose interest is free from state and local income taxes.

BARRON'S CONFIDENCE INDEX: A market index that measures investors' willingness to take risks according to yields on rated bonds. See Confidence Theory.

BASIC: An acronym for the Banking and Securities Industry Committee, a financial industry group formed to promote standardization in operation and certificate processing systems.

BASIS PRICE ODD-LOT ORDER: An odd-lot order executed on a fictitious round-lot price somewhere between the prevailing bid and offering, if (1) the issue doesn't trade throughout the day; (2) the spread is at least two full points; and (3) the customer requests such an execution.

BASIS POINT: One one-hundredth of a percentage point. For example if a Treasury Bill yielding 7.17% changes in price so that it now yields 7.10%; it is said to have declined seven basis points.

BEAR MARKET: A declining securities market in terms of prices. See Bull Market.

BEAR RAIDERS: Groups of speculators who pooled capital and sold short to drive prices down, then bought to cover their short positions—thereby pocketing large profits. This practice was outlawed by the Securities Exchange Act of 1934.

BEAR SPREAD: An option spread so designed that a profit will result if the underlying security declines in market value.

BEARER BONDS: Bonds that do not have the owner's name registered on the books of the issuing corporation and that are payable to the bearer.

BEARER FORM: Securities issued in such a form as not to allow for the owner's name to be imprinted on the security. The bearer of the security is presumed to be the owner who collects his interest by clipping and depositing coupons semi-annually.

BENEFICIAL OWNER: The owner of securities who receives all the benefits, even though they are registered in the "street name" of a brokerage firm or nominee name of a bank handling his account.

BID-AND-ASKED QUOTATION (OR QUOTE): The bid is the highest price anyone has declared that he wants to pay for a security at a given time; the asked is the lowest price anyone will accept at the same time. See Offer.

BIG BOARD: A popular slang term for the New York Stock Exchange.

BLOCK POSITIONER: A broker/dealer who takes positions for his own account and risk in order to facilitate the large purchase or sale of securities by customers which would otherwise be disruptive to the market. A block positioner may be given relief under Regulation T to assist his financing of such positions.

BLUE LIST: A publication of Standard & Poor's Corporation advertising Municipal Bonds available in the secondary market.

BLUE ROOM: One of the small trading areas just off the main trading floor of the New York Stock Exchange.

BLUE-SKY LAWS: State securities laws pertaining to registration requirements and procedures for issuers, broker/dealers, their employees, and other associated persons of those entities.

BOARD BROKER: A member of an options exchange appointed by that exchange to handle public limit orders left in his care by floor brokers. In performing this function he is said to be running the "public book." It is his prime responsibility to insure that a fair, orderly and competitive market exists in the classes of options to which he is assigned. He is compensated by earning floor brokerage on orders he executes, and may not trade for his own account or risk.

BOILER ROOM SALES: The use of high pressure sales tactics to promote purchases and sales of securities.

BONA FIDE ARBITRAGE: Arbitrage transactions by professional traders that take profitable advantage of prices for the same or convertible securities in different markets. The risk is usually minimal and the profit correspondingly small. *See* Risk Arbitrage, Special Arbitrage Account.

BOND: A certificate representing creditorship in a corporation and issued by the corporation to raise capital. The company pays interest on a bond issue at specified dates and eventually redeems it at maturity, paying principal plus interest due. *See* Bearer Bond; Collateral Trust Bond; Equipment Trust Bond; Income Bond; Mortgage Bond; Receiver's Certificate; Registered Bond; Serial Bond; Tax-Exempt Securities; United States Government Securities.

BOND AND PREFERRED STOCK COMPANIES: Investment companies that emphasize stability of income. In the case of municipal bond companies, income exempt from federal taxation is the chief goal.

BOND ANTICIPATION NOTE: A short-term municipal debt instrument usually offered on a discount basis. The proceeds of a forthcoming bond issue are pledged to pay the note at maturity.

BOND BROKER: A member of the NYSE who executes orders in the bond room as a continuing practice.

BOND INTEREST DISTRIBUTION: Bonds that are traded at a market price "and interest" require an adjustment for the interest on the settlement date. The buyer therefore pays the seller the price plus interest accrued since the last payment date, and the buyer is thereby entitled to the next full payment of interest. The interest due is calculated by multiplying Principal $\times$ Rate $\times$ Time. *See* Ex-Dividend Date.

BOND POWER: *See* Stock (or Bond) Power.

BOND RATIO: The relationship of all bonds outstanding to the total capitalization of a corporation.

BOND ROOM: The room at the New York Stock Exchange where bonds are traded.

BOOK VALUE PER SHARE: Equal to the Common stockholders' equity minus intangible assets, divided by number of common shares outstanding.

BOX (THE): A section of a cashiering department where securities are stored temporarily. Its responsibilities are sometimes subdivided to monitor both an active box and a free box for securities held by the firm.

BREADTH INDEX: The net securities advanced or declined for a given day's trading divided by the total issues traded. For example:

Advances	500
Declines	600
Unchanged	200
	1,300

$$\frac{600 - 500}{1,300} = -7.69\%$$

BREAKOUT: The rise or fall of a security's market price through level that had been containing it.

BROKER: An agent, often a member of a stock exchange firm or an exchange member himself, who handles the public's orders to buy and sell securities and commodities, for which service he charges a commission. The definition does not include a bank. *See As Agent; As Principal.*

BROKER'S COLLATERAL (CALL) LOANS: A broker's loan from a commercial bank using margin account customers' securities or firm-owned securities as the bank's protection. It is sometimes referred to as a "call" loan because either party can terminate it on twenty-four hour notice. *See Call Money.*

BUCKET SHOP: An organization that accepts customer orders but does not immediately execute them. It waits until, and if, the market acts contrary to the customer's expectations, then executes the order but confirms it to the customer at the price prevailing originally. This practice is outlawed by the National Association of Securities Dealers.

BULK IDENTIFICATION, BULK SEGREGATION: A system of segregating customer securities in accordance with SEC Rule 15c3-3 in which all certificates and/or depository positions of an issue are identified as belonging to all customers. For example, a broker has ten customers each owning 100 shares and the broker keeps one certificate for 1,000 shares segregated.

BULL MARKET: A rising securities market in terms of prices. *See Bear Market.*

BULL SPREAD: An option spread so designed that a profit will result if the underlying security increases in market value.

BUNCHING ODD-LOT ORDERS: The combination of several odd-lot orders into round lots so they can be handled by a commission house broker, specialist, or two-dollar broker, thereby eliminating the odd-lot differential.

BUSINESS DAY: Defined by the Federal Reserve as any day the New York Stock Exchange is open for business. Defined by the New York Stock Exchange as any day the New York banks are open for business.

BUY-IN PROCEDURE: On any day, on or after a prescribed settlement date, the purchasing firm who has failed to receive the certificates can give written notice to the selling firm that the contract is in default, and (1) after giving notice, purchase the security in the marketplace, and (2) hold the seller responsible for any money loss that may be incurred. *See Sellout Procedures.*

BUYER'S OPTION: *See Call Option.*

BUYER'S OPTION CONTRACT: A securities contract in which the seller's delivery of the certificates is due at the purchaser's office on the date specified at the time of the transaction. For example, "Buyer's 10," means delivery is due ten calendar days after the transaction date. *See Cash Contract; Regular Way Contract; Seller's Option Contract; When Issued/When Distributed Contract.*

BUYER POWER: The dollar amount of equity securities a customer could purchase without additional funds and continue to meet the initial margin requirements of Regulation T of the Federal Reserve.

BW: An abbreviation for *bid wanted* indicating that the broker/dealer is soliciting buyers of the stock or bond.

BYLAWS: (1) Rules of operation for members of the association in the over-the-counter market, established and maintained by the Board of Governors of the NASD. *See Schedule C.* (2) The internal rules governing the operations of a corporation

"CABINET" CROWD: *See* Inactive Bonds.

CAGE (THE): A slang expression used to describe a location where brokerage Cashiering Department responsibilities are satisfied.

CALENDAR SPREAD: The simultaneous purchase and sale of options of the same class having the same striking price but different expiration dates.

CALL FEATURE: (1) A feature of preferred stock through which it may be retired at the corporation's option by paying a price equal to or slightly higher than either the par or market value; (2) A bond feature by which all or part of an issue may be redeemed by the corporation before maturity and under certain specified conditions.

CALL LOAN: *See* Broker's Collateral (Call) Loan.

CALL MONEY RATE: The percentage of interest a broker/dealer pays on a broker's collateral loan.

CALL OPTION: A privilege giving its holder the right to demand the purchase of 100 shares of stock at a fixed price any time within a specified period (the lifetime of the option). Also sometimes referred to as a buyer's option.

CALL PROTECTION: A term used to describe a bond or preferred stock without a call feature or with a call feature which cannot be activated for a period of time.

"CAN" CROWD: *See* Inactive Bonds.

CANCELLATION: Revocation of a buy or sell order, an action that is permissible at any time prior to execution. After execution, it is allowed only with the consent of the other party to the trade and with the approval of a NYSE floor official.

CAPITAL GAIN (OR LOSS): Profit (or loss) from the sale of a capital asset. Capital gains may be short-term (one year or less) or long-term (more than one year). Capital losses are used to offset capital gains to establish a net position for tax purposes.

CAPITALIZATION: *See* Total Capitalization.

CAPITAL SURPLUS: *See* Paid-In Capital.

CASH CONTRACT: A securities contract by which delivery of the certificates is due at the purchaser's office the same day as the date of the trade. *See* Buyer's Option Contract; Regular Way Contract; Seller's Option Contract; When Issued/When Distributed Contract.

CASH FLOW: Reported net income of a corporation plus amounts charged off for depreciation, depletion, amortization, and other non-cash expenses.

CASH ON DELIVERY (COD): See Delivery versus Payment.

CASHIERING DEPARTMENT: A department of a broker/dealer organization responsible for the physical handling of securities and money, delivery and receipt, collateral loans. borrowing, lending, and transfer of securities, and other financial transactions.

CENTRAL BANK: (1) A Federal Reserve Bank situated in one of twelve banking districts in the United States; (2) The Federal Reserve System.

CERTIFICATE: The actual piece of paper that is evidence of ownership or creditorship in a corporation. Water-marked certificates are finely engraved with delicate etchings to discourage forgery.

CERTIFICATE OF INCORPORATION (CHARTER): A state-validated certificate recognizing a business organization as a legal corporate entity.

CERTIFICATE OF INDEBTEDNESS (CI): A federal bearer debt instrument in denominations of $1,000 to $500 million at a fixed interest rate, with maturities up to one year; they are fully marketable at a price reflecting their average rate of return.

CERTIFICATES OF DEPOSIT (CDs): Negotiable securities issued by commercial banks against money deposited with them for a specified period of time. They vary in size according to amount of deposit and maturity period and may be redeemed before maturity only by sale in a secondary market. The maximum interest is fixed by the Federal Reserve Board for CDs under $100,000.

CHARTER: *See* Certificate of Incorporation (Charter).

CHECK KITING: The illegal practice of drawing a check upon a demand deposit account that contains no money or has insufficient funds. It is so called even if the person deposits someone else's check into his account prior to clearance of the check he previously drew and presented as payment for an obligation.

CHIEF EXAMINER'S DEPARTMENT: The Department of the New York Stock Exchange responsible for the auditing of member firms.

CHURNING: A term used to denote a registered representative's improper handling of a customer's account. It implies that he buys and sells securities for a customer intent only upon the amount of commissions generated as a result, while ignoring the customer's suitable interests and objectives.

CLEARANCE: (1) The delivery of securities and monies in completion of a trade; (2) The comparison and/or netting of trades prior to settlement.

CLEARING HOUSE FUNDS: (1) Money represented by a person's demand deposit account at a commercial bank. Withdrawals are accomplished by means of a check, which notifies the bank to transfer a sum to someone else or to another bank; (2) Funds used in settlement of equity, corporate bond and municipal bond settlement transactions; (3) A term used to mean "next day availability" of funds.

CLEARING MEMBERS OF THE NYSE: A member organization of the NYSE whose clearance operations are handled through the Stock Clearing Corporation.

CLIMAX: A large increase or decrease in the price of a security accompanied by large volume. The price change should gap, indicating a completion of a price increase or decrease cycle.

CLOSE: The final transaction price for an issue on the stock exchange during the course of a trading day.

CLOSE-OUT PROCEDURE: The procedure taken by either party to a transaction when the contra-broker defaults; the disappointed purchaser may "buy in," and the rejected seller may "sell out" or liquidate. *See* Reclamation; Rejection.

CLOSED-END INVESTMENT COMPANY: A management company whose equity capitalization remains constant unless special action is taken by the directors to alter it (by the issuance of new shares).

CLOSED-END PROVISION: A mortgage bond provision in the indenture that, in the event of default or liquidation, entitles first bondholders to a claim upon assets senior to second and subsequent bondholders, whenever the same real assets are used as collateral for more than one issue of debt.

CLOSING PURCHASE TRANSACTION: The purchase of a listed option so as to close or eliminate an existing short position.

CLOSING QUOTATION: A market-maker's final bid and asked prices for an issue as he ceases trading activities at the end of the business day.

CLOSING SALE TRANSACTION: The sale of a listed option so as to close or eliminate an existing long position.

CLOSING THE UNDERWRITING CONTRACT: The finalizing of contractual terms between an issuing corporation and the underwriters. Usually one week after the effective date the certificates are given over to the underwriters and payment in full is made to the corporation.

C.O.D. TRADE: "Cash on delivery," a general term to describe a transaction in which a seller is obliged to deliver securities to the purchaser or his agent in order to collect his payment thereof. *See* DVP Trade.

C.O.D. TRANSACTION: A purchase of securities in behalf of a customer promising full payment immediately upon delivery of the certificates to an agent bank or broker/dealer.

CODE OF ARBITRATION: Rules established and maintained by the NASD Board of Governors to regulate arbitration of intra-member and customer/member disputes involving securities transactions. *See* Board of Arbitration.

COLLATERAL: Securities or other property pledged by a borrower to secure repayment of a loan.

COLLATERAL TRUST BOND: A bond issue that is protected by a portfolio of securities held in trust by a commercial bank. The bond usually requires immediate redemption if the market value of the securities drops below or close to the value of the issue.

COLLECTION RATIO: An analysis of the average number of days it takes a corporation to receive payment for merchandise it has sold.

COMMERCIAL PAPER: Unsecured, short-term (usually a maximum of nine months) bearer obligations in denominations from $100,000 to $1 million, issued principally by industrial corporations, finance companies, and commercial factors at a discount from face value.

COMMINGLING: The act of using various customer securities in the same loan arrangement with firm securities. The practice is prohibited.

COMMISSION: A broker's fee for handling transactions for a client in an agency capacity.

COMMISSION HOUSE BROKER: A member of the NYSE executing orders in behalf of his own organization and its customers.

COMMITTEE OF CORPORATE FINANCING: A standing national committee of the NASD that examines all appropriate documents regarding the issuance of new securities, reviewing and approving their terms and conditions.

COMMITTEE ON UNIFORM SECURITY IDENTIFICATION PROCEDURES (CUSIP): An agency of the NASD responsible for issuing identification numbers for virtually all publicly-owned stock and bond certificates.

COMMON STOCK: A unit of equity ownership in a corporation. Owners of this kind of stock exercise control over corporate affairs and enjoy any capital appreciation. They are paid dividends only after preferred stock. Their interest in the assets, in the event of liquidation, is junior to all others.

COMMON STOCK EQUIVALENTS: (1) Debt and/or equity-type securities capable of subscription, exchange, or conversion into common stock of the company; (2) Convertible bonds and convertible preferred stock may be so classified at the time of issuance, based on many factors. Once so classified they must be considered as common stock when computing primary earnings per share.

COMMON STOCKHOLDERS' EQUITY: Common stock plus paid-in capital plus retained earnings.

COMMON STOCK RATIO: The relationship of common stock outstanding to the total capitalization of a corporation.

COMPARISON: A confirmation of a contractual agreement citing terms and conditions of a transaction between broker/dealers. This document must be exchanged by the contra firms shortly after trade date. See Confirmation.

COMPETITIVE BIDDING: A sealed envelope bidding process employed by various underwriter groups interested in handling the distribution of a securities issue. The contract is awarded to one group by the issuer on the basis of the highest price paid, interest rate expense, and tax considerations.

COMPETITIVE TRADER: A member of an organized exchange who may, subject to certain rules and restrictions, trade for his own account and risk while on the trading floor.

CONDUIT: Under NASD interpretations regarding hot issues, it refers to bank, trust or similar affiliations not disclosed.

CONDUIT THEORY: See Pipeline (Conduit) Theory.

CONFIDENCE THEORY: A market theory stating that stock price movements are affected by increases or decreases in investor confidence in future economic trends in the country. See Barron's Confidence Index.

CONFIRMATION: An announcement of transaction terms and conditions and other pertinent information that is prepared for customer trade activities. It serves as a bill for customer purchases and as an advisory notice for sales.

CONFLICT OF INTEREST: A legal term used to describe the situation in which a person or group of people are placed in a position of authority so that they may personally profit from a disservice to those to whom they are responsible.

CONSOLIDATED TAPE: A system of reporting all trades in New York Stock Exchange listed securities on one tape, called Tape A, and all other exchange-listed securities on another tape, called Tape B, regardless of where the trade takes place.

CONSTANT DOLLAR PLAN: Similar to a constant ratio plan, this is an investment plan by which an investor keeps a constant dollar value of different securities in his portfolio—either through purchases and sales or by depositing additional funds as necessary.

CONSTANT RATIO PLAN: A formula investment plan requiring a fixed percentage balance between stocks and bonds in a portfolio. The ratio is determined by the owner's investment objectives, and purchases and sales are effected to maintain the predetermined percentages.

CONSTRUCTION AND DEVELOPMENT REIT: An REIT primarily engaged in providing short-term financing during the construction period to builders.

CONSUMER CREDIT: Credit extended to the ultimate users of goods and services.

CONTINUING COMMISSIONS: The practice of paying commissions to registered representatives after they have left the employment of the broker/dealer or to their heirs after a registered representative has died.

CONTINUOUS NET SETTLEMENT: A procedure used by all clearing corporations to simplify processing daily transactions and correspondingly to reduce the number of certificate deliveries required. The Clearing Corporation interposes itself on each transaction, crediting or debiting each member's total holdings in each issue. The net balance is carried forward from day to day.

CONTRA-BROKER: A term used to describe the broker with whom a trade was made.

CONTRACT SHEET: A complete list of each member's daily transactions arranged by issue and prepared by the clearing house for members to check for accuracy of detail and approval of settlement terms.

CONTRACTUAL (PERIODIC PAYMENT) PLAN: An investment plan for a mutual fund by which an investor agrees to invest a fixed sum of money at specified intervals over a ten or fifteen-year period. *See* Front-End (Prepaid Charge) Plan.

CONTROL PERSON: A person subject to special rules of the SEC when acquiring or selling control stock. A Control Person is one who: (1) owns or controls 10% or more of the voting stock of a corporation; (2) holds a position as an officer or director of a corporation; or (3) is in a position to influence the decision-making process of a corporation.

CONTROL STOCK: Stock owned by a control person in the corporation over which he has control.

CONTROLLER'S DEPARTMENT: The department of any business responsible for keeping the accounting records, preparing and filing reports with various government and regulatory bodies, and preparing financial reports for management.

CONVENTIONAL OPTION: (1) An option contract entered into by two parties which is not standardized as to striking price and/or expiration date and is not cleared through the Options Clearing Corportion; (2) an over-the-counter or not listed option.

CONVERSION: (1) A bond feature by which the owner may exchange his bonds for a specified number of shares of stock. Interest paid on such bonds is lower than the usual interest rate for straight debt issues. *See* Conversion Parity; Conversion Price; Conversion Ratio; (2) A feature of some preferred stock by which the owner is entitled to exchange his preferred for common stock, usually of the same company, in accordance with the terms of the issue; (3) A feature of some mutual fund offerings allowing an investor to exchange his shares for comparable value in another fund with different objectives handled by the same management group; (4) A term used to describe the creation of a Call Option from a Put Option by means of taking a long position in the underlying equity.

CONVERSION PARITY: The equal dollar relationship between a convertible security and the underlying stock trading at or above the conversion price.

CONVERSION PRICE: In the case of convertible bonds, this is the price of the underlying stock at which conversion can be made. The price is set by the issuing corporation and is printed in the indenture.

CONVERSION RATIO: The ratio indicating how many underlying shares may be obtained upon exchange of each convertible security.

CONVERTIBLE PREFERRED STOCK: *See* Conversion (2).

COOLING-OFF PERIOD: *See* Twenty Day (Cooling-Off) Period.

CORNERING THE MARKET: A situation in which a party or group has acquired a substantial quantity of the available shares and, as a result, exerts considerable influence on its market price.

CORPORATION: A business organization chartered by a state secretary as a recognized legal institution of and by itself and operated by an association of individuals, with the purpose of ensuring perpetuity and limited financial liability.

COST OF GOODS SOLD: The expense of inventory marketed in a particular accounting period.

COUPON BOND: A bond with interest coupons attached. The coupons are clipped as they come due and are presented by the holders to their banks for payment. *See* Bearer Bond; Registered Bond.

COVERED WRITE: The writing (selling) of a call option against a position in the underlying stock or its equivalent.

COVERING: Buying a security previously sold short to eliminate that open position.

CREDIT: (1) Time allowed for the payment of goods and services; (2) Power to buy or borrow on trust; (3) In bookkeeping the right hand side of an account; Opposed to a debit; (4) A deposit against which one may draw.

CREDIT AGREEMENT: A document containing the complete terms and arrangements by which financing will be conducted in a customer's account. It emphasizes when and how interest is charged for the lending service provided.

CREDIT BALANCE: (1) In a customer's account of a broker/dealer it indicates that the broker/dealer owes money to the customer either conditionally or unconditionally; (2) The opposite of debit balance.

CREDIT DEPARTMENT: *See* Margin Department.

CROSS (CROSSING STOCK): A broker/dealer's pairing off of a purchase order with a sell order in the same security at the same time and price for different customers.

CUM-DIVIDEND: A term applied to stock at a time when the purchaser will be entitled to a forthcoming dividend.

CUM RIGHTS: A term applied to a stock trading in the marketplace "with subscription rights attached" and reflected in the price of that security.

CUMULATIVE PREFERRED STOCK: A preferred stock which accrues any omitted dividends as a claim against the company. This claim must be paid in full before any dividends may be paid on the company's common stock.

CUMULATIVE VOTING: A voting privilege in which a stockholder multiplies the shares he owns by the number of vacancies to be filled on the board (or proposals to be resolved), allowing him to apportion his total votes accordingly in the manner he so prefers. This procedure is particularly advantageous for minority stockholders.

CURRENCY IN CIRCULATION: Paper bills and coins used by the general public to pay for goods and services.

CURRENT ASSET: Cash or an item of value expected to be converted into cash within one year or one operating cycle, whichever is longer.

CURRENT LIABILITY: An obligation of a corporation payable within one year or one operating cycle, whichever is longer.

CURRENT MARKET VALUE: (1) According to Regulation T of the Federal Reserve Board, this is the latest closing price (or quotation, if no sale occurred); (2) According to NYSE rules, this is the up-to-the-minute last sale price of a security.

CURRENT RATIO: Current assets divided by current liabilities; also known as working capital ratio.

CURRENT YIELD: The annual dollar interest paid by a bond divided by its market price. Example: any bond carrying a 6% coupon and trading at 95 is said to offer a current yield of 6.3%.

CUSHION BOND: A higher-than-current coupon debit instrument with a deferred call provision in its indenture offering a better current return and minimal price volatility (as compared with a bond without call protection).

CUSHION THEORY OF INVESTMENT: A theory of investment that views the short seller as a stabilizing influence on either a bull or bear market.

CUSIP: *See* Committee on Uniform Security Identification Procedure (CUSIP).

CUSIP NUMBER: A unique identifying number appearing on the face of publicly-traded securities.

CUSTODIAN: A person or institution legally charged with the responsibility of safeguarding the property of another.

CUSTOMER: For purposes of disclosure of financial condition under SEC Rule 17a-5, a customer is any person for whom, or with whom, the broker/dealer firm (1) has executed a transaction; or (2) holds or owes monies or securities for that month or the month following which the firm's financial report is to be prepared.

CUSTOMER ASSISTANCE PROGRAM: A $125 million trust fund established and developed beginning in 1960 by the NYSE for the purpose of making restitution to the customers and creditors of member firms that failed prior to 1970.

CUSTOMER'S AGREEMENT: A document that explains the terms and conditions under which a brokerage firm consents to finance a customer's credit transaction. No margin account should be opened or maintained unless the customer signs such an agreement. *See also* Margin Agreement.

D.K.: A slang expression for "Don't Know" which applies to a securities transaction on which fundamental data is missing.

DAISY CHAIN: A series of purchases and sales of the same issue at successively higher (or lower) prices, by the same group of people. Its purpose is to manipulate prices and draw unsuspecting investors into the market, leaving them defrauded of their money or securities.

DATE OF RECORD: The date set by the corporate board of directors for the transfer agents to close their books to further changes in registration of stock and identify the recipients of the distribution. *See* Ex-Dividend Date.

DAY ORDER: A transaction order that remains valid only for the remainder of the trading date on which it is entered.

DEALER: An individual or firm in the securities business acting as a principal rather than as an agent. *See As Agent; As Principal.*

DEBENTURE: An unsecured debt offering by a corporation, promising only the general assets as protection for these creditors; sometimes these general assets referred to are only goodwill and reputation.

DEBIT BALANCE: The balance owed by a customer in his account as reflected on the brokerage firm's ledger statement of settled transactions only.

DEBT/EQUITY RATIO: The ratio of long-term debt to shareholder's equity.

DEEP IN THE MONEY: (1) A term used to describe a securities option with a strike price that is already profitable and relatively far from the market price of the underlying security. (2) In certain regulatory contexts more than 5 points in the money.

DEEP OUT OF THE MONEY: (1) A term used to describe a securities option with a strike price that is unprofitable and relatively far from the market price of the underlying security. (2) In certain regulatory contexts more than 5 points out of the money.

DEFAULT: The failure of a corporation to pay principal and/or interest on outstanding bonds or dividends on its preferred stock.

DEFERRED CHARGE: Expenses incurred by a corporation to improve or promote the long-term prospects of business. They may be apportioned and charged off against earnings over a period of years.

DEFICIENCY LETTER: A letter from the SEC to an issuer stating the nature of material omissions or misrepresentations in the corporation's registration statement. The effective date is postponed until such deficiencies are corrected.

DELIVERY DATE: The day delivery of securities is made which may be on or subsequent to settlement date.

DELIVERY VERSUS PAYMENT: The purchase of securities in a cash account with instructions that payment will be made upon the delivery of the securities, usually to an agent bank.

DEMAND DEPOSIT: A loan or checking account that gives its owner the right to withdraw funds from a commercial bank at his own discretion.

DEPLETION RESERVE: Obsolete term for allowance for depletion.

DEPOSITORY TRUST COMPANY (DTC):   An independent corporation owned by broker/dealers and banks responsible for: (1) holding deposit securities owned by broker/dealers and banking institutions; (2) arranging the receipt and delivery of securities between users by means of debiting and crediting their respective accounts; (3) arranging for payment of monies between users in the settlement of transactions.

DEPRECIATION RESERVE: Obsolete term for allowance for depreciation.

DESIGNATED ORDER TURNAROUND: A computerized system used by the New York Stock Exchange to match and automatically execute small market orders.

DIAGONAL SPREAD: The simultaneous purchase and sale of options of the same class having different striking prices and expiration dates.

DIFFERENTIAL: The dealer's compensation for handling an odd-lot transaction. The dealer adds the differential to the price of the first possible round-lot sale and fills a customer's buy order at that somewhat higher price (a somewhat lower price for sell order). The differential is generally one-eighth of a point and is not itemized separately on the trade confirmation.

DIGEST OF EARNINGS REPORTS: A section in the *Wall Street Journal* reporting in summary form the earnings of publicly-held corporations soon after the information has been released.

DIGITS DELETED: A ticker tape announcement to signify that trade information is falling one minute behind activity on the trading floor. Only the last digit and fraction of a transaction price is then printed until the tape catches up with its timely reporting responsibilities.

DIGITS RESUMED: An announcement stating that the condition of *digits deleted* is no longer in effect.

DISCOUNT BOND: Any bond that sells in the marketplace at a price below its face amount. *See* Premium Bond.

DISCOUNT RATE (THE): A rate of interest associated with borrowing reserves from a central bank by member banks in the Federal Reserve district. The rate is set by the officials of that central bank.

DISCOUNT, TRADING AT: A term used to describe debt instruments trading at a price below their face value. For example, trading at 99 would mean that for $990 one could purchase a bond which would pay $1,000 principal at maturity.

DISCOUNT WINDOW: A tellerlike cage at which member banks may borrow reserves from a central bank upon pledge of acceptable collateral.

DISCRETIONARY ACCOUNT: A customer's account in which an employee of a member firm has authority to act arbitrarily. The meaning of this term does not include authorized use of judgment as to time or price of execution for an order prompted by a customer.

DISCRETIONARY ORDER: An order that empowers a registered representative or other brokerage firm employee to use his own judgment on the customer's behalf with respect to choice of security, quantity of security, and whether any such transaction should be a purchase or sale. *See* Discretionary Accounts; Fractional Discretionary Orders.

DISPROPORTIONATE IN QUANTITY: Under NASD interpretation with regard to hot issues, certain customers may not be allocated securities disproportionately compared to bona fide public customers.

DISTRIBUTOR: *See* Underwriter.

DISTRICT BANK: One of 12 Federal Reserve Banks acting as the central bank for its district.

DISTRICT BUSINESS CONDUCT COMMITTEE: An NASD district subcommittee responsible for supervising and enforcing the Board of Governors' Rules of Fair Practice; it consists of the officials of the district committee itself.

DISTRICT COMMITTEE: The governing body of each of the 13 districts of the NASD.

DISTRICT UNIFORM PRACTICES COMMITTEE: One of 13 district committees within the NASD whose function is the dissemination of information regarding the Uniform Practice Code.

DIVERSIFICATION: Spreading investments among different companies in different fields of endeavor. Another type of diversification is offered by the securities of many individual companies because of the wide range of companies they own or in which they have holdings.

DIVERSIFIED COMMON STOCK COMPANY: A diversified management company that invests substantially all of its assets in a portfolio of common stocks in a wide variety of industries.

DIVERSIFIED MANAGEMENT COMPANY: A management company that has at least 75 percent of its assets represented by: (1) cash and cash items; (2) government securities; (3) securities of other investment companies; and (4) other securities, limited to securities of one issuer having a value not greater than 5 percent of the management company's total assets and no more than 10 percent of the voting securities of the issuing corporation.

DIVIDEND PAYOUT: The percentage of dividends distributed in terms of what is available out of current net income.

DIVIDENDS: Distribution to stockholders declared by the corporate board of directors.

DIVIDENDS PAYABLE: A current liability showing the amount due to stockholders for dividends declared but not yet paid.

DO NOT REDUCE (DNR) ORDER: A limit order to buy, a stop order to sell, or a stop-limit order to sell that is not to be reduced by the amount of a cash dividend on the ex-dividend date because the customer specifically requested that it be entered that way.

DOLLAR BONDS: An identifying designation for some corporate and municipal serial bonds that are denominated and trade in currency values instead of as a percentage of face amount because of the relatively small amounts available for each maturity in the entire issue.

DOLLAR COST AVERAGING: A long-term investment plan based on investing fixed-dollar amounts at periodic intervals, regardless of security price fluctuations.

DOT: An acronym for *Designated Order Turnaround.*

DOUBLE BOTTOM: A situation where the price of a security has twice declined to its support level and risen again. It indicates a demand for securities at that level.

DOUBLE DECLINING BALANCE DEPRECIATION: A highly accelerated procedure for reducing a corporation's cost basis of a qualified asset during its useful life. A significant amount is charged off against earnings during the early years of operation.

DOUBLE TOP: A situation where the price of a security has twice risen to its resistance level and fallen back. It indicates a supply of securities at that level.

DOW-JONES AVERAGE: A market average indicator consisting (individually) of (1) thirty industrial, (2) twenty transportation, and (3) fifteen public utility common stocks; the composite average includes these sixty-five stocks collectively.

DOW THEORY: A theory predicated on the belief that the rise or fall of stock prices is both a mirror and a forecaster of business activities.

DOWN AND OUT OPTION: A block of at least ten call options with the same striking price and expiration date that carries a provision for immediate cancellation of the exercise privilege if the underlying stock declines by a predetermined, agreed-upon amount in the marketplace.

DRAFT: A debt instrument payable on sight, or at a specific time in the future, upon presentation to a paying agent, usually a bank.

DUAL PURPOSE (LEVERAGED) COMPANIES: Closed-end investment companies that initially distribute two classes of securities in equal amounts in a single offering, each class having different objectives and privileges: income shares and capital shares. Holders of either class of shares receive a benefit from at least $2 worth of portfolio for each $1 of personal investment.

DUE BILL: A legal document that evidences the indebtedness of one party to another with regard to a dividend or other distribution.

DUE BILL CHECK: A due bill relating only to a cash dividend on stock or accrued interest on registered bonds. A due-bill check is a post-dated check depositable on the corporation's payment date.

DUE DILIGENCE MEETING: A meeting between corporation officials and the underwriting group to (1) discuss and review detailed information in the registration statement; (2) prepare a final prospectus; and (3) negotiate a formal underwriting agreement.

DVP TRADE: "Deliver versus payment," a transaction in which a broker/dealer sends securities to a contra-dealer or agent of a customer with a requirement for immediate payment therefrom. *See* C.O.D. Trade.

E & OE: "Errors and omissions excepted," this legend often appears on a customer's statement. It is intended to absolve the firm of liability if it makes a mistake in preparing that statement.

EARLY WARNING SYSTEM: A system of financial reports made by broker/dealers under various exchange and SEC rules designed to provide information on the broker/dealer's financial condition.

EARNED INCOME: For Federal income tax purposes, personal service income earned through salary, wages and the like. The maximum effective tax rate on earned income is 50%.

EARNED SURPLUS: *See* Retained Earnings.

EARNINGS PER SHARE: The amount of net profit attributable to each share of common stock outstanding.

EARNINGS REPORT: A financial statement—also called an income statement—issued by a company showing its revenues and expenses over a given period.

EASTERN ACCOUNT: *See* Severally and Jointly.

EFFECTIVE DATE: The date on which a security can be offered publicly, if no deficiency letter is submitted to the issuer by the SEC. It is generally no earlier than the twentieth calendar day after filing the registration statement.

EFFECTIVE LIFETIME: The period of time for which an order is valid.

EFFECTIVE SALE: A round-lot transaction consummated on the floor of the New York Stock Exchange after entry of an odd-lot order by a customer. Its price is used to determine the execution price for the odd-lot order after consideration of the dealer's fee. *See* Differential.

EITHER/OR ORDER: *See* Alternative (Either/Or) Order.

ELECTING SALE: The round-lot transaction that activates (triggers) a stop order.

EQUIPMENT TRUST BOND: A serial bond collateralized by the machinery and/or equipment of the issuing corporation.

EQUITY: (1) The ownership interest of common and preferred stockholders in a company. (2) The excess of value of securities over the debit balance in a margin (general) account.

EX-CLEARING HOUSE: A transaction processed without benefit of clearing corporation facilities.

EX-DISTRIBUTION: The security is trading so that the buyer will not be entitled to a distribution that will be made to holders.

EX-DIVIDEND DATE: (Synonymous with "without dividend") A date set by the Uniform Practice Committee or appropriate stock exchange, upon which a given stock will begin trading in the marketplace without the value of pending dividend included in the contract price. It is closely related to and dependent on the date of record. It is often represented as "X" in the stock listing tables in the newspapers. *See* Bond Interest Distributions.

EX-RIGHTS: A term applied to stocks trading in the marketplace for which the value of the subscription privilege has already been deducted and which, therefore, no longer bears such a right; it is literally trading "rights off."

EX-WARRANTS: The security is trading so that the buyer will not be entitled to warrants that will be distributed to holders.

EXCHANGE DISTRIBUTION: The marketing of a large block of stock by one or two member organizations under special terms and conditions. Buy orders are solicited informally and then crossed with the large block of stock at the current market price on the floor of the Exchange.

EXCHANGE-TYPE COMPANY: An investment company created to take advantage of a specific individual tax ruling obtained by the Investment Company that enables an investor to swap "paper profits" on securities owned for shares in a more diversified investment company and still be able to defer payment of capital gains taxes on this exchange of assets.

EXECUTOR: A court-appointed person charged with the maintenance and distribution of the assets and liabilities of a deceased.

EXEMPTED SECURITIES: As defined in the 1934 act, issues not subject to margin regulations, borrowing restrictions, registration requirements, proxy solicitations, and periodic statements of ownership. In general, these securities include any obligations of the U.S. Government, any of its territories, possessions, states, or municipalities.

EXEMPTED TRANSACTION: Transaction involving an exempted security.

EXERCISE AN OPTION: To require the seller of an option to perform a securities transaction as agreed upon in the terms of his contract. The seller of a call option must deliver stock, whereas the seller of a put option must purchase it from the holder of that privilege.

EXERCISE NOTICE: A document delivered to the Options Clearing Corporation for listed options, or to the guarantor of a conventional option, legally requiring the writer of an option to perform his contracted obligations.

EXERCISE OF CALL: (1) The full or partial retirement of a bond issue through the use of a call privilege provided for in the terms of that security. The redemption price is usually higher than the face value if the option is exercised in the early years after the distribution; (2) The action of the owner of a Call Option when delivery of the underlying security is demanded.

EXERCISE PRICE: *See* Striking Price.

EXPENSE RATIO: For a mutual fund annual operating expenses (including management fees) ÷ average annual net assets. In some cases, the management company may reimburse the mutual fund should the ratio exceed a certain percentage. *See also* Operating Ratio.

EXTRAORDINARY ITEM: An income or expense item of an unusual nature not expected to occur again nor affect future years' operations.

FACE-AMOUNT CERTIFICATE COMPANY: An investment company that issues a debt instrument obligating itself to pay a stated sum of money (face amount) on a date fixed more than twenty-four months after issuance, usually in return for deposits made by an investor in periodic installments.

FACE VALUE: The redemption value of a bond or preferred stock appearing on the face of the certificate, unless that value is otherwise specified by the issuing corporation. It is also sometimes referred to as par value.

FAIL CONTRACT: A transaction between brokerage concerns that is not completed by delivery and payment on a settlement date.

FAIR AND REASONABLE: *See* Five Percent Guideline.

FAIR TREATMENT: Under the NASD Rules of Fair Practice members have a business relationship with their customers and a fiduciary responsibility in handling their accounts.

FANS: *See* Free Account Net Settlement.

FEDERAL FUNDS: (1) Excess reserve balances of a member bank on deposit at a Central Bank in the Federal Reserve System. This money may be made available to eligible borrowers on a short-term basis. (2) Funds used for settlement of money market instruments and U.S. Government securities transactions. (3) A term used to mean "same day availability" of money. See Clearing House Funds.

FEDERAL FUNDS RATE: A rate of interest associated with borrowing a member bank's excess reserves. The rate is determined by the forces of supply and demand.

FEDERAL HOME LOAN BANKS (FHLB): A Government-sponsored agency that finances the home-building industry with mortgage loans from monies raised on offerings of bond issues; interest on these bonds is free from state and local income tax.

FEDERAL INTERMEDIATE CREDIT BANKS (FICB): An agency under the supervision of the Farm Credit Administration that makes loans to agricultural credit and production associations, with revenues derived from five-year bond issues. The interest on those bonds is free from state and local income tax.

FEDERAL LAND BANKS (FLB): Government-sponsored corporations that arrange primary mortgages on farm properties for general agricultural purposes; interest on their bonds is exempt from state and municipal taxes.

FEDERAL NATIONAL MORTGAGE ASSOCIATION (FNMA): A publicly-owned, Government-sponsored corporation that purchases and sells mortgages insured by the Federal Housing Administration (FHA) or Farmers' Home Administration (FHDA); or guaranteed by the Veterans' Administration (VA). Interest on these bonds is fully taxable.

FEDERAL OPEN MARKET COMMITTEE: See Open Market Operations.

FEDERAL RESERVE BANK: One of the banks forming the Federal Reserve System.

FEDERAL RESERVE BOARD (FRB): A United States government agency empowered by Congress to regulate credit in the country. Its members are appointed by the President of the United States.

FEDERAL RESERVE REQUIREMENTS: Each commercial bank must set aside a certain percentage of its deposits, as determined by the Federal Reserve, in order to limit its potential credit-granting capability.

FEDERAL RESERVE SYSTEM: A system of Federal Reserve Banks in the U.S. forming 12 districts under the control of the Federal Reserve Board which regulate the extension of credit as well as other banking activities.

FHLB: See Federal Home Loan Banks (FHLB).

FICB: See Federal Intermediate Credit Banks (FICB).

FIDELITY BOND INSURANCE: See Blanket (Fidelity) Bank Insurance.

FIDUCIARY: A person or institution to whom property is entrusted for the benefit of another.

FIFO: "First in, first out," a popular inventory cost accounting procedure in which it is assumed that the first item manufactured is the first one sold by the company.

FILL-OR-KILL (FOK) ORDER: An order that requires immediate purchase or sale of a specified amount of stock, though not necessarily at one price. If the order cannot be filled immediately, it is automatically cancelled (killed).

FINANCIAL AND OPERATIONAL COMBINED UNIFORM SINGLE REPORT: A report required periodically of brokers by various regulatory authorities giving vital statistics regarding the firm's capabilities to handle its business.

FINANCIAL PRINCIPAL: A registered principal of the NASD who is qualified to participate in the preparation and approval of a member firm's financial statement and net capital computations, besides all other phases of the business's operations. See Principal Registration.

FIRM MARKET: In the OTC market, a quotation on a given security rendered by a market-maker at which he stands ready and able to trade immediately.

FIVE PERCENT GUIDELINE: A general guideline established by the NASD Board of Governors to define "fair" in a random trading transaction; it is not a rule or regulation and is used only as a rough criterion for markups, markdowns, and commissions.

FIXED ANNUITY: An annuity paying a fixed or predetermined amount of money periodically.

FIXED ASSET: An item of value used in current operations that would normally be of use for more than one year.

FIXED CHARGE COVERAGE: The degree by which a corporation is able to earn its interest obligations from total income.

FIXED LIABILITY: An obligation of a corporation payable more than a year hence.

FIXED TRUST: A unit investment company that issues shares reflecting units in a packaged portfolio of securities, such as U.S. Government or tax-exempt obligations.

FLASH PRICES: When reporting falls six or more minutes behind activity on the stock exchange floor, transactions in 30 representative issues are periodically culled from their proper sequence and immediately published on the ticker tape.

FLAT: A transaction involving bonds (most income bonds and all obligations for which interest has been deferred) in which accrued interest is not added to the contract price.

FLOOR: The securities trading area of an exchange. *See* Trading Ring.

FLOOR BROKERAGE: A fee paid to a broker on the floor for executing a trade.

FLOOR DEPARTMENT: The department of the NYSE responsible for the administration and supervision of trading rules and regulations on the floor of the Exchange.

FLOOR ORDER TICKETS: Abbreviated forms of order tickets, used on the floor of the exchange for recording execution.

FLOOR TRADER: *See* Registered (Floor) Trader.

FLOWER BOND: A type of Treasury bond selling at a discount with a special privilege attached permitting redemption after the death of the owner at par value in satisfaction of his Federal estate taxes. These bonds were issued prior to April 1, 1971, and will be in circulation up to final maturity in 1998.

FORMULA INVESTING: Securities investments in the market using a fixed set of criteria.

FORWARD PRICING: The means of determination of purchase or redemption prices after receipt of a mutual fund order from a customer.

FOURTH MARKET: A term referring to the trading of securities between investors without the use of broker/dealers.

FRACTIONAL DISCRETIONARY ORDER: An order to buy or sell at specified prices but with a fraction of a point leeway, to be exercised at the disretion of the broker if necessary. *See* Discretionary Order.

FRANCHISE: *See* Seat (Franchise).

FREE ACCOUNT NET SETTLEMENT: A securities depository organized and promoted by the NASD for use by its members in OTC transactions. Its purpose is to immobilize certificate movement and reduce opportunities for theft of these valuable documents.

FREE BOX: A bank vault or other secure location used to store fully paid customer securities. The depositories of the NCC and DTC serve as a free box for many member firm customers.

"FREE" CROWD: *See* Active Bonds (the "Free" Crowd).

FREE-RIDING: As used in credit activities within the securities industry, the illegal practice of purchasing and selling an issue without showing ability and intent to pay for the transaction. The penalty for this practice is to freeze the account for ninety days.

FREE-RIDING AND WITHHOLDING: As defined by the NASD in distributions of hot issues, the failure of a member to make a bona fide offering of a security he is distributing as underwriter or selling group member.

FREE SECURITIES: A term used to describe securities unencumbered by a lien.

FRONT-END (PREPAID CHARGE) PLAN: A contractual investment plan in which most of the sales charges are applied to payments made in the early years of operation.

FROZEN ACCOUNT: A special cash account in which a customer sells a security he had purchased but not paid for, and then either: (1) fails to pay by the seventh business day after the transaction; or (2) withdraws any portion of the proceeds before payment for the purchase. Full payment is required before any further purchase executions for ninety days thereafter.

FULL DISCLOSURE ACT: An acronym for the Securities Act of 1933.

FULL REGISTRATION: A form of NYSE representative status that enables an employee to engage in the solicitation of all aspects of securities business in which the firm participates.

FULL TRADING AUTHORIZATION: See Power of Attorney, Unlimited.

FULLY DILUTED EARNINGS PER SHARE: A computation of earnings applicable to each share of common stock outstanding based upon the supposition that all convertible securities were exchanged for common stock at the beginning of that accounting period.

FULLY REGISTERED BONDS: Bonds registered as to both principal and interest.

FUNDED DEBT: The aggregate of a corporation's liabilities with maturities exceeding five years.

FUNGIBLE: Interchangeable in law. The concept that one unit of a security is interchangeable with any other unit of the same security. For example, one share of A.T.&T. common stock is interchangeable with any other share of A.T.&T. common stock.

GARAGE: One of the small trading areas just off the main trading floor of the New York Stock Exchange.

GENERAL ACCOUNT: See Margin (General) Account.

GENERAL OBLIGATION (GO) BOND: A tax-exempt bond whose pledge is the issuer's good faith and full taxing power.

GENERAL PARTNER: A member of a partnership whose participation, especially in liabilities, is unlimited. Such a member may have his personal assets attached to satisfy a business-related liability.

GIVE UP: The practice of the payer of a commission or fee directing the recipient to "give up" part of the fee to another broker. In some situations the practice may be illegal.

GOOD DELIVERY: Proper delivery by a selling firm to the purchaser's office of certificates that are negotiable without additional documentation and that are in units acceptable under the Uniform Practice Code.

GOOD FAITH DEPOSIT: (1) An amount of money given by members of an underwriting syndicate to the syndicate manager to guarantee their financial performance under the syndicate agreement; (2) An amount of money deposited by a customer upon opening a new account.

GOOD NAME: A slang expression used to denote the registration of securities so as to permit good delivery (i.e., not in legal form).

GOOD-'TIL-CANCELLED (GTC, or OPEN) ORDER: An order that remains valid indefinitely, until executed or cancelled by the customer.

GOVERNMENT NATIONAL MORTGAGE ASSOCIATION (GNMA): An offshoot of the FNMA, a wholly-owned government corporation (operated by the Department of Housing and Urban Development—HUD) that provides primary mortgages through bond issuances carrying no tax exemptions.

GROUP SALES: Sales of securities by a syndicate manager to institutional purchasers from "the pot."

GTC: *See* Good-'Til-Cancelled (GTC or Open) Order.

GUARANTEE LETTER: A letter issued by a member of the Options Clearing Corporation to an options exchange guaranteeing the financial performance of a market-maker.

GUARANTEED ACCOUNT: An agreement whereby the equity of one account guarantees the financial integrity of another account.

GUARANTEED ANNUITY: *See* Fixed Annuity.

GUARANTEED BONDS: Bonds issued by a subsidiary corporation and guaranteed as to principal and/or interest by the parent corporation.

HEAD-AND-SHOULDERS-DOWNWARD (UPWARD) TREND: A technical theory founded on the belief that a market trend may be predicted by plotting price fluctuations of securities on graph paper. A downward trend would be indicated by horizontal movement, followed by another decline. An upward trend would be indicated by horizontal movement, decline, rise, horizontal movement followed by another rise in price.

HEDGE: Any combination of long and/or short positions taken in securities, options or commodities where one position tends to reduce the risk of the other.

HEDGE CLAUSE: A statement that appears on a securities valuation, research report, or market letter, in which the writer disclaims responsibility for inadvertent errors or omissions in the contents of the material.

HEDGE FUND: An investment partnership that aggressively buys securities of certain companies while at the same time selling short shares of other companies engaged in the same industry.

"HITCHBALLING": The illegal act of swapping securities with a customer at price levels above that prevailing for those same issues under competitive conditions.

HOLDER OF RECORD: The party whose name appears on a company's stockholder register at the close of business on the record date. That party will receive a dividend or other distribution from the company in the near future.

HOLDING COMPANY: An investment company formed to own a controlling interest in one or more subsidiary companies.

HORIZONTAL SPREAD: The term is used interchangeably with Calendar Spread.

HOT ISSUE: A security that is expected to trade in the aftermarket at a premium over the public offering price. *See* Withholding.

HOUSING AUTHORITY BOND: A municipal bond whose payment of interest and/or principal is contingent upon the collection of rents and other fees from users of a Housing Facility built with the proceeds of the issuance of the bond.

$100 RULE: Same-day purchases and sales of different securities by the same customer, resulting in a cash deficiency of $100 or less, do not mandate satisfaction under Regulation T.

HYBRID ANNUITY: An annuity which is partly fixed and partly variable.

HYPOTHECATION: The act of borrowing money to finance purchasing or carrying securities using those securities as collateral for the loan.

HYPOTHECATION AGREEMENT: *See* Customer's Agreement.

IMMEDIATE FAMILY: Defined differently under various industry regulations, generally it means: husband or wife, children, grandchildren, grandparents, parents, in-laws, or any other relative in the same household.

IMMEDIATE OR CANCEL (IOC) ORDER: An order that requires immediate execution at a specified price of all or part of a specified amount of stock, with the unexecuted portion required to be cancelled by the broker.

IN THE MONEY: An expression used to denote a securities option with a striking price that is profitable in comparison with the current market value of the underlying stock.

INACTIVE BONDS: Debt instruments that are expected by the NYSE Floor Department to trade only infrequently. All bids and offers, therefore, are filed in a "cabinet" or "can" (on cards colored to reflect effective lifetimes) until they are cancelled or executed.

INCOME (ADJUSTMENT) BONDS: In the event of bankruptcy, long-term debt obligations are offered in exchange for outstanding bonds by the court-appointed receiver. The interest requirement associated with such debt will be paid by the corporation only when, as, and if earned.

INCOME COMPANIES: Investment companies that stress higher-than-average current income distributions without regard to quality or class of security in their portfolios.

INCOME SHARES (STOCKS): A class of securities issued by dual-purpose investment companies that entitles owners to net dividends and interest earned by the company's entire portfolio with a minimum amount guaranteed.

INCOME STATEMENT: An accounting document—also called an earnings report—that reflects revenues and expenses incurred by a corporation over a specific period of time.

INDENTURE: A written agreement between corporation and creditors by which the terms of a debt issue are set forth, such as rate of interest, means of payment, maturity date, terms of prior payment of principal, collateral, priorities of claims, trustee.

INDENTURE QUALIFICATION STATEMENT: For publicly offered debt instruments not subject to registration under the Securities Act of 1933 but subject to the Trust Indenture Act of 1939, the statement required to be filed with the SEC to comply with the latter act.

INDEX: A stock market indicator, derived in the same way as an average, but from a broader sampling of securities.

INDICATION: On the ticker tape means an approximation of the current quotes.

INDICATION OF INTEREST: An expression of consideration by an underwriter's circle of customers for investment in a new security expected to be offered soon It is not a binding commitment on the customer or the underwriter.

INDIVIDUAL IDENTIFICATION: A system for segregating customer securities in accordance with SEC Rule 15c3-3 where each stock certificate is specially identified as belonging to a particular customer.

INDIVIDUAL PROPRIETORSHIP: The simplest, most common form of business organization, typified by the personal management and ownership by one individual.

INDIVIDUAL RETIREMENT ACCOUNT: Under certain circumstances, individuals not enjoying a qualified retirement plan at their place of employment may qualify to deduct up to $1,500 per year from their Federal taxable income and set that amount aside for their retirement.

INDUSTRIAL DEVELOPMENT BONDS: Industrial Revenue Bonds issued to improve the environment and subject to certain Internal Revenue Service regulations with regard to the tax-exempt status of the interest payments.

INDUSTRIAL REVENUE BONDS: Municipal bonds issued for the purpose of constructing facilities for profit-making corporations. The tax-exempt feature of these bonds may be restricted by certain Internal Revenue Service regulations. The Corporation, rather than the Municipality, is liable for the payment of interest and principal.

INFLATION: A general rise in prices.

INITIAL MARGIN REQUIREMENT: The minimum equity requirement, as established by various Federal Reserve regulations and New York Stock Exchange Rules, required at the time a security is purchased.

INSIDE MARKET: The favorable, wholesale market price for a security available only to a market-maker and other members of the NASD.

INSIDER: An officer, director, or principal stockholder of a publicly-owned corporation, and members of their immediate families. This category may also include people who obtain nonpublic information about a company and use it for personal gain.

INSUBSTANTIAL QUANTITY: Under NASD interpretations regarding hot issues, 100 shares or $5,000 face value in bonds may be allocated to certain restricted parties.

INTANGIBLE ASSET: An item of value whose true worth is hard, or even impossible, to determine, such as goodwill, reputation, patents, and so on.

INTEREST COVERAGE: Total income divided by interest on bonds.

INTER-VIVOS TRUST: A legal instrument that appoints some person or institution to perform a specific function with a designated sum of money. The terms of this incumbency become effective during its creator's lifetime.

INTERNATIONAL BANK FOR RECONSTRUCTION AND DEVELOPMENT: An international bank (25% controlled by the U.S.) designed to loan monies to its members (some 90 countries) to develop and modernize industry.

INTERPOLATION: The calculation of a figure, using ratio techniques, which exists between two known figures.

INTERPOSITIONING: An unethical and unfair practice by a broker/dealer of needlessly employing a third party between the customer and the best available market, so that the customer pays more on a purchase or receives less on a sale than he should.

INVENTORY TURNOVER: An indicator of the rapidity with which a corporation's inventory is manufactured and sold.

INVESTMENT ADVISOR: A person, company or institution registered with the SEC under the Investment Advisors Act of 1940 to manage the investments of third parties.

INVESTMENT BANKER: A broker/dealer organization that provides a service to industry through counsel, market-making, and underwriting of securities.

INVESTMENT COMPANY: An institution engaged primarily in the business of investing and trading in securities; includes only (1) face-amount certificate companies, (2) unit investment trust companies, and (3) management companies.

INVESTMENT HISTORY: Under NASD interpretation with regard to a hot issue, certain customers must have made at least 10 purchases over a three-year period with an average dollar value equal to the hot issue allocated.

INVESTMENT LETTER: A written agreement between a seller and buyer, in a private placement of securities, stating that the buyer's intentions are for investment only and that he does not intend to re-offer the securities publicly.

INVESTMENT "SKELETON": A slang expression denoting a speculative security in an investor's portfolio that failed to meet his expectations or financial objective.

INVOLUNTARY (STATUTORY) UNDERWRITER: An individual or corporation that purchases an unregistered security and offers it in a public distribution without an effective registration statement. Such parties are subject to fine and/or imprisonment.

IOC ORDER: *See* Immediate or Cancel (IOC) Order.

IRA: *See* Individual Retirement Account.

ISSUE: Any of a company's class of securities, or the act of distributing them.

ISSUED-AND-OUTSTANDING STOCKS: That portion of authorized stock distributed among investors by a corporation.

ISSUER: A corporation, trust, or association engaged in the distribution of its securities.

JOINT ACCOUNT: An arrangement whereby two or more people pool their money and abilities to buy, sell and/or carry securities collectively.

JOINT TENANTS IN COMMON: An account in which the several people participating have a fractional interest in its assets, and that percentage of the assets that will become part of each person's estate upon his death.

JOINT TENANTS WITH RIGHTS OF SURVIVORSHIP (W/R/O/S): An account in which several people have an ownership interest and whose assets are inherited by the survivors upon the death of any participant.

KEOGH PLAN: Initiated under the provisions of the Self-Employed Individuals Tax Retirement Act of 1962, this term applies to programs that enable an individual to defer payment of any income taxes on the lesser 15% of annual earned income, or $7,500 (with a minimum of the first $750 earned) until the individual retires and begins to withdraw funds from this accumulated pool of capital.

KNOW YOUR CUSTOMER RULE: *See* Rule 405.

LAY-OFF: Under the terms of a Standby Underwriting Agreement, an issuer of securities may sell any or all unsubscribed shares in a rights offering to the Underwriters at the subscription price.

LEGAL DELIVERY: A delivery of securities which is not good delivery due to the registration of the certificates.

LEGAL INVESTMENTS: Securities investments deemed eligible for inclusion in portfolios of certain fiduciaries whose activities are monitored by state banking and/or insurance departments.

LEGAL LIST: A list of securities published annually by some state banking and/or insurance departments that indicates items deemed suitable for investment by certain fiduciaries with their departments' jurisdiction.

LENDING AT A PREMIUM: When securities cannot be obtained through the typical sources to cover a short sale, the short-seller is obliged to pay lenders a fee for the use of their certificates in addition to the cash collateral normally provided. Lending at a premium usually brings a deluge of certificates into the market thereby eliminating the need for the premium entirely. *See* Lending at a Rate.

LENDING AT A RATE: A situation in which the short-seller, with his pick of lenders demands interest for his cash collateral. *See* Lending at a Premium.

LETTER OF INTENT: A statement of intent by a mutual fund investor announcing his desire to invest over a period of thirteen months a sum of money sufficient to qualify for a load discount.

LETTER SECURITY: An unregistered security offered privately in which the purchaser is obliged to sign an investment letter to complete the transaction and to forestall disciplinary action against the seller under the Securities Act of 1933.

LEVEL LOAD VOLUNTARY ACCUMULATION PLAN: A method of selling mutual fund shares by which sales commission per dollar of investment is the same throughout the plan and future investments may be stopped without penalty.

LEVERAGE: A financial condition brought about by the assumption of a high percentage of debt in relation to the equity in a corporation's capital structure.

LEVERAGED COMPANIES: *See* Dual Purpose (Leveraged) Companies.

LIABILITIES: All the outstanding claims against a corporation: accounts payable, wages and salaries, dividends declared payable, accrued taxes, fixed or long-term liabilities such as mortgage bonds, debentures, and bank loans. *See* Assets; Balance Sheet; Equity.

LIFO: "Last in, first out," an inventory cost accounting procedure in which it is assumed that the last item manufactured is the first one sold by the company.

LIMIT ORDER: An order in which a customer sets a maximum price he is willing to pay as a buyer and a minimum price he is willing to accept as a seller. *See* Market Order; Stop Order.

LIMITED ACCESS TO BOOKS AND RECORDS: A shareholder's right to inspect financial information made public in accordance with federal, state, exchange, and NASD regulations.

LIMITED DISCRETION: A term used in the maintenance of customer option accounts. Normally a customer will give a registered representative discretion in trading options limited to selling or exercising options which are in the money and about to expire.

LIMITED PARTNER: A member of a partnership whose participation in liabilities and/or profits and losses has been limited by written agreement.

LIMITED PARTNERSHIP: A partnership with one or more limited partners.

LIMITED REGISTRATION: A form of temporary NYSE representative status in which a firm employee is permitted to solicit business and service customers only in selected mutual funds and MIP accounts. This representative must qualify for full registration within seven months thereafter.

LIMITED TRADING AUTHORIZATION: *See* Power of Attorney, Limited.

LIQUIDATION: The voluntary or involuntary closing out of security positions.

LIQUIDITY: (1) The ability of the market in a particular security to absorb a reasonable amount of trading at reasonable price changes. Liquidity is one of the most important characteristics of a good market. (2) The easy ability of investors to convert their securities holdings into cash and vice versa.

LIQUIDITY RATIO: A proportion of quick assets to current liabilities, indicative of a corporation's ability to weather an immediate financial crisis. Also known as the acid test ratio or the quick asset ratio.

LISTED BOND TABLE: A daily publication appearing in many newspapers showing a summary of transactions by exchange (or OTC) by security.

LISTED COMPANY: *See* Listed Stock.

LISTED OPTIONS: (1) Options traded on an organized exchange or system having standardized striking prices and expiration dates, and which are cleared through the Options Clearing Corporation; (2) Not conventional options.

LISTED STOCK: The stock of a company traded on a securities exchange and for which a listing application and registration statement have been filed with the SEC and the exchange itself.

LISTED STOCK TABLE: A daily publication appearing in many newspapers showing a summary of transactions by exchange (or OTC) by security.

LIVING TRUST: *See* Inter-Vivos Trust.

LOAD: The portion of an offering price of shares in an open-end investment company that covers sales commissions and all other costs of distribution. The load is incurred only on purchases, since there is generally no charge when the shares are sold (redeemed).

LOAN VALUE: The maximum permissible credit extended on securities in a margin account, presently 50 percent of the current market value of eligible stock in the account.

LONG MARKET VALUE: The market value of securities owned by a customer (long in his account).

LONG POSITION: An expression signifying ownership of securities.

LONG-TERM CAPITAL TRANSACTION: A purchase and subsequent sale more than one year later.

LONG-TERM DEBT: The debt of a company due and payable more than one year hence.

M: Abbreviation for one thousand. For example 5M means 5,000; 25M means 25,000. Usually used to denote bond face value.

M 1: The basic money supply, defined as total currency in circulation plus all demand deposits in commercial banks.

M 2: M 1 plus savings and time deposits of less than $100,000 in commercial banks.

MAINTENANCE CALL: A notice to a customer of a broker/dealer that the customer must deposit additional equity in his account to meet either New York Stock Exchange or the broker/dealer's own minimum maintenance requirements.

MAJOR BRACKET PARTICIPANT: A member of an underwriting syndicate who will handle a large part of the issue in relation to other members of the syndicate.

MALONEY ACT: Federal legislation passed in 1938 authorizing the registration of an association of securities broker/dealers with the SEC. The NASD and Municipal Securities Rulemaking Board are registered under this act.

MANAGEMENT COMPANY: An investment company that conducts its business in any manner other than as a face-amount certificate company or unit investment company. *See* Diversified Management Company; Closed-end Investment Company; Nondiversified Management Company; Open-End Management Company.

MANAGEMENT GROUP: An organization that serves an open-end investment company as an investment advisor.

MARGIN: The amount of equity required to be deposited in an account carried on credit.

MARGIN (GENERAL) ACCOUNT: An account in which a customer uses credit from a broker/dealer to take security positions; the extension of credit by broker/dealers is regulated by the Federal Reserve Board.

MARGIN AGREEMENT: *See* Customer's Agreement.

MARGIN CALL: A demand on the customer to deposit money or securities with the broker when a purchase is made or when the customer's equity in a margin account declines below a minimum standard set by an exchange or the firm.

MARGIN DEPARTMENT: A group within a securities firm that monitors all trade activities, insuring that payment and delivery procedures are in account with Federal, exchange, and NASD regulations to which it is subject.

MARGIN OF PROFIT RATIO: The quotient of operating income divided by net sales.

MARGIN REQUIREMENT: *See* Margin Call.

MARGIN SECURITY: According to Regulation T of the Federal Reserve Board, a margin security is (1) any stock, right, or warrant traded on one of the registered stock exchanges in the U.S.; (2) an OTC stock specifically declared eligible for credit by the Federal Reserve Board; (3) a debt security traded on one of the registered stock exchanges that either (a) is convertible into margin stock or (b) carries a right or warrant to subscribe to a margin stock. Regulations U and G include in this category investment company securities and any warrants to purchase a margin security—whether or not they are traded on a registered stock exchange.

MARK TO THE MARKET: As the market value of a borrowed security fluctuates, the lender may demand more in cash collateral for a rise in value, or the borrower may demand a partial refund of collateral for a decline. The written notice for either demand is a "mark" to the market.

MARKDOWN: The fee charged by a broker/dealer—acting as a dealer—when he buys a security from a customer and sells it, at a higher price, to a market-maker. The fee, or markdown, is included in the sale price and is not itemized separately in the confirmation. *See* As Principal; Five Percent Guideline.

MARKETABLE SECURITIES: (1) Those which may be readily purchased or sold. (2) Government bonds freely traded in the open market. *See* Certificate of Indebtedness; Treasury Bill; Treasury Bond; Treasury Note

MARKET-IF-TOUCHED ORDER: An order allowable only on the CBOE. Such a buy order is activated when a series declines to a predetermined price or below. Such a sell order is activated when a series rises to a predetermined price or higher.

MARKETING DEPARTMENT: The Department of the New York Stock Exchange responsible for public relations.

MARKET-MAKER: (1) A member of an options exchange who trades for his own account and risk. He is charged with the responsibility of trading in such a manner as to add to the maintenance of a fair, orderly and competitive market. He may not act as agent. (2) A firm actively making bids and offers in the OTC market.

MARKET ORDER: An order to be executed immediately at the best available price.

MARKET VALUE: The price that would be paid for a security or other asset.

MARKUP: The fee charged by a broker/dealer—acting as a dealer—when he buys a security from a market-maker and sells it to his customer at a higher price. The fee, or markup, is included in the sale price and is not itemized separately in the confirmation. *See* As Principal; Five Percent Guideline.

MATCHED SALE/PURCHASE TRANSACTION (REVERSE REPURCHASE AGREE-MENT): A Federal Open Market Committee sale of Treasury bills or other Government securities for cash settlement with a provision for repurchase at the same price plus interest on a specific date in the future.

MATURITY: The date on which a loan, bond or debenture comes due; both principal and any accrued interest due must be paid.

MEMBER: A term used to describe a member of the New York Stock Exchange or other organized exchange or clearing corporation.

MEMBER FIRM: A term used to describe a company which has as an officer or partner a member of the New York Stock Exchange or other organized exchange or clearing corporation.

MEMBER FIRMS DEPARTMENT: A department of the NYSE responsible for policing the practices and operations of member organizations.

MEMBER FIRMS SURVEILLANCE DEPARTMENT: The Department within the New York Stock Exchange responsible for the conduct of member firms.

MESSAGE SWITCHING: An automated communication procedure that links sales, operations, and trading locales by means of a computer. This electronic device routes orders, stores information, and relays execution reports to the proper departments and offices.

MINIMUM MAINTENANCE MARGIN: The minimum equity a customer must have in his account as defined by various Federal Reserve Regulations and New York Stock Exchange Rules.

MINIMUM TRADING VARIATION: The minimum amount of variation allowable in the trading values in an exchange, usually one-eighth of a point. See Point.

MINUS TICK: A transaction on the Exchange at a price below the previous transaction in a given security.

MISSING THE MARKET: The failure by a member of the exchange to execute an order due to his negligence. The member is obliged to promptly reimburse the customer for any losses due to his mistake.

MIXED ACCOUNT: A margin account containing both long and short positions in securities.

MONEY: Coin or certificates generally accepted in payment of debts for goods and services.

MONEY MARKET INSTRUMENTS: Short-term debt usually issued at a discount and not bearing interest. For example, Treasury Bills, Commercial Paper, or Bankers' Acceptances.

MORAL SUASION: An expression used to denote the Federal Reserve Board's ability to influence member bank financial policies by threatening to employ drastic powers in order to gain compliance with its own preferences.

MORTGAGE BOND: The most prevalent type of secured corporate bond. The bondholders are protected by the pledge of the corporation's real assets evaluated at the time of issuance. See Closed-end Provision; Open-end Provision.

MORTGAGE REIT: An REIT primarily engaged in the financing of new construction.

MULTIPLIER EFFECT: The leveraged power of loan expansion enjoyed by commercial banks using reserve balances as a base requirement.

MUNICIPAL SECURITIES RULEMAKING BOARD: Registered under the Maloney Act in 1975, the Board consists of industry and public representatives. It is designed to create rules and regulations for municipal bond trading among brokers, dealers and banks. Its powers are similar to those of the NASD.

MURPHY'S LAW: (1) The theory that if it can be done wrong, someone will find a way. (2) Gordon Variation: The theory that if something is designed to be foolproof, someone will design a better fool.

MUTILATION: A term used to describe the physical condition of a bond or coupon where the instrument is no longer considered negotiable. Such missing items as the signature of the authorized officer, the serial number of the instrument, the amount or the payable date would cause the instrument to be considered mutilated. The issuing authority, or its agent, must be contacted to obtain certain documents needed to make the instrument negotiable again.

MUTUAL FUND COMPANY: See Open-End Management (Mutual Fund) Company.

MUTUAL FUND CUSTODIAN: A commercial bank or trust company with certain qualifications that holds in safekeeping monies and securities owned by an open-end investment company and accumulation plans of its shareholders.

MUTUAL FUNDS: Shares offered by an open-end management, or mutual fund, company. See No-Load Mutual Fund; Plan Company.

NAKED OPTION: An option that is written without any corresponding security or option position as protection in the seller's account.

NASD: See National Association of Securities Dealers (NASD).

NASDAQ: See National Association of Securities Dealers Automated Quotations (NASDAQ).

NASDAQ LEVEL 1: Provides only the arithmetic mean of the bids and offers entered by members.

NASDAQ LEVEL 2: Provides the individual binds and offers next to the name of the member entering the information.

NASDAQ LEVEL 3: Available to NASD members only, the member may enter his bids and offers and receive Level 2 service.

NASDAQ-OTC PRICE INDEX: *See* National Association of Securities Dealers Automated Quotations-Over-The-Counter Price Index.

NATIONAL ASSOCIATION OF SECURITIES DEALERS (NASD): An association of broker/dealers in over-the-counter securities organized on a nonprofit, non-stock-issuing basis. Its general aim is to protect investors in the OTC market.

NATIONAL ASSOCIATION OF SECURITIES DEALERS AUTOMATED QUOTA-TIONS (NASDAQ): An electronic data terminal service furnishing subscribers with instant identification of market-makers and their current quotations, updated continuously, thus obviating the need for "shopping in the street."

NATIONAL ASSOCIATION OF SECURITIES DEALERS AUTOMATED QUOTATIONS OVER-THE-COUNTER PRICE INDEX: A computer-oriented, broad-based indicator of activity in the unlisted securities market, updated every five minutes.

NATIONAL CLEARING CORPORATION: An NASD affiliate organization responsible for arranging a daily clearance of transactions for members by means of a continuous net settlement process. Although its principal office is in New York City, it operates electronic satellite branches in major U.S. cities.

NATIONAL MARKET ADVISORY BOARD: Mandated by the Securities Act of 1975, the Board is responsible to advise the SEC regarding the operations and regulations of the nation's security markets. The Board is comprised of 15 members, serving terms of between 2 and 5 years, with a majority coming from the securities industry.

NATIONAL QUOTATION BUREAU, INC. (NQB): A subsidiary of Commerce Clearing House, Inc. that distributes to subscribers several lists a day of broker/dealers making bids and/or offerings of securities traded over-the-counter.

NATIONAL QUOTATIONS COMMITTEE: A national committee of NASD that sets minimum standards for the publication of quotations furnished to newspapers, radio, or television.

NATIONAL SECURITIES CLEARING CORPORATION: A corporation organized to consolidate clearing securities nationally regardless of where the trade occurred. Designed to, among other things, consolidate SIAC and NCC.

NCC: *See* National Clearing Corporation.

NEGOTIABILITY: In reference to securities, the easy ability to transfer title upon delivery.

NEGOTIATED MARKETPLACE: A term used to describe the over-the-counter market since transactions are negotiated between two parties. Opposite of Auction Marketplace.

NET ASSET VALUE PER SHARE: (1) Net assets divided by number of outstanding shares; (2) For an open-end investment company, often the net redemption price per share; (3) For a no-load open-end investment company both the net redemption price per share and the offering price per share.

NET CHANGE: The last column in the listed stock and bond table showing the difference between the closing prices of that day and the last day the security traded adjusted for dividends and other distributions.

NET COST: Actual cost minus salvage value.

NET CURRENT ASSETS: *See* Working Capital.

NET EARNINGS: *See* Net Income.

NET INCOME: The income of a company after deducting all expenses from all revenues.

NET INTEREST COST: The net cost to the issuer of a debt instrument taking into account both the coupon and the discount or premium on issue.

NET LIQUID ASSETS: Loosely defined as the excess of cash, readily marketable securities and accounts receivable over all liabilities. *See* Acid Test Ratio.

NET PRICE: The proceeds of a sale or the gross payment on a purchase after deducting or adding respectively all expenses.

NET PROCEEDS: The contract price less all expenses incurred on a sale execution. *See* Net Price.

NET PROFIT MARGIN: The ratio of net profit divided by net sales.

NET QUICK ASSETS: Quick assets minus all current liabilities.

NET SALES: Gross revenues realized less discounts, refunds, and returns of merchandise.

NET TANGIBLE ASSET VALUE PER SHARE (BOOK VALUE): It is all tangible assets of a corporation minus total liabilities, and divided by the total number of shares outstanding. For a mutual fund, it is portfolio value plus all other assets minus management group fees and all other liabilities, divided by the number of shares of that fund outstanding.

NET WORKING CAPITAL: The excess of current assets over current liabilities. *See* Working Capital.

NET WORTH: *See* Shareholders' Equity.

NEW ACCOUNT REPORT: A mandatory document for broker/dealers who conduct a customer business, this is a record of inquiry probing into the essential facts relative to the background, financial circumstances, and investment objectives of each customer.

NEW YORK STOCK EXCHANGE GRATUITY FUND: A fund created to provide $20,000 death benefits to the next of kin of each deceased member by means of voluntary contributions; coverage is limited to NYSE members exclusively.

NEW YORK STOCK EXCHANGE INDEX: A "weighted" market index consisting of all common stocks listed on the Big Board, further broken down into (1) industrial, (2) transportation, (3) utilities, and (4) finance. The index is updated and printed on the ticker tape every half-hour.

NEW YORK TIMES MARKET INDICATORS: A report in that newspaper of vital statistics regarding the previous day's stock market conditions.

NEXT DAY CONTRACT: A security transaction calling for settlement the day after trade date.

NH: *See* Not Held (NH) Order.

NINE BOND RULE: Unless prior consent of the NYSE can be obtained, all orders for nine listed bonds or less must be sent to the floor for a diligent attempt at execution.

NO-LOAD MUTUAL FUNDS (NL): Mutual funds offered directly to the public at net asset value with no sales charge.

NO-PAR VALUE: Stock with no dollar value assigned on the issuance of certificates but with an arbitrary equity interest assigned nevertheless for use in preparing financial statements.

NOMINAL QUOTATION: A quote given which is not to be considered as firm in the event that a purchase or sale is consummated. An approximation of the price which could be expected on a purchase or sale.

NOMINAL YIELD: The annual interest rate payable on a bond, specified in the indenture and printed on the face of the certificate itself.

NOMINEE NAME: A certificate registration in the name of a partnership acting in a fiduciary capacity. This form of registration is useful to facilitate delivery of certificates that would otherwise require supporting documentation.

NONCLEARING MEMBER: A member firm of the NYSE whose clearing operations are not handled by the Stock Clearing Corporation.

NONCUMULATIVE PREFERRED STOCK: Preferred stock on which omitted dividends do not accrue and the shareholders have no claim to them any time in the future.

NONDIVERSIFIED MANAGEMENT COMPANY: Any management company that declares itself not subject to the limitations defining a diversified management company.

NONPURPOSE LOAN: A loan involving securities as collateral that is arranged for any purpose other than to purchase, carry, or trade margin securities. *See* Purpose Loan.

NONRECURRING ITEM: *See* Extraordinary Item.

NORMAL INVESTMENT PRACTICES: As defined by the NASD Board of Governors, the history of investment practices between the member firm and its customers. For customers subject to the NASD definition of restricted categories, no new accounts may be opened with the broker/dealer to purchase a hot issue. For customers not so restricted, the customer's investment objectives and financial circumstances must be considered.

NORMAL TRADING UNIT: The accepted unit of trading in a given marketplace: on the NYSE it is 100 shares (round lot) for stocks and $1,000 par value for bonds. In some relatively inactive stocks, the unit is 10 shares. For NASDAQ traded securities it is 100 shares for stocks and $10,000 par value for bonds. *See* Odd Lot; Round Lot.

NOT HELD (NH) ORDER: An order that does not hold the executing member financially responsible for using his personal judgment in the execution price or time of a transaction.

NQB: *See* National Quotation Bureau, Inc.

NSCC: *See* National Securities Clearing Corporation.

OCC: Acronym for the Option Clearing Corporation.

ODD LOT: An amount of stock less than the normal trading unit.

ODD-LOT DIFFERENTIAL: Generally, the dealer who facilitates an odd-lot transaction will buy the securities ⅛ or ¼ point below the next round lot trade; or sell the securities ⅛ or ¼ above the next round lot trade.

ODD-LOT THEORY: A theory of market activity stating that the small (odd-lot) investor frequently becomes a heavy buyer as the market peaks and sells heavily on balance in a declining market, just prior to a rally.

OFF-BOARD: An expression that refers either to transactions over-the-counter in unlisted securities or to transactions involving listed shares that were not executed on a national securities exchange.

OFFER: The price at which a person is ready to sell. *See* Bid and Asked.

OFFICE OF SUPERVISORY JURISDICTION (OSJ): An office set up by individual member firms in compliance with Section 27 of the NASD Rules of Fair Practice, managed by a registered principal, to review a firm's supervisory responsibilities.

OFFICE ORDER TICKETS: Transaction order forms filled out in great detail at each sales office of member firms. *See* Floor Order Tickets.

ON-THE-QUOTATION ODD-LOT ORDER: An odd-lot order that must be executed immediately; the price is therefore based on the existing round-lot quotation on the floor of the New York Stock Exchange.

ON THE TAPE: A trade reported on one of several ticker tapes.

ONE-CANCELS-THE-OTHER ORDER: Two or more orders to be treated as a unit. If one order is executed, the other order is cancelled.

OPD: Appearing next to a ticker symbol, three letters indicate an issue's initial transaction during a trading session if the price is significantly different from the previous day's closing transaction, or the ticket price of the transaction did not get published shortly after execution.

OPEN BOX: See Active Box.

OPEN-END MANAGEMENT (MUTUAL FUND) COMPANY: A management company that offers shares (mutual funds) continuously after an initial offering, thereby altering its capitalization from day to day.

OPEN-END PROVISION: A mortgage bond provision that enables a corporation to use the same real assets as collateral for more than one bond issue. In the event of default, creditors on all issues have equal claims.

OPEN INTEREST: The total number of option or commodity contracts issued and outstanding by the responsible clearing corporations.

OPEN MARKET OPERATIONS: The activity of the Federal Open Market Committee, in behalf of the Federal Reserve Banking System, to arrange outright purchases and sales of government and agency securities, matched sale/purchase agreements, and repurchase agreements, in order to promote monetary policy of the Federal Reserve Board.

OPEN ORDER: See Good-'till-Canceled (GTC or Open) Order.

OPENING ONLY ORDER: See At the Opening (Opening Only) Order.

OPENING PURCHASE TRANSACTION: The buying of a listed option so as to establish a new long position.

OPENING SALE TRANSACTION: The writing or selling of a listed option so as to establish a new short position.

OPERATING INCOME: Net sales less cost of sales, selling expenses, administrative expenses and depreciation. The pre-tax income from normal operations.

OPERATING RATIO: A comparison of operating expenses to net sales.

OPERATIONS DEPARTMENT: A department of the NYSE responsible for (1) the listing and delisting of corporate and government securities, and (2) all trading activity and ancillary services.

OPTION: A contract wherein one party (the option writer) grants another party (buyer) the right to demand that the writer perform a certain act. See Call Option; Put Option.

OPTION CLASS: All Call Options or all Put Options (not both) having the same underlying security.

OPTION PREMIUM: The fee paid by a purchaser of an option to entice someone to give him the right of exercise anytime within a specified time period.

OPTION SERIES: All options having the same type (either as a put or a call) of underlying security, striking price and expiration date.

OPTION SPREADING: A system of strategies calling for the simultaneous purchase and sale of options of the same class in order to establish hedged positions.

OPTION TYPE: The type of option as defined in the Options Clearing Corporation prospectus; calls are one type of option and puts are another.

OPTION WRITER: The seller of securities option who receives an immediate fee for providing a purchaser with the right to demand performance in a securities transaction.

OPTION CLEARING CORPORATION (OCC): A Corporation owned jointly by all the exchanges trading listed options. Based on compared trades submitted by various exchanges, the OCC issues the option to the buyer and holds the writer to his obligation. OCC is therefore the issuer of all listed options and a holder must exercise against the OCC, not the original writer. The OCC maintains a system for collecting and remitting funds in settlement of option trades, and holds collateral deposited by option writers to guarantee their performance.

ORDER BOOK OFFICIAL: An employee of an options exchange who performs all the duties of a board broker. He is compensated by salary paid by the exchange.

ORDER DEPARTMENT: A group that routes buy and sell instructions to the trading floors of the appropriate stock exchanges and executes orders in the OTC market for customer and firm trading accounts.

ORDER ROOM: The area occupied by the Order Department.

OUT OF THE MONEY: An expression used to denote a securities option with a striking price that is unprofitable in comparison with the current market value of the underlying stock.

OVER-THE-COUNTER (OTC): A market for securities made up of securities dealers who may or may not be members of a securities exchange. "Over-the-counter" is mainly a market conducted over the telephone. Thousands of companies have insufficient shares outstanding, stockholders, or earnings to warrant application for listing on a national exchange. Securities of these companies are therefore traded in the over-the-counter market between dealers who act either as agents or as principals for their customers. The over-the-counter market is the principal market for U.S. Government and municipal bonds and for stocks of banks and insurance companies.

OVERTRADING: A practice of violation of NASD principles by which a broker/dealer overpays a customer for his security to enable him to subscribe to a security offered by that broker/dealer at a higher markup than the loss to be sustained when the firm sells the customer's security at prevailing market prices.

OW: An abbreviation for Offer Wanted indicating that the broker/dealer is soliciting sellers of the stock or bond.

P/E RATIO: *See* Price-Earnings Ratio.

P & S DEPARTMENT: An acronym for the Purchase and Sales Department. An operations group responsible for comparing transaction details with contra dealers, and for preparing confirmation notices for customers.

PAID-IN CAPITAL: The difference between par, or bookkeeping value of a security, and the amount realized from sale or distribution of those shares by the corporation.

PAPER LOSS: An unrealized loss on a security still held. Paper losses become actual when a security position is closed out by a purchase or sale.

PAPER PROFIT: An unrealized profit on a security still held. Paper profits become actual when a security position is closed out by a purchase or sale.

PAR: A dollar amount assigned to a share of stock by the corporation's charter. At one time, it reflected the value of the original investment behind each share, but today it has little significance except for bookkeeping purposes. Many corporations do not assign a par value to new issues. In preferred shares or bonds, it has importance insofar as it signifies the dollar value on which the dividend/interest is figured and the amount to be repaid upon redemption.

PAR VALUE: *See* Par; Face Value.

PARITY: (1) If no priority exists, the right of an execution is awarded to the broker who can at least completely fill the contra order. If more than one broker can fill the order, they match coins to determine which one will satisfy the contra broker. (2) Options are considered to be at parity when the striking price plus the premium (less the premium for a Put Option) equals the market price of the underlying stock.

PARTICIPATE BUT DO NOT INITIATE (PNI) ORDER: An order to obtain an overall favorable price through gradual and intermittent transactions, usually by a customer with substantial holdings who does not want to upset price equilibrium.

PARTICIPATING PREFERRED STOCK: Preferred stock that is entitled to its stated dividend and also to additional dividends on a specified basis if declared after payment of dividends on common stock.

PARTICIPATING TRUST: A unit investment company that issues shares reflecting on interest in a specified investment company.

PARTNERSHIP: A type of business organization typified by two or more proprietors.

PAYOUT RATIO: Common stock dividends divided by net income minus preferred dividends.

PENALTY SYNDICATE BID: A series of restrictive financial measures written into agreement among underwriters with the purpose of discouraging resale of securities requiring stabilization. A monetary penalty helps insure distribution to investment portfolios and not to traders and speculators seeking short-term profits at the expense of the underwriters.

PERIODIC PURCHASE DEFERRED CONTRACT: A variable annuity contract plan under which periodic payments may be applied to accumulate separate account units. Variable annuity payments are deferred until after the accumulation period.

PHILADELPHIA PLAN: An equipment trust bond calling for 20% of the original cost to be paid for by the issuer and the appointment of an independent trustee to supervise the issue.

PINK SHEETS: Named for the color of the paper used, one of the lists issued by the NQB identifying market-makers dealing in stocks of nationwide interest and giving representative bids and asks. (Yellow, green and white sheets refer to debt securities and to securities of regional interest.)

PIPELINE (CONDUIT) THEORY: A theory of investment by which tax liabilities of mutual funds are avoided by passing income and profits on to a fund's stockholders as dividends and capital distributions; the tax liabilities, ultimately, are widely dispersed and incurred among many shareholders.

PLAN COMPANIES: Companies registered with the SEC as unit investment companies who manage offerings of extended purchase contracts involving mutual fund shares, in behalf of underwriters.

PLUS TICK: A transaction on a stock exchange at a price higher than the price of the last transaction.

PNI ORDER: *See* Participate But Do Not Initiate (PNI) Order.

POINT: In stocks, a point means $1; in bonds, since a bond is quoted as a percentage of $1,000, it means $10. In market averages, it means simply a point—a unit of measure.

POINT AND FIGURE CHARTING: A method of technical analysis where significant price changes are plotted without regard to the timing of such changes.

PORTFOLIO: Holdings of securities by an individual or institution, which may include bonds and preferred and common stocks of various enterprises.

(THE) POT: A pool of securities, aside from those distributed among individual syndicate members, that is allocated by the manager for group sales. When "the pot is clean," the portion of the issue reserved for institutional (group) sales has been completely sold.

POWER OF ATTORNEY: (1) The legal right conferred by a person or institution upon another to act in the former's stead; (2) In the securities industry, a limited power of attorney given by a customer to a representative of a broker/dealer would normally give a registered representative trading discretion over the customer's account. The power is limited in that neither securities nor funds may be withdrawn from the account; (3) In the securities industry, an unlimited power of attorney given by a customer to a representative of a broker/dealer would normally give a registered representative full discretion over the conduct of the customer's account.

PRECEDENCE: If an execution of an order cannot be awarded to a broker on the basis of priority or parity, then precedence (the order filling the largest part of the contra order) assumes that right before any others.

PRE-EMPTIVE RIGHT: See Subscription Privilege (Pre-emptive Right).

PREFERENCE: If a broker with a parity can prove he was in the trading crowd before his competitors, prior to the appearance of the contra order that initiated the trading activity, he assumes the privilege of executing his order first without matching coins.

PREFERENCE INCOME: Taxable income which may be subject to additional Federal income tax known as the minimum tax computation.

PREFERENCE STOCK: See Prior Preferred (Preference) Stock.

PREFERRED DIVIDEND COVERAGE: Net income divided by total preferred dividends.

PREFERRED STOCK: Owners of this kind of stock are entitled to a fixed dividend to be paid regularly before dividends can be paid on common stock. They also exercise claims to assets, in the event of liquidation, senior to common stockholders but junior to bondholders. Preferred stockholders normally do not have a voice in management.

PREFERRED STOCK RATIO: The relationship of preferred stock outstanding to the total capitalization of a corporation.

PRELIMINARY AGREEMENT: An agreement between an issuing corporation and an underwriter drawn up prior to the effective date and pending a decision by the underwriter on the success potential of the new securities. See Indication of Interest.

PREMIUM: (1) The price of an option; (2) The time value portion of the price of an "in the money" option or warrant; (3) The difference between the strike price of an option plus the price paid for the option and the market value of the underlying stock of an "out of the money" option or warrant. Strike Price + Option Price − Market Value = Premium.

PREMIUM BOND: Any bond that sells at a price above the face amount. See Discount Bond.

PREMIUM, TRADING AT: A term used to describe debt instruments trading at a price above their maturity value (usually 100, or $1,000 per bond). For example: trading at 101 would mean that for $1,010 one could purchase a bond which would pay $1,000 principal at maturity.

PREPAID EXPENSE: Payments or deposits made for services, facilities or materials in advance of receipt or utilization. Prepaid expense is treated as an asset.

PRICE-EARNINGS RATIO: An equation used by some investors to gauge the relative value of a security in light of current market conditions. Ratio = Market Price ÷ Earnings Per Share.

PRICE/EQUITY RATIO: The ratio of the market place of a common share to the book value of a common share.

PRICE SPREAD: This option term is used interchangeably with Vertical Spread.

PRIMARY DISTRIBUTION (OFFERING): The original sale of a company's securities.

PRIMARY EARNINGS PER SHARE: A computation of earnings applicable to each share of common stock outstanding based upon the supposition that all common stock equivalent securities were exchanged for common stock at the beginning of that accounting period.

PRIMARY MARKET: (1) A term referring to organized stock exchanges; (2) A term used to define the new issue market as opposed to the secondary market.

PRIMARY MOVEMENT: A long-term (one to five years) movement or direction in the market.

PRIME RATE: The interest rate charged by a bank on loans made to its most creditworthy customers.

PRINCIPAL REGISTRATION: A form of registration with the NASD entitling the registrant to participate in all phases of the member organization except preparation and approval of the financial statements and net capital computations. *See* Financial Principal: Representative Registration.

PRINCIPAL TRANSACTION: *See* As Principal.

PRINCIPALS (STOCKHOLDERS):   The investors in a corporation with an equity interest, entitled to voting privileges, dividends, access to books and records, ready transferability of stock, proportionate shares of assets in liquidation, and subscription privileges.

PRIOR PREFERRED (PREFERENCE) STOCK: A kind of preferred stock entitling the owner to prior claim to forthcoming dividends or claims to assets in liquidation proceedings.

PRIORITY: The privilege of the first broker in the trading crowd at a particular price to execute his order before any of his competitors. If no priority exists, then parity, precedence, or preference may be used to award the execution.

PRIVATE PLACEMENT: The distribution of unregistered securities to a limited number of purchasers without the filing of a statement with the SEC. Such offerings generally require submission of an investment letter to the seller by all purchasers.

PROCEEDS SALES: *See* Switch (Contingent or Swap) Order.

PROFIT AND LOSS STATEMENT (P & L):   *See* Income Statement.

PROFIT MARGIN RATIO: A comparison of operating income to net sales.

PROPORTIONATE SHARE OF ASSETS IN LIQUIDATION: A common stockholder's right to assets in proportion to his interest, upon liquidation, after all liabilities have been satisfied.

PROPRIETARY: Refers to the assets of a brokerage firm and those of its principals that have been specifically pledged as their capital contribution to the organization.

PROPRIETARY ACCOUNT: An account used by broker/dealers for trading securities, options, or commodities for their own account and risk, as opposed to trading for their customers.

PROSPECTUS: A document stating material information for an impending offer of securities (containing most of the information included in the registration statement) that is used for solicitation purposes by the issuer and underwriters.

PROXY: A formal authorization from a stockholder that empowers someone to vote in his behalf.

PROXY CONTEST: A term used to describe the situation in which a person or group of people, other than a company's management, attempts to solicit shareholders' proxies, usually to change the management of the company.

PROXY DEPARTMENT: The department in a brokerage firm responsible for soliciting proxies from beneficial owners, collecting proxies from various sources, and voting those proxies in accordance with the rules of various authorities, including the SEC and the New York Stock Exchange.

PROXY STATEMENT: Material information required by the SEC to be given to a corporation's stockholders as a prerequisite to solicitation of votes. It is required for any issuer subject to the provisions of the Securities Exchange Act of 1934.

PRUDENT MAN INVESTMENT: A transaction in a quality security in such a fashion that is exemplified by the conduct of a conservative person managing his own assets.

PUBLIC RELATIONS AND INVESTOR SERVICES DEPARTMENT: The department of the NYSE responsible for, besides publc relations and investor services, almost all advertising and public communications practices of members and member organizations.

PURCHASE AND SALES DEPARTMENT: The department in operations responsible for the first processing of a trade. Responsibilities include the recording of order executions, figuring monies due and payable as a result of trades, preparing customer confirmations, and trade comparison with other brokers.

PURCHASING (BUYING) POWER: The amount of security value acquirable in a margin account solely from use of existing equity in excess of current Federal requirements.

PURPOSE LOAN: A loan, using corporate securities as collateral, that is used to purchase, trade, or carry margin securities. See Nonpurpose Loan.

PUT OPTION: A privilege giving its holder the right to demand acceptance ofhis delivery of 100 shares of stock at a fixed price anytime within a specified lifetime. Sometimes referred to as a seller's option.

QUICK ASSET RATIO: See Acid Test Ratio.

QUICK ASSETS: Cash, cash equivalents and accounts receivable.

QUOTATION OR QUOTE: See Bid and Asked (Quotation or Quote).

RALLY: A brisk rate following a decline in the general price level of the market or for an individual stock.

RAN: See Revenue Anticipation Note.

RANGE: A set of prices consisting of the opening sale, high sale, low sale, and latest sale of the day for a given security.

READY TRANSFERABILITY OF SHARES: A shareholder's right to give away or sell shares without prior consultation with corporate directors.

REAL ESTATE INVESTMENT TRUST: A closed end investment company investing in various ventures related to the field of real estate.

RECEIVER-IN-BANKRUPTCY: An impartial, court-appointed administrator of a corporation that has sought protection from its creditors' claims under Federal bankruptcy laws. He is appointed to help the court decide between liquidation or reorganization and is remunerated out of the remaining assets of the corporation.

RECEIVER'S CERTIFICATES: Short-term (90 to 120 days) debt obligations issued by a receiver for a bankrupt corporation to supply working capital during the receiver's inquiry. These obligations take priority over the claims of all other creditors.

RECLAMATION: The privilege of a seller in a transaction to recover his certificates and return the contract money, or of a buyer to recover his contract money and return the certificates, should any irregularity be discovered upon delivery and settlement of the contract. See Rejection.

RECORD DATE: The day on which a company closes its stockholder register for the purpose of identifying the recipients of a forthcoming dividend distribution or other right.

RED HERRING: A preliminary prospectus for securities to be offered publicly by a corporation or underwriter. It is the only form of written communication allowed between a broker and potential purchaser before the effective date. The Securities Act of 1933 requires a red-lettered caveat on the front page; hence, the derivation of the name.

REDEMPTION: (1) For bonds, the retirement of these securities by repayment of face value or above to their holders; (2) For mutual funds, the shareholder's privilege of converting his interest in the fund into cash—normally at net asset value.

REFUNDING (REFINANCING): The issuance of a new debt security (bond) using the proceeds to redeem older bonds at maturity or outstanding bonds issued under less favorable terms and conditions.

REG. T CALL: A notice to a customer of a broker/dealer that additional equity is needed in his account to meet the minimum standards set by Regulation T of the Federal Reserve.

REG. T EXCESS: The amount of equity in a customer's account above the minimum requirements of Regulation T of the Federal Reserve.

REGISTERED AS TO INTEREST ONLY: Bonds which are registered as to interest and on which interest checks are sent to the registered owner, but which are payable to the bearer at maturity.

REGISTERED AS TO PRINCIPAL ONLY: Bonds which are registered and which are payable at maturity to the registered holder; but which have coupons attached that must be presented by the bearer periodically for payment.

REGISTERED BONDS: Outstanding bonds whose owners' names are recorded on the books of the issuing corporation. Legal title may be transferred only when endorsed by the registered owner.

REGISTERED FORM: Securities issued in a form to allow the owner's name to be imprinted on the certificate and which allow the issuer to maintain records as to the identity of the owners. Opposite of Bearer Form.

REGISTERED OPTIONS PRINCIPAL: An individual who has been approved by an options exchange to supervise the conduct of customers' accounts in which there are listed options transactions.

REGISTERED SECONDARY DISTRIBUTIONS: Offerings of securities by affiliated persons that require an effective registration statement on file with the SEC before distribution may be attempted.

REGISTERED (FLOOR) TRADER: A member of the NYSE who buys and sells stocks for his own account and risk.

REGISTERED PRINCIPAL: *See* Principal Registration.

REGISTRAR: Often a trust company or bank, the registrar is charged with the responsibility of preventing the issuance of more stock than authorized by the company. It insures that the transfer agent issues exactly the same number of shares canceled with each reregistration of certificates.

REGISTRATION STATEMENT: A document required to be filed with the SEC by the issuer of securities before a public offering may be attempted. The Securities Act of 1933 mandates that it contain all material and accurate facts. Such a statement is required also when affiliated persons intend offering sizable amounts of securities. The SEC examines the statement for a 20-day period, seeking obvious omissions or misrepresentations of fact.

REGULAR SPECIALIST: A specialist of the NYSE who continually solicits and executes orders in listed stocks assigned to him. He also maintains an orderly market and provides price continuity via transactions for his own account and risk. *See* Associate Specialist; Relief Specialist.

REGULAR WAY CONTRACT: The most frequently used delivery contract. For stocks and corporate and municipal bonds, this type of contract calls for delivery on the fifth business day after the trade. For U.S. Government bonds, delivery must be made on the first business day after the trade.

REGULATED COMPANIES: Investment companies that meet certain criteria for eligibility and are, therefore, exempted by the IRS from paying taxes on investment income, after expenses.

REGULATION G: A Federal Reserve Board regulation requiring any person, other than a bank or broker/dealer, who extends credit secured directly or indirectly with margin securities to register and be subject to Federal Reserve Board jurisdiction.

REGULATION T: A Federal Reserve Board regulation that explains the conduct and operation of general and special accounts within the offices of a broker/dealer firm, prescribing a code of conduct for the effective use and supervision of credit.

REGULATION U: A Federal Reserve Board regulation that regulates the extension of credit by banks where securities are used as collateral. *See* Nonpurpose Loan; Purpose Loan.

REGULATION W: The regulation of the Federal Reserve Board regulating consumer installment loans.

REGULATION X: Rules established by the Federal Reserve Board that place equal burdens of responsibility for compliance with Regulations G, T, and U on the borrower as well as the lender.

REHYPOTHECATION: A broker's practice of pledging customer securities from a margin account to serve as collateral at a bank in order to finance the customer's debit balance in this account.

REJECTION: The privilege of the purchaser in a transaction to refuse a delivery lacking in negotiability or presented in the wrong denominations, without prejudice to his rights in the transaction. *See* Reclamation.

RELIEF SPECIALIST: A specialist of the NYSE affiliated with regular specialists and capable of substituting for that specialist for a limited period of time. He has the same responsibility as the regular specialist while substituting for him.

REORGANIZED DEPARTMENT: The department in a brokerage firm responsible for effecting the conversion of securities. For example, the Department would accomplish conversion for a customer owning convertible bonds to be converted and used to fulfill his sale of the underlying common stocks.

REPEAT PRICES OMITTED: A ticker tape announcement to signify that the tape has fallen three minutes behind transactions on the trading floor. Sequential transactions at the same price are then purposely eliminated from the tape; only the first trade prices in a string of transactions appears.

REPO: *See* Repurchase Agreement.

REPRESENTATIONS TO MANAGEMENT: When any member of the NYSE or person associated with a member wishes to represent a corporation or its stockholders, he must meet certain rules established by the Exchange.

REPRESENTATIVE REGISTRATION: The minimum NASD qualification for solicitors of investment banking or securities business, traders, assistant officers of member firms, and training directors and assistants. *See* Financial Principal; Principal Registration.

REPURCHASE AGREEMENT (REPO): (1) A Federal Open Market Committee arrangement with a dealer in which it contracts to purchase a government or agency security at a fixed price, with provision for its resale at the same price at a rate of interest determined competitively; (2) A method of financing inventory positions by sale to a non-bank institution with the agreement to buy the position back.

RESERVE CITY BANK: A commercial bank with its main office in a city where a Central Bank or branch is located that has net demand deposits exceeding $400 million.

RESERVE FOR DEPLETION: *See* Allowance for Depletion.

RESERVE FOR DEPRECIATION: *See* Allowance for Depreciation.

RESERVE REQUIREMENT: The obligation of a commercial bank to set aside and refrain from lending a percentage of its available currency. This is a form of protection for depositors.

RESTRICTED ACCOUNT: (1) A margin account in which the equity is less than the current Federal requirement; (2) A cash account which has failed to pay for a purchase under Regulation T and must have cash in the account prior to executing a buy for a period of 90 days.

RESTRICTED CATEGORIES: Five categories of people outlined by the NASD Board of Governors and declared ineligible for allocations of hot issues, along with their immediate families.

RETAINED EARNINGS: An account reflecting net income earned by a corporation over a period of years, that has not been distributed to the stockholders as dividends.

RETENTION REQUIREMENT: The amount of money necessary to be withheld in a loan after sale or withdrawal of a portion of the collateral, presently 70 percent of the proceeds of the sale, or current market value of the securities to be withdrawn.

RETIREMENT OF DEBT SECURITIES: The repayment of principal and accrued interest due to the holders of a bond issue.

RETURN: *See* Yield.

RETURN OF CAPITAL DIVIDEND: A dividend paid by a corporation, in cash or kind, which is not paid from retained earnings. The striking price of a listed option will be reduced by such a distribution to the nearest ⅛th dollar. The striking price of a conventional option will be reduced by the exact amount of the dividend.

RETURN ON COMMON EQUITY: Net profit divided by book value per share of common stock.

RETURN ON EQUITY: Net income divided by shareholder's equity.

RETURN ON INVESTED CAPITAL: Net income plus interest expense divided by total capitalization.

REVENUE ANTICIPATION NOTE: A short-term municipal debt instrument usually offered on a discount basis. Proceeds of future revenues are pledged as collateral to the payment of the note at maturity.

REVENUE BONDS: Tax-exempted bonds whose interest payment is dependent upon, secured by, and redeemable from the income generated by a particular project financed by their issuance.

REVERSE CONVERSION: A term used to describe the creation of a Put Option from a Call Option by means of taking a short position in the underlying equity.

REVERSE REPURCHASE AGREEMENT: (1) For Federal Open Market Committee transactions, synonymous with matched sale/purchase agreements; (2) A transaction by which a broker/dealer provides funds to his customers by means of purchasing a security with a contract to sell it at the same price plus interest.

REVERSE SPLIT: A means by which a corporation reduces the number of shares outstanding by issuing one new share for more than one old share. For example, a corporation calls all of its old shares and issues one new share for each five old shares held. The purpose of such a move would be to increase the price per share in the market.

RIGHT: *See* Subscription Right.

RIGHTS OF ACCUMULATION: A privilege offered by some investment companies that allows the investor to include the total market value of shares already owned in calculating sales charges when a new investment is made in additional shares.

RISK ARBITRAGE: A purchase and short sale of potentially equal securities at prices that may realize a profit. *See* Bona Fide Arbitrage.

RISKLESS TRANSACTION: *See* Simultaneous (Riskless) Transactions.

ROLLOVER: (1) The reinvestment of funds received from the maturity of a debt instrument into another debt instrument; (2) A term used to describe moving funds in a tax-free transaction from one retirement plan to another.

ROP: An acronym for Registered Options Principal.
ROUND LOT: A unit of trading or a multiple thereof. On the NYSE, stocks are traded in round lots of 100 shares for active stocks and 10 shares for inactive ones. Bonds are traded in units of $1,000. *See* Normal Trading Unit; Odd Lot.
RULE 15c2-11:   An SEC rule regulating submission and representation of quotations of little-known securities whose asset value is questionable.
RULE 15c3-1:   An SEC rule pertaining to definition and calculation of a registered broker/dealer's minimum net capital.
RULE 15c3-3:   An SEC rule pertaining to a registered broker/dealer's requirements for protecting his customers' money and securities from improper use by the firm in the conduct of its own business.
RULE 144:   An SEC rule permitting the occasional sale of restricted ("letter") securities in modest amounts by certain persons without registration with the SEC.
RULE 237:   An SEC rule that permits nonaffiliated holders of restricted ("letter") securities to sell them publicly under certain conditions, if they cannot dispose of them privately due to circumstances beyond their control.
RULE 405:   An NYSE rule requiring its membership to perform a proper investigation into the financial affairs of each customer prior to, and during, a business relationship with that party. This directive is also referred to as the "know your customer" rule.
RULES OF FAIR PRACTICE: A set of rules established and maintained by the NASD Board of Governors regulating the ethics employed by members in the conduct of their business.
RUN ON A BANK: A situation in which substantial numbers of depositors, fearing for the safety of their funds, seek withdrawal of their balances in currency.
RVP TRADE: "Receive versus payment," this signifies a transaction in which a broker/dealer is obliged to make payment upon receipt of securities from a customer or contra dealer. *See also* C.O.D. Trade.

S: A symbol on the ticker tape meaning 100 shares if preceded by a single digit— or the actual quantity if preceded by more than one digit. For example: T means 200 shares of A.T.&T. at 50½.   2s50½
S.   A symbol on the ticker tape meaning actual quantity in a security which trades
S'   in round lots of 10 shares.
S.   A symbol on the ticker tape meaning stopped.
T
SAFEKEEPING: A protected condition maintained as a service by a brokerage firm for its customers' fully-paid securities registered in the customers' own names. The practice entails use of vault space to store those certificates until they are withdrawn or sold.
SAME DAY SUBSTITUTION: A provision of Regulation T of the Federal Reserve which allows a customer to sell securities and buy securities of a lesser or equal amount without meeting initial margin requirements on the purchase.
SAVINGS DEPOSIT: An interest-earning deposit in a commercial bank subject to immediate withdrawal.
SCALE ORDERS: Multiple limit orders entered by investors at various prices but at the same time. The purpose is to obtain an overall, or average, favorable purchase or sale price. Multiples of round lots may be bought at prices scaled down from a given value, or sold at prices scaled up from a given value.
SCC: *See* Stock Clearing Corporation (SCC).
SCHEDULE C: A set of criteria contained in the NASD by-laws whereby various

persons associated with a member organization must qualify and register with the association as principal, financial principal, or representative.

SEAT (FRANCHISE): A membership in the Exchange. A seat must be owned by an individual who is a U.S. citizen and at least twenty-one years of age; it may be sold at auction to the highest bidder or transferred for a nominal consideration, both means subject to approval by the Exchange's Board of Directors. See Allied Member.

SEC: The Securities and Exchange Commission, a Government agency responsible for supervision and regulation of the securities industry.

SEC STATEMENT OF POLICY: A policy set forth by the SEC, governing fair and proper sales representations of mutual funds to the public. It encompasses both verbal and written practices employed to solicit or distribute those shares.

SECO MEMBER: A broker/dealer who is not a member of a registered stock exchange or of the NASD. The initials stand for Securities and Exchange Commission Organization, to denote its registration with the commission.

SECONDARY DISTRIBUTION (OFFERING): A public offering of stock by selling stockholders. If listed on the NYSE, a member firm may be employed to facilitate such an offering in an over-the-counter net transaction for a purchaser, with prior approval of the Exchange. Both member and nonmember broker/dealer can participate in this distribution.

SECONDARY MARKET: (1) A term referring to the trading of securities not listed on an organized exchange; (2) A term used to describe the trading of securities other than a new issue.

SECONDARY MOVEMENT: A short-term movement in the market in the opposite direction from the primary movement.

SECONDHAND OPTION: See Special Option.

SECURED OBLIGATION: A debt whose payment of interest and/or principal is ensured by the pledge of physical assets.

SECURITIES: Any note, stock bond, evidence of debt, interest or participation in a profit-sharing agreement, investment contract, voting trust certificate, fractional undivided interest in oil, gas, or other mineral rights, or any warrant to subscribe to, or purchase, any of the foregoing or other similar instruments.

SECURITIES ACT OF 1933: Federal legislation designed to protect the public in the issuance and distribution of securities by providing full and accurate information about an issue to prospective purchasers.

SECURITIES EXCHANGE ACT OF 1934: Federal legislation designed to protect the public against unfair and inequitable practices on stock exchanges and in over-the-counter markets throughout the United States.

SECURITIES INDUSTRY AUTOMATION CORPORATION: A corporation owned two-thirds by the New York Stock Exchange and one-third by the American Stock Exchange. The Corporation is under contract to receive trade information from the two exchanges and from their members for the purpose of assisting in final settlement. To perform this function SIAC will issue balance orders and Continuous Net Settlement information to the members.

SECURITIES INVESTOR PROTECTION CORPORATION (SIPC): A Government-sponsored private corporation that guarantees repayment of money and securities in customer accounts valued at up to $100,000 per separate customer, in the event of a broker/dealer bankruptcy.

SECURITY DISTRICTS: Administrative districts (thirteen in number, that encompass the United States) established by the NASD, each governed by a district committee and represented on the association's Board of Governors.

SEGREGATED SECURITIES: Customer-owned securities fully paid for or representing excess collateral in a margin account that are locked away and cannot be used in the conduct of the firm's business.

SEGREGATION: A protected condition maintained by a brokerage firm for its customers' fully-paid securities and those representing excess collateral in margin accounts. *See* Rule 15c3-3.

SELLER'S OPTION: (1) In stocks or bonds, a settlement contract by which delivery of the certificates is due at the purchaser's office on a specific date (usually within sixty calendar days of the trade date) stated in the contract at the time of purchase; expressed as "Seller's 24," "Seller's 39," and so forth; (2) A Put Option.

SELLING CONCESSION: A fraction of an underwriter's spread, granted to a selling group member by agreement. It is payment for services as a sales agent for the underwriters.

SELLING DIVIDENDS: The unfair and unethical practice of soliciting purchase orders for mutual fund shares solely on the basis of an impending distribution by that fund.

SELLING GROUP: Selected broker/dealers of the NASD who contract to act as selling agents for underwriters and who are compensated by a portion of the sales charge (selling concession) on newly issued stocks. They assume no personal responsibility for financial liability to the issuer.

SELLING-OUT PROCEDURE: Upon failure of the purchasing firm to accept delivery of the security and lacking proper rejection form, the seller can, without notice, dispose of that security in the marketplace at the best available price and hold the buyer responsible for any financial loss resulting from the default. *See* Buy-In Procedure.

SELL-PLUS: A market or limit order to sell a security at a price higher than the previous different-priced transaction for that security.

SELL-STOP ORDER: A memorandum that becomes a market order to sell if and when someone trades a round lot at, or below, the memorandum price.

SENIOR OPTIONS PRINCIPAL: The senior partner or officer of a member firm holding the ultimate responsibility for the conduct of the firm's options business.

SEPARATE ACCOUNT: A specialized legal entity created by an insurance company to incorporate contracts offered by the company under a variable annuity plan.

SEPARATE CUSTOMER: As defined by SIPC, the accounts of a given customer at a single brokerage firm. Different types of accounts held by the same person do not constitute "separate customers."

SERIAL BOND: An issue that matures in relatively small amounts at periodic stated intervals.

SERIES E SAVINGS BONDS: Nonmarketable Federal savings bonds of various denominations (minimum of $50) offered at a price below face value and redeemed at face value five years later; they have a ballooning interest rate averaging 6 percent yearly.

SERIES H SAVINGS BONDS: Nonmarketable Federal savings bonds of various denominations (minimum of $500) offered and redeemed at face value, bearing interest every six months during a lifetime of ten years.

SETTLEMENT (DELIVERY) DATE: The day on which certificates involved in a transaction are due at the purchaser's office.

SEVERALLY AND JOINTLY: A phrase included in a typical corporate underwriting agreement by which each member of the syndicate agrees to be liable only for his allocation of the issue and not for allocations that his fellow underwriters failed to dispose of. Such a relationship is called a "divided" or "western" account.

SHAREHOLDERS: See Principals (Shareholders).

SHAREHOLDERS' EQUITY: The financial interest of the stockholders in the net assets of a company. It is the aggregate of the preferred and common stockholders' accounts as depicted on a balance sheet.

SHELF DISTRIBUTION: A privilege written into a registration statement by an affiliated person, by which he may dispose of sizable amounts of securities from his portfolio (shelf) over a nine-month period following the effective date. For OTC transactions, order tickets must be marked "distribution stock"; for exchange sales, "DIST."

SHELL COMPANY: A corporation without assets or any apparent business activity.

SHOPPING THE STREET: In the OTC market, the canvassing by a broker/dealer of competing market-makers for quotations to determine a basis for price negotiation. See Firm Market; Subject Market; Workout Market.

SHORT-AGAINST-THE-BOX: A situation in which a person is both long and short in the same security at the same time in his account, a practice usually employed to defer tax liability on capital gains.

SHORT INTEREST THEORY: Short Interest (positions) are reported each month as of the fifteenth. There is a theory which postulates that an increase in the short interest is bullish since those customers who are short must buy back that position causing a demand for securities. Conversely, a decline in short interest would be bearish.

SHORT MARKET VALUE: The market value of security positions which a customer owes to a broker/dealer (short in his account).

SHORT POSITION: One of three conditions: (1) The number of shares in a given security sold short and not covered as of a particular date; (2) the total amount of stock sold short by all investors and not covered as of a particular date; (3) a term used to denote the writer of an option.

SHORT SALE: The sale of a security that is not owned at the time of the trade, necessitating its purchase some time in the future to "cover" the sale. A short sale is made with the expectation that the stock value will decline, so that when the sale is finally covered, it will be at a price lower than the original sale, thus realizing a profit. Before the sale is covered, the broker/dealer borrows stock (for which he puts up collateral) to deliver on the settlement date.

SHORT SELLING POWER: The dollar amount of equity securities a customer may sell short without additional funds and continue to meet the initial margin requirements of Regulation T of the Federal Reserve. Computed as Reg. T excess ÷ Reg. T initial margin requirements. For example, $10,000 ÷ 50% = $20,000.

SHORT-STOP (LIMIT) ORDER: A memorandum that becomes a limit order to sell short when someone creates a round-lot transaction at, or below, the memorandum price (electing sale); the short sale may or may not be executed since the rules then require that it be sold at least one-eighth above the electing sale as well as high enough in value to satisfy the limit price.

SHORT-TERM CAPITAL TRANSACTION: A purchase and subsequent sale in one year or less; or a short sale and a purchase to cover at a profit within any time period.

S I A C: An aconym for Securities Industry Automation Corporation.

SILENT PARTNER: A member of a partnership represented only by capital and not entitled to a voice in management.

SIMULTANEOUS (RISKLESS) TRANSACTION: A transaction in which the broker/dealer takes a position in a security only after receipt of an order from a customer, and only for the purpose of acting as principal so as to disguise his remuneration from the transaction.

SINGLE PURCHASE IMMEDIATE CONTRACT: A variable annuity contract plan under which a single payment is made for units of the separate account and variable annuity payments commence immediately.

SINKING FUND: An annual reserve of capital required to be set aside out of current earnings to provide monies for retirement of an outstanding bond issue. Such a feature has favorable effect on the market value of that issue.

SIPC: *See* Securities Investor Protection Corporation (SIPC).

SLD: *See* Sold Sale.

SMA: *See* Special Miscellaneous Account (SMA).

SOLD LAST SALE: A ticker tape identification for a transaction that has fluctuated volatilely between sales. It appears for an issue that has moved one or more points if its previous sale as 19⅞ or below, two or more points if its previous sale was 20 or above.

SOLD SALE: A transaction appearing on the ticker tape out of its proper sequence.

SOP: *See* Senior Options Principal.

SPECIAL ARBITRAGE ACCOUNT: An account in which a customer purchases a security and, at about the same time either (1) sells it in a different market; or (2) sells an equal security in the same or different market, to take advantage of a difference in prices. Such an account is entitled to special margin requirements under Regulation T of the Federal Reserve.

SPECIAL BID: A procedure on the New York Stock Exchange to facilitate bids for a large block of stock. Regulations are similar to those regarding a special offer.

SPECIAL BOND ACCOUNT: An account in which a customer may favorably finance his purchase of (1) exempted securities or (2) nonconvertible bonds traded on registered stock exchanges in the U.S. The account is defined in Regulation T of the Federal Reserve.

SPECIAL CASH ACCOUNT: An account in which the customer is required to make full payment on the fifth business day after the trade date, and in no case later than the seventh calendar day (see Frozen Account), or arrange for C.O.D. payment on the fifth business day. The account is defined in Regulation T of the Federal Reserve.

SPECIAL CONVERTIBLE SECURITY ACCOUNT: An account used to finance activity in debt securities traded on a registered stock exchange and that (1) are convertible into a margin stock or (2) carry a warrant or right to subscribe to a margin stock. The account is defined in Regulation T of the Federal Reserve.

SPECIAL DEALS: A mutual fund underwriter's improper practice of disbursing anything of material value (more than $25 in value per person annually) in addition to normal discounts or concessions associated with the sale or distribution of investment company shares.

SPECIAL MISCELLANEOUS ACCOUNT (SMA): An account defined under Regulation T used to record a customer's excess margin and buying power.

SPECIAL OFFERING: The disposal of a large block of stock in accordance with certain terms and conditions, by inviting members of the Exchange to place buy orders on the floor to be executed by crossing in the normal procedure. The seller pays a special commission.

SPECIAL OMNIBUS ACCOUNT: A brokerage account maintained by one broker/dealer in behalf of customer transactions of another broker/dealer. Execution and clearing services are provided by the carrying firm without ever knowing the identities of the introducing firm's customers, whose activities are processed under the introducing firm's name. The account is defined in Regulation T of the Federal Reserve.

SPECIAL OPTION: Also known as a secondhand option, this is an over-the-counter option with some remaining lifetime that is offered for resale by a put and call broker or dealer in a secondary market transaction.

SPECIAL SUBSCRIPTION ACCOUNT: An account under Regulation T of the Federal Reserve in which a customer can receive favorable financing arrangements for the purpose of subscribing to new issue securities.

SPECIAL TAX BOND: A municipal bond whose payment of interest and/or principal is contingent upon the collection of a tax imposed against those who will benefit from the use of the funds obtained from the issuance of the bond.

SPECIALIST: A member of the NYSE with two essential functions. First, he maintains an orderly market, insofar as reasonably practicable, in the stocks in which he is registered as a specialist. To do this, he must buy and sell for his own account and risk, to a reasonable degree, when there is a temporary disparty between supply and demand. In order to equalize trends, he must buy or sell counter to direction of the market. Second, he acts as a broker's broker, executing orders when another broker cannot afford the time. At all times the specialist must put his customer's interest before his own. All specialists are registered with the NYSE as regular, substitute, associate, or temporary.

SPECIALIST BLOCK PURCHASE/SALE: With the approval of a floor official, a specialist may transact business with another member firm representing an institutional investor for a large block of stock for his own portfolio in a private over-the-counter transaction. If he buys, he buys at a price lower than the prevailing floor price. If he sells, he sells at a price somewhat higher.

SPECIALIST BOOK: The notebook a NYSE specialist in a given security uses to keep a record of the buy and sell orders he receives for execution at specified prices.

SPECIAL UNITS: Units of three or more fully-qualified specialists who have banded together in a partnership or corporation for the purpose of maintaining an orderly market in specific stocks.

SPECIALIZED COMPANIES: Investment companies that concentrate their investments in one industry, group or related industries, or a single geographic area of the world for the purpose of long-term capital growth.

SPECULATION: The employment of funds for relatively large and immediate gains, in which the safety of principal is of secondary importance.

SPIN OFF: A distribution of stock in a company that is owned by another corporation and that is being allocated to the holders of the latter institution.

SPLIT: A division of the outstanding shares of a corporation into a large number of shares, by which each outstanding share entitles its owner to a fixed number of new shares. The shareholder's overall equity remains the same, though he owns more stock, since the total value of the shares remains the same. For example, the owner of a hundred shares, each worth $100, would be given two hundred shares, each worth $50, in a two-for-one split.

SPLIT DOWN: A corporate reorganization whereby the holder of a security must return his certificate to the issuer and receive proportionately fewer shares in exchange.

SPLIT OFFERING: (1) An offering combining both a primary and secondary distribution; (2) A term used to describe a Municipal Bond Offering, part of which are serial bonds and part of which are term bonds.

SPLIT RATING: A term used to describe the situation where a Corporation has been given different credit quality ratings by different services.

SPLIT UP: A corporate recapitalization in which the holder of a security receives proportionately more shares from the issuer in relation to his current ownership in the company.

SPONSOR: *See* Underwriter.

SPOT SECONDARY DISTRIBUTION: A secondary distribution that does not require an SEC registration statement and may be attempted on the spot, without delay.

SPREAD: (1) The difference in value between the bid and offering prices; (2) The simultaneous purchase and sale of the same class of options; (3) underwriting compensation.

SPREAD OPTION: (1) In the OTC market one put and one call option carrying the same expiration date but different striking prices. The call is written with a strike price above that current value of the underlying stock, while the put is written with a strike price below that value; (2) The simultaneous purchase and sale of listed options of the same class.

SPREAD ORDER: An order to execute the simultaneous purchase and sale of options of the same class for either a net debit or a net credit without regard to the prices of the individual options.

SPREAD POSITION: *See* Spread Option.

STABILIZATION: The syndicate manager is empowered by the members of his group to maintain a bid in the aftermarket at or slightly below the public offering price, thus "stabilizing" the market and giving the syndicate and selling-group members a reasonable chance of successfully disposing of their allocations. This practice is a legal exception to the manipulation practices outlawed by the Securities and Exchange Act of 1934.

STANDARD & POOR'S INDEX: A market index consisting of 425 industrial, 20 transportation, and 55 public utility common stocks.

STANDARD AND POOR'S STOCK REPORTS: Periodically-issued information on publicly-held corporations and their common stocks.

STAND-BY UNDERWRITING AGREEMENT: An agreement between an investment banker and a corporation, whereby the banker agrees for a negotiated fee to purchase any or all shares offered as a subscription privilege that are not bought by the rights holders by the time the offer expires.

STATED PERCENTAGE ORDER: An order by institutional or other substantial investors to buy or sell a certain percentage of the market volume of a given security. The purpose is to avoid upsetting prices that reflect normal supply and demand conditions.

STATEMENT OF PURPOSE: A document required of a borrower who is using margin securities as collateral for a loan, stating the purpose of the loan.

STATUTORY UNDERWRITER: *See* Involuntary (Statutory) Underwriter.

STATUTORY VOTING: A means by which a stockholder is given the right to cast one vote for each share owned in favor of or against each of a number of proposals or director/nominees at a formal meeting convened by the corporation.

STOCK AHEAD: An expression used on the floor of the New York Stock Exchange to signify that one or more brokers has made a prior bid (or offer) at the same price as an order you have entered.

STOCK CLEARING CORPORATION: Formerly a NYSE subsidiary responsible for arranging daily transaction clearances, preparation of balance orders to receive and deliver, a singular money settlement for members, and a centralized location for making physical deliveries of certificates. The Stock Clearing Corporation was merged into the National Securities Clearing Corporation.

STOCK DIVIDEND DISTRIBUTION: A distribution to shareholders made upon declaration of a corporation's board of directors. This distribution differs from the usual disbursement in that it is given in the form of additional shares of stock instead of money.

STOP LIMIT ORDER: A memorandum that becomes a limit order only if a transaction takes place at or through the price stated in the memorandum. The sale that activates the memorandum is called the electing sale.

STOCK LIST DEPARTMENT: A department of the NYSE responsible for (1) examining the eligibility of corporations applying for listing and trading on the Exchange; (2) supervising distributions of proxies to beneficial owners of shares held in street name by member organizations.

STOCK (OR BOND) POWER: A legal document, either on the back of registered stocks and bonds or attached to them, by which the owner assigns his interest in the corporation to a third party, allowing that party the right to substitute another name on the company records in place of the original owner's.

STOCK RECORD: The records of a brokerage firm showing the beneficial owner (long) and the location (short) of every security entrusted to the firm. Longs and shorts must be equal (in balance) since for every beneficial owner there must be a location.

STOCK RECORD DEPARTMENT: The department in a brokerage firm responsible for maintaining a balanced stock record.

STOCKHOLDER: See Principals (Shareholders).

STOCKHOLDERS' EQUITY: See Shareholders' Equity.

STOCKS: Certificates representing ownership in a corporation; they may yield dividends and can appreciate or decline in value. *See* Authorized Stock: Common Stock; Issued Stock; Preferred Stock; Treasury Stock; Unissued Stock.

STOP LIMIT ORDER: A memorandum that becomes a limit (as opposed to a market) order immediately after a transaction takes place at or through the indicated (memorandum) price.

STOP ORDER: A memorandum that becomes a market order only if a transaction takes place at or through the price stated in the memorandum. The sale that activates the memorandum is called the electing sale. *See* Market Order; Sell-Stop Order.

STOPPED OUT: An expression reflecting a broker's unsuccessful attempt to improve upon the price of a transaction after having been guaranteed an execution price by the specialist.

STOPPING STOCK: A specialist's guarantee of price to a broker, thus enabling the broker to try to improve upon that price without fear of missing the market.

STRADDLE OPTION: One put and one call option on the same underlying security carrying the same striking price and expiration date.

STRAIGHT-LINE DEPRECIATION: An accounting procedure for apportioning a corporation's cost of a qualified asset in equal increments over its useful lifetime.

STRAP OPTION: In the OTC market one put and two call options on the same underlying security carrying the same striking price and expiration date. The total premium for this quantity transaction is generally cheaper than if the options were purchased separately.

STREET NAME: When securities have been bought on margin or when the customer wishes the security to be held by the broker/dealer, the securities are registered and held in the broker/dealer's own firm name.

STRIKING PRICE: The contract price of a stock at which the holder of an option may require its writer to perform a transaction as agreed upon in the original privilege.

STRIP OPTION: In the OTC market, one call and two put options on the same underlying security carrying the same striking price and expiration date. The total premium for this quantity transaction is generally cheaper than if the options were purchased separately.

SUBJECT MARKET: In the OTC market, a range of buying or selling prices, quoted by a market-maker, at which he is unable to trade immediately. Such prices are "subject to verification" by the party whose market he represents.

SUBORDINATED DEBT INSTRUMENTS: A debt instrument where repayment of principal may not be made until another debt instrument senior to it has been repaid in full.

SUBSCRIPTION PRIVILEGE (PRE-EMPTIVE RIGHT): A shareholder's right to purchase newly-issued shares or bonds (before the public offering). It must be exercised within a fixed period of time, usually thirty to sixty days, before the privilege expires and becomes worthless.

SUBSCRIPTION RATIO: The ratio of old stock to new stock offered as a subscription privilege.

SUBSCRIPTION RIGHT: A privilege granted to the owner of certain stocks to purchase newly-issued securities in proportion to his holdings, usually at values below the current market price. Rights have a market value of their own and are actively traded. They differ from warrants in that they must be exercised within a relatively short period of time.

SUBSTANTIAL NET CAPITAL: Each member of the New York Stock Exchange is required to maintain substantial net capital as defined by NYSE Rule 325.

SUBSTANTIVE INTEREST: A term referring to a matter raised at a corporate meeting that affects stockholder participation in the company. It includes a contest of control, changing the purpose of powers of the corporation, altering its capitalization, authorizing the expenditure of capital funds, and the like.

SUBSTITUTION: The sale of one security in an account to use the proceeds to pay for the purchase of another security on the same trade date. See Switch (contingent, or Swap) Order.

SUM-OF-YEARS DIGITS DEPRECIATION: A somewhat accelerated accounting procedure used to write off the cost of a qualified asset over the period of its useful lifetime to the corporation.

SUMMARY COMPLAINT PROCEEDINGS: In the event of a minor infraction of NASD Rules of Fair Practice, the Business Conduct Committee may offer the accused member a penalty of censure and/or fine up to $1,000, if he wishes to plead guilty, waive formal hearings, and all rights of appeal.

SUNDRY ASSET: An item of value to be held by a corporation for an indefinite time. This category includes unimproved land and investments in subsidiary concerns.

SUPER-RESTRICTED ACCOUNT: A margin account in which the equity is less than 30 percent of the market value of the collateral in the account.

SUPPORT AND RESISTANCE: A technical market theory that attempts to predetermine price levels at which eager investor purchases will develop (support) or aggressive selling may appear (resistance), based upon previous fluctuations for a particular security.

SUSPENSE ACCOUNT: A record maintained by a broker/dealer to reflect unreconciled money and securities differences in its business activities.

SWAP ORDR: See Switch (Contingent, or Swap) Order.

SWITCH (CONTINGENT, OR SWAP) ORDER: An order to buy one security and then sell another at a limit, or to sell one security and then to buy another at a limit. The transaction may also be called a proceeds sale, if as is usually the case the proceeds of the sell order are applied against the expenses of the buy order.

SYNDICATE: A group of investment bankers, usually organized along historical or social lines, with one member acting as manager, that collectively insures the successful offering of a corporation's securities.

TAN: *See* Tax Anticipation Note.

TAX ANTICIPATION BILLS (TAB): Treasury bills with maturity dates fixed several days after a major tax payment date with a proviso enabling their holders to tender them at face value in satisfaction of their tax requirement and earn a little extra interest in the process.

TAX ANTICIPATION NOTE: A short-term municipal note usually offered on a discount basis. The proceeds of a forthcoming tax collection are pledged to repay the note.

TAX-EXEMPTED SECURITIES: Obligations issued by a state or municipality whose interest payments (but not profits via purchase or sale) are exempted from Federal taxation. The interest payment may be exempted from local taxation, too, if purchased by a state resident. *See* General Obligation (GO) Bond; Revenue Bond.

TAX REFORM ACT OF 1976: Federal legislation which created several changes in the Federal income tax code.

TAX-SHELTERED PROGRAMS: A term used to describe investment programs which have only limited economic value compared with high risk, but which are profitable from the standpoint of reducing Federal income tax.

TECHNICAL ANALYSIS: An approach to market theory stating that previous price movements, properly interpreted, can indicate future price patterns.

TELEPHONE BOOTHS: Booths or cubicles ringing the stock exchange trading rooms that are used by member organizations to (1) receive orders from their offices; (2) distribute orders to brokers for execution; (3) transmit details of the executed orders back to their offices.

TEMPORARY SPECIALIST: An experienced member of the Exchange appointed by a floor official to act as a specialist only in an emergency situation. His responsibilities are the same as those of a regular specialist. *See* Associate Specialist; Relief Specialist.

TENANTS BY ENTIRETY: In certain states a securities account owned jointly by husband and wife in which the assets legally transfer to the spouse upon the death of either party.

TENDER OFFER: A formal proposition to stockholders to sell their shares in response to a large purchase bid. The buyer customarily agrees to assume all costs and reserves the right to accept all, none, or a specific number of the shares presented for acceptance.

TENNESSEE VALLEY AUTHORITY (TVA): A Government-sponsored agency whose bonds are redeemable from the proceeds of the various power projects in the Tennessee River area. Interest payments on these bonds are fully taxable to investors.

TERM BOND: (1) A U. S. Treasury bond with a call privilege that becomes effective generally five years prior to maturity; (2) a large municipal bond issue with all of the bonds maturing on the same date.

TESTAMENTARY TRUST: A legal instrument that appoints an individual or an institution to perform a specific function with a designated sum of money. The trust relationship becomes effective upon the death of its creditor; its terms are spelled out in the decedent's will.

THE MARKET: A general term denoting the entire system for buying and selling securities.

THE THIRD MARKET: OTC transactions in listed stocks by nonmember broker/ dealers of that exchange.

THEORETICAL VALUE: In the absence of actual market values, the value of stock offered under a pre-emptive privilege, which is determined by (1) subtracting the price of the new stock from the price of the old stock (cum-rights); (2) dividing the difference by the number of rights needed to subscribe to one new share plus one.

THIRD-PARTY ACCOUNT: A brokerage account carried in the name of a person other than a customer. The practice is prohibited by NYSE regulation.

THIRD PARTY CHECK: A check drawn to the order of one person who endorsed it to another person, who subsequently presents it to someone else in satisfaction of his own obligation.

THIRTY-DAY RULE: See Wash Sale.

TICK: A transaction on the stock exchange. See Minus Tick; Plus Tick; Zero-minus Tick; Zero-plus Tick.

TICKER TAPE: A trade-by-trade report in chronological order of trades executed. Separate tapes exist for various markets.

TIME DEPOSIT: An account containing a currency balance pledged to remain at that bank for a specified, extended period in return for payment of interest.

TIME SPREAD: The term is used interchangeably with Calendar Spread.

TIME FIXED CHARGES EARNED: See Fixed Charge Coverage.

TOTAL CAPITALIZATION: The aggregate value of a corporation's long-term debt, preferred, and common stock accounts. Funded debt plus shareholders' equity.

TOTAL COST: The contract price plus all expenses incurred on the purchase execution.

TOTAL VOLUME: A column in the Listed Stock and Bond Tables showing for stocks total shares traded (omitting the last two zeros) and for bonds the total par value traded (omitting the last three zeros).

TRADE DATE: The date a trade was entered into as opposed to settlement date.

TRADER: A person or firm engaged in the business of buying and selling securities, options or commodities for a profit.

TRADING AUTHORIZATION: The legal right conferred by a person or institution upon another to effect the purchase and/or sale of securities in the former's account.

TRADING FLOOR: The location at any organized exchange where buyers and sellers meet to transact business.

TRADING POST: Twenty-three locations on the floor of the NYSE that are seven-foot high horseshoe shaped structures with an outside circumference from 26 to 31 feet. The one exception is a table-like structure, Post 30, in the garage, where most inactive preferred stocks are traded in multiples of ten shares.

TRADING RING: An octagonal ring in the center of the bond room floor in which all bond trading activity must take place.

TRADING ROTATION: The trading rotation is a system of opening the market on an options exchange. It is used to open trading in the morning and to reopen trading if a trading halt occurs during the day. Each option series is opened one at a time until all series in the same underlying stock have been given a chance to trade. After the rotation, simultaneous trading in all series then begins. Some exchanges use a closing rotation at the end of the day which then officially closes the market.

TRADING TO TOTAL VOLUME (TTV): The amount of trading in a security in which the specialist participates for his own account in relation to total volume in that security. The amount is computed by dividing the specialist's total dealings by twice the reported share volume.

TRANSFER AGENT: An agent of a corporation responsible for the registration of shareowners' names on the company records and the proper re-registration of new owners when a transfer of stock occurs.

TRANSFER AND SHIP: Customer instructions to have his securities transferred into his name and sent to him.

TREASURY BILL: A Federal bearer obligation issued to denominations of $10,000 to $1 million with a maturity date usually of three months to one year. It is fully marketable at a discount from face value (which determines the interest rate). *See* Tax Anticipation Bill (TAB).

TREASURY BOND: A Federal registered or bearer obligation issued in denominations of $500 to $1 million with maturities ranging from five to thirty-five years, carrying a fixed interest rate and issued, quoted, and traded as a percentage of its face value. *See* Flower Bond.

TREASURY NOTE: A Federal registered or bearer obligation issued in denominations of $1,000 to $500 million for maturities of one to ten years, carrying a fixed rate of interest. These notes are issued, quoted, and traded as a percentage of their face value.

TREASURY STOCK: Shares of stock reacquired by a corporation through purchase, and occasionally by donation, which are treated as authorized but unissued stock for dividend, voting, or earnings calculation purposes.

TRUSTEE: Generally a party (often a commercial bank) designated to supervise compliance with the terms of a legal agreement. In the case of bonds, the trustee is designated by indenture.

TWENTY-DAY (COOLING-OFF) PERIOD: A period of twenty calendar days following the filing of a registration statement with the SEC, during which (1) the SEC examines the statement for deficiencies; (2) the issuing corporation negotiates with an underwriting syndicate for a final agreement; and (3) the syndicate prepares for the successful distribution of the impending issue. The final day of the period is normally considered the effective date.

TWO-DOLLAR BROKER: A member of the NYSE who stands ready to execute orders in any security for any organization, in return for which he receives a brokerage fee.

UNCOVERING AN OPTION: The act of selling a position (or covering a short position) which had been used in conjunction with a covered option thereby leaving the option uncovered.

UNDERWRITER: Also known as an "investment banker," an underwriter is a middleman between an issuing corporation and the public. He usually forms an underwriting group, called a syndicate, to limit his risk and commitment of capital. He may also contract with selling groups to help distribute the issue-for a concession. In the case of mutual funds, he may also be known as a sponsor, distributor, or even wholesaler. Investment bankers also offer other services, such as advice and counsel on the raising and investment of capital.

UNDERWRITING COMPENSATION (SPREAD): The gross profit realized by an underwriter equal to the difference between the price he paid to the issuing corporation and the price of the public offering.

UNIFORM GIFTS TO MINORS ACT: A simplified law that enables minors to own property or securities in a beneficial fashion without need of trust instruments or other legal documents.

UNIFORM PRACTICE CODE ("the code"): A code established and maintained by the NASD Board of Governors that regulate the mechanics of executing and completing securities transactions in the OTC market.

UNIFORM PRACTICE COMMITTEE: An NASD district sub-committee that disseminates information and interpretations handed down by the Board of Governors regarding the Uniform Practice Code.

UNINCORPORATED ASSOCIATION: A group of people and/or institutions existing without the benefit of incorporating. Included in this category are partnerships and, in certain cases churches, schools and charitable organizations.

UNISSUED STOCK: That portion of authorized stock not distributed among investors.

UNIT INVESTMENT TRUST COMPANY: An investment company (1) organized under a trust indenture rather than a corporate charter; (2) directed by a body of trustees rather than a board of directors; and (3) able to issue only redeemable shares of beneficial interest to represent an undivided participation in a unit of specified securities. *See* Fixed Trust, Participating trust.

UNIFIED ACCOUNT: *See* Severally and Jointly.

UNITED STATES GOVERNMENT SECURITIES: Debt obligations of the Treasury Department, backed by the Government's unlimited power of taxation. *See* Marketable Securities.

UNSECURED OBLIGATION: A debt instrument whose repayment is backed solely by the credit worthiness of the issuer.

UP AND OUT OPTION: A block of at least ten put options with the same striking price and expiration date carrying a provision for immediate cancellation of the exercise privilege if the underlying stock rises by a predetermined, agreed-upon amount in the marketplace.

VARIABLE ANNUITY CONTRACT PLAN: An investment contract prepared by a life insurance company designed to offer continuous income through participation in a mutual fund portfolio; some life insurance is included as a death benefit and as an additional attraction.

VARIABLE RATIO HEDGING: A system of taking long and/or short positions in different securities and/or options for the purpose of creating a hedged position using other than a one-for-one relationship between the positions. Example: Buy 2 IBM Jan 260 Calls, Sell 5 IBM Jan 180 Calls.

VENTURE CAPITAL COMPANY: An investment company whose objectives are to invest in new or underdeveloped companies.

VERTICAL LINE CHARTING: A method of technical analysis where the high and low for the period (usually a day) are shown as a vertical line on the chart, with the closing price shown as a small horizontal line.

VERTICAL SPREAD: The simultaneous purchase and sale of options of the same class having the same expiration date but different striking prices.

VOLUME DELETED: A ticker tape announcement to signify that quantities of less than 5,000 shares per transaction will not appear until the ticker tape can stay abreast of trading activity on the stock exchange floor. It appears when the tape falls two minutes behind.

VOLUNTARY ACCUMULATION PLAN: An informal mutual fund investment program allowing a customer to arrange purchases in frequency and numbers of dollars at his own choosing, yet providing him with benefits normally available only to larger investors. Sales charge percentage requirements are constant throughout the life of the plan and are, therefore, "level-loaded."

VOLUNTARY ASSOCIATION: A form of business dating back to medieval England, involving a partnership with continuing existence but unlimited financial liability. The NYSE was originally a voluntary association.

VOLUNTARY UNDERWRITER: An individual or corporation that purchases a security from an issuer or affiliated person and offers it for public sale under an effective registration statement.

VOTING TRUST: The deposit of shares by shareholders with a commercial bank (trustee) for the purpose of gaining long-term corporate control.

VOTING TRUST CERTIFICATE (VTC): A certificate issued by a commercial bank in exchange for common stock deposited under terms of a voting trust. These certificates are comparable to the common stock itself but do not carry voting privileges in the affairs of the underlying corporation.

WAREHOUSING: The illegal sale of corporate security when a provision for its repurchase by the seller at some future date and at a prearranged price.

WARRANT: An inducement attached to new securities in distribution giving the purchaser a long-term (usually five to ten years) privilege of subscribing to one or more shares of stock reserved for him by the corporation from its unissued or treasury stock reserve. *See* Subscription Right.

WASH SALE: (1) For regulatory purposes—the purchase and sale of the same security at the same time and price without any change of ownership. This practice is outlawed under Section 10 of the Securities Exchange Act of 1934. (2) For tax purposes a sale at a loss and repurchase of the same, or a similar issue, within thirty days before or after intending to use that loss to offset capital gains or taxable income in that year. The loss is generally not allowed as a tax deduction under the 1954 Tax Code.

WHEN ISSUED/WHEN DISTRIBUTED CONTRACT: A delivery contract involving securities (stocks or bonds) that have been proposed for distribution but not yet issued; the date of delivery is set for some time in the future by the NASD Uniform Practice Committee or the appropriate stock exchange, as the case may be.

WHOLESALER: *See* Underwriter.

WIDGET: (1) A fictitious product used in textbook examples, especially accounting problems; (2) Slang for the plastic holder delivered through a pneumatic tube.

WINDOW SETTLEMENT: Transactions that are not cleared via the SCC or NCC and are completed in the office of the purchasing firm by means of certificate delivery versus immediately payment.

WIRE ROOM: An area in each branch office and in the home office where messages may be received and sent using machinery which creates a printed copy of the messages. Message traffic normally consists of orders, reports of execution of orders, trade settlement information and other sales data.

WITH-OR-WITHOUT A SALE (WOW): An odd-lot limit order to buy or sell either at a price derived from an effective round-lot transaction (with a sale) or at the existing round-lot quotation plus differential (without a sale) whichever occurs first in accordance with the customer's limit.

WITHHOLDING: A failure by a broker/dealer to make a bona fide distribution of a hot issue, thus encouraging demand at a premium price. This practice is a violation of the NASD Rules of Fair Practice. *See* Free-riding.

WORK-OUT MARKET: In the OTC market, a range of prices quoted by a market-maker when he is not certain that there is an existing market available, but he feels he can "work one out" within a reasonable period of time.

WORKING CAPITAL: *See* Net Working Capital.

WORKING CAPITAL RATIO: *See* Current Ratio.

WORLD BANK: Another name for the International Bank for Reconstruction and Development.

WOW ORDER: *See* With-or-Without a Sale (WOW) Order.

WRITE-OUT: An Exchange floor procedure by which a specialist is allowed to buy stock for himself from a customer's offering in his book, or sell from his account to a customer's bid. He must, however, allow the broker who entered the order to execute and "write out" the confirmation of the transaction and earn the contingent brokerage fee.

WRITER: *See* Option Writer.

YELLOW SHEETS: *See* A daily publication of the National Quotation Bureau giving markets in corporation debt securities.

YIELD: The percentage return on an investor's money in terms of current prices. It is the annual dividend/interest per share/bond divided by the current marketprice of that security.

YIELD TO MATURITY: The calculation of an average rate of return on a bond if held to its maturity date.

ZERO-MINUS TICK: A transaction on the Exchange at a price equal to that of the preceding transaction but lower than the last different price.

ZERO-PLUS TICK: A transaction on the Exchange at a price equal to that of the preceding transaction but higher than the last different price.

Index

Entries in this index exclude the defined terms in the Glossary, which are listed in alphabetical order.